JOHN H. LINNER M.D.

NORMANDY
TO OKINAWA

*A Navy Medical Officer's Diary
and Overview of World War Two*

All maps adapted from A World At Arms by Gerhard Weinberg—reprinted with permission of Cambridge University Press, July 15, 2000.

ISBN 13: 978-1-59298-204-2

ISBN 10: 1-59298-204-2

Library of Congress Catalog Number: 2007933281

Cover, book design, and typesetting: Anders Hanson, Mighty Media Inc.

Printed in the United States of America

First Printing: 2007
Second Printing: 2009

13   12   11   10   09   6   5   4   3   2

7104 Ohms Lane, Suite 101
Edina, Minnesota 55439 USA
(952) 829-8818
www.BeaversPondPress.com

To order, visit www.BookHouseFulfillment.com or call
1-800-901-3480. Reseller and special sales discounts available

*Dedicated to the wonderful women in my life:
My wife, Evodia, and our daughters, Kristin,
Jennifer, Andrea, Victoria, and Elizabeth.*

*Also, to all my great shipmates on the LST-6,
LST-52, and the* Rankin *(AKA-103).*

Eternal father, strong to save,
Whose arm has bound the restless wave,
Who bade the mighty ocean deep,
Its own appointed limits keep.

Oh Holy Spirit who didst brood,
Upon the chaos dark and rude,
And bid its angry tumult cease,
And give for wild confusion, peace.

Oh hear us when we cry to thee,
For those in peril on the sea.

W. Whiting

TABLE OF CONTENTS

....

PREFACE

....

BEING IN GOOD HEALTH AND ABOUT HALFWAY THROUGH THE UNIVERSITY of Minnesota Medical School at the time of Pearl Harbor, I knew that I would be drafted as a medical officer upon completion of my internship. Realizing the magnitude of this event, I determined to keep a daily diary of my experience in the war, and, if lucky enough to survive, to some day write my war memoirs for my family. After reading the diary, it occurred to me that if I were to combine my personal experience as a medical officer in the Normandy and Okinawa invasions, in the context of the war as a whole, its genesis, as well as its broad multi-focal course from 1939 to V-J Day, September 2, 1945, it might be of greater interest and value.

This account is not a detailed, comprehensive document of this immense historical event. Rather it is a synopsis, or overview, of the critical period between the two world wars (1918 to 1938) and the principal turning points and battles of the war.

Such an overview offers the reader an opportunity to grasp the wide-flung interrelated parts and to put them into a more unified perspective. A condensed version of the war, such as this, must of necessity leave out many military actions and background political events that to some readers may seem too important to exclude. It deals more with putative causes of World War II and military campaigns in the broad sense rather than individual actions within each campaign. For those interested in greater details for any particular battle, or other aspects of the war, the bibliography contains many excellent references where this information can be found. This bit of history has not suffered from lack of coverage. There have been over 50,000 books written about WWII.

ACKNOWLEDGMENTS

....

During a rainy vacation week in Rio Verde, Arizona, in 1997, Andrea was a great inspiration to me in the early stage of this manuscript with her insightful reading of the text. I also wish to thank Victoria for her edits and help with captions.

Many thanks to Marianne Fearon, who, before I was knowledgeable with the word processor, assumed the daunting task of deciphering my handwritten text and transcribing it.

Great appreciation and thanks are due my son-in-law, Dr. John McClure, who not only gave me his retired computer, but also took on the challenge of teaching me to use it.

I'm particularly grateful to Evodia for her help in picture arrangement and her dogged persistence in helping me to complete this project before the start of the new millennium.

INTRODUCTION

....

The Spanish-American War of 1898, a little-remembered event, importantly affected the strategy and conduct of the United States in WWII.

This has been of particular interest to me because my father, Henry P. Linner, at age 19, to earn money for college and to see the world, enlisted in the U.S. Army at the beginning of that war. Unfortunately, as far as his travel plans were concerned, because the war lasted only four months from late April to early August, 1898, he never left the country. Instead, he was sent with an army unit to Leech Lake near Walker, Minnesota to quell an Indian uprising which became known as the *Battle of Sugar Point*. The sanitary conditions in this camp were so bad that a large number of men developed gastroenteritis and other communicable diseases. What the soldiers thought were raisins in the oatmeal turned out to be flies. Although seven U.S. troops were killed and ten wounded, there were many more casualties from disease than from fighting. Author John M. Barry in his book, *The Great Influenza*, reported that six times as many soldiers, roughly 5000 young men, died of some disease (predominately typhoid fever in the Spanish American war) than were killed in battle or died of their wounds. My father almost died of typhoid or para-typhoid fever, but fortunately recovered and later received his BA degree from Gustavus Adolphus College in St. Peter, Minnesota. He then taught school for two years in the Chisago Lakes District to earn money for the University of Minnesota Graduate School. After one year in law school, he switched to medicine and became a very successful and much beloved physician and surgeon in Minneapolis.

The Spanish American War was remarkable not only for its brevity and low cost in men and material, but also for the territorial gains that accrued to the United States as a result of that war. The Philippine Islands were purchased from Spain for $20 million, and Guam, Puerto Rico, and the Hawaiian Islands were acquired at no cost. Cuba was granted independence from Spain.

Theodore Roosevelt, assistant secretary of the Navy under President William McKinley during the Spanish American War, has been credited with keeping the U.S. Navy ships in top operating condition and readiness. Unlike President McKinley, he was strongly in favor of declaring war on Spain after the sinking of the *U.S.S. Maine* in Havana harbor on February 17, 1897. Two hundred sixty-six American seamen were killed in that explosion, allegedly (but never proved to be) a Spanish torpedo. The superior strength of the U.S. Navy over that of Spain, plus Roosevelt's strong desire to fight Spain for the Philippines, was in large part responsible for the overwhelming victory of the United States.

Even though Spain lost the war of 1898, including the loss of its colonies, the redirection of its energy and economy to the home front exclusively strengthened it and greatly improved its standard of living, at least up until the devastating Spanish Civil War of 1936–1939. By contrast, for the first time in its history, the United States had become a major imperial power in the world with new bases in both the Caribbean and the Pacific Ocean.

This new reality gave huge impetus to long dormant plans to build a canal across Central America, either through Nicaragua (first choice at that time) or Panama, where the French had been toiling on a sea-level canal since 1870. A canal across the Isthmus of Panama would cut 8,000 nautical miles from the usual route around South America's Cape of Good Hope, saving at least one month's sailing time for most vessels going from New York to San Francisco. This not only lowered the cost of transporting goods, but was of great strategic importance militarily.

Building the canal became a top priority on the national agenda, and President William McKinley initiated extensive canal studies to this end. Unfortunately, he was assassinated on September 6, 1901, during a speech in Buffalo, New York, only nine months into his second term. Vice President Theodore Roosevelt then took over as president and made the Panama Canal project one of his major goals. He is considered to have been the most influential force in the planning and ultimate construction of the Panama Canal, one of the world's greatest engineering feats.

WWI, The Versailles Treaty, and Influenza

....

After four years (1914 to 1918) of brutal, bloody warfare, with mounting mortality from increasingly lethal weapons such as heavier cannon, machine guns, tanks, air bombardment, poison gas, and in 1918 the frighteningly deadly influenza pandemic, a welcomed armistice was declared on November 11, 1918. From that time until the signing of the Versailles Treaty on June 28, 1919, peace terms were hammered out in Paris by the three principle Allied leaders: Premier and War Minister of France, Georges Clemenceau, Prime Minister of England, Lloyd George, and the twenty-eighth President of the United States, Woodrow Wilson.

Clemenceau and Wilson were at loggerheads for months trying to settle on mutually acceptable terms for the final treaty. Wilson strongly favored a moderate program of restitution and sustainable goals, whereas Clemenceau demanded huge reparations and painful territorial concessions that Germany would find virtually impossible to fulfill. Wilson championed the enlightened concept of "peace without victory." France, of course, having been involved in the war for four long years (the U.S. for less than two years), and having suffered the greatest loss of life and destruction of property, understandably had greater grievances. Wilson was thinking in terms of a durable peace achieved through "fairness to all."

During the entire period of the peace treaty process, the world was bedeviled by a sudden, deadly influenza pandemic that apparently started in an army barracks in Haskell County, Kansas. With global troop movements, the flu spread rapidly throughout the world. Its virulence was far more deadly than the Black Death of the Middle Ages. Epidemiologists estimate that at least 50 million people, and due to incomplete mortality statistics, more likely one hundred million people died world wide of this disease, a much greater mortality than for the entire war from all causes for all participants. For baffling reasons it had a predilection for young people in their prime of life. In October, 1918 alone, 4,574 Parisians died of influenza.

Influenza had a more immediate impact on the Paris peace deliberations, however, when at 6:00 PM on April 3, 1919, President Wilson was struck down by a sudden, explosive illness, so violent, with paroxysms of coughing, nausea, vomiting, and diarrhea, that his physician, Carey Grayson, thought he had been poisoned by an assassin. Grayson soon realized it was an especially severe attack of influenza.

Wilson was confined to his bed for several days and could barely move when after four days, negotiations were resumed in his sick room. His thinking was definitely affected by the influenza, and suddenly, unexpectedly, he abandoned the principles he had previously insisted upon, yielding all to Clemenceau. Most historians have attributed this sudden illness and reversal in character to a stroke. However, historian Alfred Crosby, cited by Barry, reviewed all reports concerning this illness, and concluded, along with Wilson's physician, that it was not a stroke. Rather, it was influenza with a cerebral component which frequently accompanied this pandemic. Four months later, back in the United States, Wilson suffered a severe stroke which was thought by Crosby to probably be related to the brain damage he had suffered back in April.

Wilson's sudden abrogation of his principles caused a great furor among many British and American diplomats, scholars and pacifists. They felt betrayed. John Maynard Keynes, British economist at the peace conference, was stunned and called Wilson "the greatest fraud on earth." He predicted that the Versailles Treaty would seriously disrupt the entire world economy.

Other disenchanted world figures were William Bullitt, Adolph Berle Jr., Christian Herter, John Foster Dulles, Lincoln Steffens, and Walter Lippmann.

Berle wrote Wilson a bitter letter of resignation from his post as Assistant Secretary of State.

"I am sorry that you did not fight our fight to the finish and that you had so little faith in the millions of men like myself, in every nation who had faith in you. Our government has consented now to deliver the suffering peoples of the world to new oppressions, subjections and dismemberment: a new century of war."

According to John Barry, "Wilson had influenza, only influenza."

The predominant theory fostered by most historians has been that the inception, early development, and growth of Hitler, of the Nazi party, and ultimately of the causes of World War II was due to the harshness of the Versailles Treaty. This had been my belief until my recent rediscovery of two outstanding war historians, Gerhard L. Weinberg and Lynn Montross. They totally disagree with this view. Both provided strong evidence that the Versailles Treaty, as actually applied, was not adhered to by Germany and had nothing to do with the rise of Hitler or Nazism. Though Hitler used the treaty as a propaganda tool, he was well aware that it posed no obstruction to his plan to build a new and larger military and ultimately a new German empire, The Third Reich.

In his book, *A World at Arms*, Weinberg contends that "Contrary to the pablum of most history books today, Germany was not crushed." Modifications to the treaty included reduction in reparation payments that for the most part were covered by money borrowed from Britain and the United States and never paid back, an earlier end to the occupation, and farcical war crime trials, conducted by Germany. He characterized the period from WWI to WWII as a quiet, though politically turbulent, part of one continuous war, reflected in his chapter heading for that time: "From One War to the Next."

Montross entitles his chapter for the same period, "Germany Wins the Peace." Although the armistice of November 11, 1918 demanded immediate immobilization, the German Republic within four months signed up volunteers for a new "civilian" army. This "Freicorps" grew to 450,000 members the first winter. Former military officers resumed their WWI authority. Of 200 million dollars loaned to Germany under the U.S. Dawes Plan, 10 million was diverted by Germany to the Krupp's munition works, and 12 million to Herr Thysen, Chairman of the German United Steel Works, who endowed Hitler.

Montross: "Future generations will doubtless find this period one of the most incredible chapters in history. For the years from 1918 to 1938, when viewed in perspective, can only appear as a brief and troubled truce linking two phases of the same war."

While post-war Germany was adapting the Armistice and the Versailles Treaty to its own purposes, the Allied Powers were struggling with their own versions of how best to shape the post-war world for peaceful coexistence.

The League of Nations, one of the products of the peace process in Paris, was established to give truth to the slogan that WWI was the "war to end all wars." It was a brilliant, if idealistic concept, designed to embrace most of the developed countries of the world, including all the belligerents. The purpose of President Woodrow Wilson's 14 Points and of the League was to provide a forum for discussion and adjudication of grievances, and to prevent another war, through collective action, such as applying sanctions against an aggressor nation. To be effective, the threat of sanctions would have to be backed up by the credible threat of military action on the part of member nations.

Concerned that the League of Nations could drag the United States into another European war and could obligate our soldiers to fight under a foreign military leader, Senator Henry Cabot Lodge led the fight in the U.S. Senate to block our entry into the League. The Senate's unwillingness to ratify the League deeply wounded its effectiveness, and greatly disappointed President Wilson, its author and principal proponent.

With this weakening of the League, the major allied powers, England, France, and the United States, pinned their hopes on maintaining peace in the world on disarmament and isolationism. Many officials and citizens believed that disarmament on the part of all countries would somehow prevent another war. Unfortunately, for their own nefarious reasons, Germany, Japan, and Italy did not disarm. They actually increased their armed strength in direct violation of the Versailles Treaty and the covenants of the League.

Basic tenets of the League and the Locarno pacts were violated when Japan invaded Manchuria in 1931, Italy invaded Ethiopia in 1935, and Germany occupied the Rhineland in 1936, but there was no collective action among the world's leading powers to halt these flagrant transgressions. This, in effect, encouraged Germany to make more illegal and brutal acquisitions. The United States, determined to stay out of Europe's wars, withdrew into a cocoon of "America First" isolationism.

Russia became so involved in its own Bolshevik revolution during the latter part of WWI that they were unable to contribute any significant military help to the Allied Powers. The Communists in Russia fully expected a comparable Bolshevik revolution in Germany and in other European countries. This Bolshevik scare fed into Hitler's hatred and distrust of all Communists in Germany and in Russia.

Although they were briefly hoodwinked by Hitler's rise to power in Germany, initially considering him to be a great new leader for the downtrodden German nation, Winston Churchill and Anthony Eden were among the first of the world's leaders who began to see Hitler as a predatory dictator bent on conquering all of Europe.

The majority of the population of England and France favored British Prime Minister Neville Chamberlain's policy of appeasement through concessions, as exemplified in the Munich Pact of 1938. The popular belief was that if they conceded the Rhineland and the German speaking Sudetenland of Czechoslovakia to Hitler, he would then be satisfied and war could be averted.

Unfortunately, Hitler had much grander designs. In his book, *Mein Kampf*, which touted his belief in the superiority of the Aryan race, and the inferiority of Jews, Slavs, and Blacks, Hitler also made it clear that Germany needed more *lebensraum* (living room) for its growing population. Germany would gain this land at the expense of eastern territory, (namely Russia) where the indigenous population would be used as common laborers. He blamed the Jews and the Bolsheviks for most of Germany's financial difficulties, and he vowed to eliminate them from the land. His hatred for the Allied countries and the avowed motivation for his drive to power stemmed from his selective perception of the inequity of the Versailles Treaty, the pinched economic conditions in Germany that stemmed from this, and the collapse of the home front in Germany in 1918. Hitler attributed this collapse to the labor unions, the Communists, and the Jews. In his view the war was not lost by the German Army, but by the undermined home front.

One other important condition of the Versailles Treaty enraged Hitler. He vowed to rectify the territorial concessions exacted from Germany, particularly the creation of the Polish corridor which stretched north from Poland to include the port city of Danzig and which separated Germany from East Prussia by thirty to forty miles. Danzig had belonged to Germany for 266 years and to Poland for 638 years. The great majority of the population of Danzig was

German, but it was now considered to be a "free" city. He was equally irritated by the loss of the Rhineland to France.

Many students of history, as alluded to earlier, believe that had the Versailles Treaty been less harsh, Hitler would never have successfully ascended to power. I now believe Montross and Weinberg: that Hitler would still have been driven to achieve his dream of a pure Aryan race and a Europe dominated by Germany. The Versailles Treaty, in all likelihood, stoked the fires of his paranoia, but mainly served as a useful oratorical prop.

With this backdrop to some of the events leading up to World War II, I will now relate how these events in Europe were affecting my life in Minnesota.

EDUCATION
AND WAR

....

IN 1934 AND 1935 AT WASHBURN HIGH SCHOOL IN SOUTH MINNEAPOLIS, I took a course in German from a wonderful teacher, Miss Denison. These were the years of Hitler's rise to power in Germany, his succession to the chancellorship of Germany on January 30, 1933, and the birth of the Third Reich. In spite of these monumental changes in Germany, I don't recall one allusion to Hitler or to German politics during that entire two-year course. Miss Denison adhered strictly to teaching the language and acquainting us with Germany's literary giants: Heine, Goethe, Schiller, and many others. Her course was so fascinating, that I'm happy now we didn't get involved in lengthy political discussions. I have a feeling that Miss Denison knew all about German politics, but deliberately avoided discussing them with her classes.

At home, over dinner, my family would frequently discuss world events and European politics, but during these early years we considered Hitler an asset to Germany and Winston Churchill a warmonger. We were in accord with Neville Chamberlain's avowed policy of "peace in our time" through cooperation with Germany. German propaganda was subtle but effective in the United States during those early years.

From January 1936 to June 1939, at Gustavus Adolphus College in St. Peter, Minnesota, where I received a BS degree, I took a course in medical German from professor Nels Langsjoen. He also refrained from discussing German politics, and adhered to translations from a German medical text book. Although newspapers and magazines covered war news extensively, there was little or no reference to the startling events in Europe in any of my classes, all of them in science or mathematics and none in political science or current events.

I do remember a striking chapel talk by Dr. Walter Judd, U.S. congress-man and former missionary to China. His spellbinding speech condemned the United States' policy of selling scrap iron to Japan and urged a boycott on Japanese goods.

"All that scrap iron will soon be returned to us as bullets and bombs, and women wearing Japanese silk hose will feel American blood running down their legs."

He also warned of Germany's rearmament. Chapel was usually a time to relax, but during this chapel period everyone sat in rapt attention and utter silence.

One of my best friends at Gustavus, Floyd Peterson, majored in German history and language, preparing to become a college professor. Through his extensive studies he developed friendships in Germany through the "pen pal" program. Based on this correspondence, Floyd became enamored of the Jugend (young people's) program and of Adolph Hitler. Those of us who read some of the letters he received were impressed with the devotion to Hitler exhibited by these eager young Germans. They talked about how much better economic conditions were becoming, improving unemployment, and the many fun pro-grams for young people since the formation of the Third Reich. Floyd wore a white sweatshirt bearing a large black swastika on the front, which I think was a gift he received from one of his pals.

With Hitler's acquisition of Austria, and Germany's march into Sudetenland in violation of the Munich Pact, it became apparent that Hitler was a dictator bent on expansion at the expense of other European countries. It was only somewhat later in 1939 that several of us were able to convince Floyd that he had better look at the entire European picture and not just the biased view he received from his German friends.

Floyd abandoned his quest to become a German professor after his disil-lusionment with Hitler. He entered medical school at the University of Minnesota, where he and I became partners in anatomy. We worked on many projects together, including studying for comprehensive examinations at the end of each year.

Floyd was investigated at length by the FBI as a possible German spy or a misguided propagandist. Of course the FBI found that he was not a spy, but that he had been deceived and was an unwitting dupe of Nazi propaganda.

After graduation from Gustavus, for the next three and one-half years, September 1939 to March, 1943, my time was almost totally devoted to the study of medicine. The demands of medical school diverted my attention from political events, except to be aware that my family and most of my friends were against getting involved in the new European war. Though we sensed that President Franklin Roosevelt, by urging Congress to ban the strict Neutrality Act, wanted an involvement to some degree, we were much more in sympathy with the majority of Americans who wished to remain strictly neutral. Our views found expression in such voices as the America First Committee, Father Charles Coughlin, and Colonel Charles Lindbergh.

For a time, Lindbergh also was one of the many misguided Americans. He received the distinguished German Flying Cross from Herman Göring, Germany's air force chief in 1938, and he warned the world at that time of the tremendous growth and strength of the German Air Force. During 1940 and 1941 Lindbergh took a firm stand for strict neutrality by the United States, and for this position was called a "Copperhead" (traitor) by President Roosevelt. Because of his status as a sterling, "All American hero," Lindbergh fueled the isolationist, antiwar sentiment in America more than anyone else. After the Pearl Harbor debacle on December 7, 1941, however, Lindbergh, along with most isolationists, immediately recanted his antiwar stance, and over the ensuing war years made significant contributions to the United States air war against Japan, at considerable risk to himself.

After the United States' entry into the war, medical students were given the option of volunteering for one of the armed services with active duty following internship, or being drafted upon graduation. I elected to volunteer for the U.S. Naval Reserve and was accepted as an ensign. To provide more doctors for military service as quickly as possible, the usual four-year medical course was shortened by one quarter, and the internship from one year to nine months.

Provision for specialty training following internship was made via the so-called "Berry" plan which permitted deferment for three nine-month periods prior to entering the service, or continued deferment in an academic setting. Essential department heads, research directors, and a few other categories were deferred for the entire war.

BOSTON CITY HOSPITAL

On recommendation of Dr. Cecil Watson, Chief of Medicine at the University of Minnesota, I applied for an internship on the Harvard Service of the Boston City Hospital. This entailed taking an oral examination at the Boston City Hospital in the summer of 1942.

On the flight to Boston I lost my wallet. It was hot on the plane, and when I gave my suit coat to the stewardess to hang up, I didn't think to first remove my billfold. Upon return of my coat, I was horrified to find that my wallet was gone. The stewardess was almost as chagrined as I. When she folded the coat over her arm, the billfold must have slipped out into the aisle, and someone picked it up. In any event, I arrived in Boston without a cent in my pocket nor any means of identification. Fortunately, the man seated next to me was willing to risk loaning me twenty dollars which permitted me to stay in a cheap boarding house overnight and call Dad to wire money the next day.

I was so upset about this episode and also about the drabness of the Boston I saw on this first visit, that I cancelled my Boston internship plan. I decided instead to take my training at the University of Minnesota, where I had been promised a position if I weren't accepted in Boston.

My negative feelings about Boston weren't improved at all upon visiting the Boston City Hospital later that day. It had a forbidding look about it with 20 or more various sized and shaped buildings scattered around one super-sized square block. The hospital wards each had 25 to 30 beds, separated only by privacy curtains. The hospital also had a large infectious disease building for patients with tuberculosis, meningitis, streptococcus infections, and typhoid fever. Other facilities included laboratories, X-ray units, a children's contagious disease building, and others I never had time to enter. Boston University, Tufts, and Harvard had medical or surgical services at the hospital. Harvard had total responsibility for the Thorndike Memorial Research Laboratory as well. These buildings were connected by a maze of very dark and forbidding underground tunnels, like the catacombs of Rome. Exaggerated stories were told about patients getting lost in the tunnels for a week or more.

The next morning I met with Dr. George Minot, Nobel Laureate, and Chief of the Harvard Medical Service and of the world famous Thorndike Laboratory.

I almost told him that I would like to withdraw my application, but he was so kind and friendly that I just didn't have the heart (or the guts) to do so. However, as he sent me to be individually examined by the rest of the department heads, I was in a perfect frame of mind. I would rather not have passed and so was totally relaxed. I didn't suffer the mental block that can sometimes occur when one fears failure or tries too hard.

George Minot shared the Nobel Prize in medicine in 1934 with Dr. William B. Murphy and Dr. George H. Whipple for the discovery of the cause, prevention, and cure of pernicious anemia, heretofore a fatal disease. My maternal grandmother Anderson died of pernicious anemia just prior to Minot's discovery. Several years later my uncle Walter Anderson was "cured" by eating raw liver, which was the treatment for this disease before the active ingredient was extracted.

There were five or six examiners that followed Minot, each asking questions in their field. I remember Dr. William B. Castle, internationally famous hematologist, who worked on pernicious anemia, hemophilia, and other blood diseases in Dr. Minot's laboratory. He became Minot's successor as Chief of Medicine and Chief of the Thorndike Laboratory. Dr. Castle was over six feet tall, well built, with deep penetrating eyes, and an awe-inspiring persona. His questions were searching but fair, and he seemed quite pleased with my responses.

Following Dr. Castle was Dr. Maxwell Finland, who was as short as Dr. Castle was tall. He was dark haired with a prominent forehead, dark brown eyes, and a direct but gentle manner. I don't remember any of the specific questions he asked, but I do recall being asked a few very obscure ones. To those I cheerfully announced, "I just don't know," instead of guessing as I might have done were I anxious to pass.

The remaining professors were Dr. Charles Davidson, who later took Dr. Castle's place as Chief of Medicine. He was tall, with brown wavy hair, blue eyes, and a most gracious and friendly personality. He made important contributions to the development of parenteral (intravenous) nutrition and to the management of severe burn victims such as inundated the Boston City Hospital and other Boston hospitals following the horrible Coconut Grove fire in 1942. He was also an authority on liver disease.

Next was Dr. Robert Williams, an endocrinologist who did pioneer work in diabetes mellitus, diabetes insipidus, and thyroid disease. He had a southern drawl and seemed to enjoy asking questions. I later discovered that he was always a lot of fun and enjoyed meeting people. He later became Chief of Medicine at the University of Washington in Seattle.

Dr. Hale Ham, an extremely bright, energetic, and cheerful man who worked closely with Dr. Castle in hematology, was the next examiner. Dr. Henry Jackson, whose specialty was lymphomas and Hodgkin's disease, was the last. He is considered to be the father of medical oncology, responsible for developing new insights into the patho-physiology and treatment of malignant lymphomas.

At the conclusion of the examination period, I was interviewed a second time by Dr. Castle. He informed me that I was on the Harvard Service first selection list. If Boston City Hospital was my first choice (the alternatives were Massachusetts General Hospital or Peter Bent Brigham), then I could definitely have the appointment and wouldn't have to await the result of the final selection process in a month or so. This sudden revelation of acceptance startled me, and instead of jumping for joy as would be normally expected, I experienced a tight feeling in my chest and a very dry mouth. It was the only time all day that I felt any pressure or anxiety. I had really hoped either to fail the selection process or have the option to turn it down by mail the following month, which would have been so much easier. I came to Boston to take a competitive examination for an appointment considered to be one of the best in the country, and I didn't want it. Worse, I had to confront the Chief of Medicine with this bizarre position.

Seated in front of this awesome figure, I finally found the courage to say, "Dr. Castle, you won't believe this, but I don't want to come here for my internship." He straightened up in his chair, stared at me incredulously, and then quietly asked, "Why is that?" This was the most difficult question I had to answer all day, and my mind was racing to formulate a reasonable reply to my negative feelings. I certainly didn't want to sound insulting. Finally, I managed to come up with, "Well, I just don't like Boston!"

"Don't like Boston?" he exploded. "And why don't you like Boston?" He seemed almost to enjoy my miserable predicament.

Trying to express the negative feelings engendered by my limited exposure to the very worst part of Boston (the blocks of red buildings, concrete, and pavement), I blurted out, "It doesn't have enough trees."

"Enough trees!" he shouted as he shot up from his chair and strode out of the room.

I was devastated. Now what do I do?

In a minute or two he returned, followed by Dr. Finland. I was quaking, not knowing what humiliation awaited me.

"Max," Dr. Castle began, "Linner has been in Boston for the first time in his life and he hasn't seen enough trees. I want you to take him out to your place on Cape Cod tonight and show him some trees!"

With that he abruptly walked out of the room. I sensed he was trying to stifle a chuckle.

Dr. Finland was very kind, and told me to meet him in front of the hospital in one hour. We then drove out to his home on the Cape, listened to his record collection of classical music, ate fried clams, drank beer, and talked for several hours. And, oh yes, we saw a lot of trees, the Boston Garden and Commons, and many lovely homes. Dr. Finland was indeed a healing balm for me.

When I left the next day, I was assured that I would receive the acceptance by mail in one month, and that I could respond either way at that time. What wonderful people! They could have squashed me for my impertinence, but instead they chose to salvage my ego, and I will be forever grateful.

When I arrived home, my concern about treeless Boston had been dispelled, but I realized that my deeper concern about going to Boston was the fear of leaving home for the first time and likely the last. After the internship would be the Navy, for how long, no one could say. This heavy feeling wouldn't leave me, and I met with Dr. Watson at the University of Minnesota to set up an internship there. He assured me of a position, but he strongly urged me to take the Boston appointment for the "experience of your life." My folks said that though they would like to have me stay home, taking the internship in Boston might be the wise thing to do. So finally, but without great joy, I accepted the Boston offer. With a heavy heart, on March 29, 1943, I left the Great Northern Railroad Station in Minneapolis on the "New England States" train bound for Boston.

Of the fourteen interns selected in 1943 for the Second and Fourth Harvard Services, only four were from medical schools other than Harvard. There was one from each of the following universities: John Hopkins (Howard Naquin), Cornell University (J. Manning), University of Iowa (George Maresh), and University of Minnesota (me). My first reaction to my fellow house officers was that they were very aloof, snobbish, and difficult to get to know. After several weeks, when the initial barriers were broken down, they all proved to be wonderfully warm and supportive. In retrospect, I realize that they were as introspective and as shy as I was. When we finally got to know each other we had a great time.

The most unusual and quite amazing characteristic of the Harvard Medical Service at the City Hospital was the collegial attitude of the top professors and the entire teaching staff toward their interns, or "house officers" as we were called. One was never insulted or put down or treated like a flunky as happens at some high-powered teaching institutions. Our service chiefs, Doctors Carleton Chapman, Robert Ebert, Canky Williams, and Gib Mebain, were demanding, but fair and extremely knowledgeable. I learned so much about clinical medicine under their tutelage.

The Second and Fourth Harvard Services prided themselves in never closing the wards to new patients regardless of how full they were. In the Peabody Building, which served the Fourth Medical Service, where I spent most of my time, beds were set up in the rotunda area or halls whenever necessary. The Peabody was an old red-brick, narrow, but deep structure with a long ward for women and an identical one on the floor above for men. On the third floor was the house officers' medical laboratory with an old lab table, a sink, and a jumble of glassware, pipettes, rubber tubing, test tubes, and lab trays.

Another absolute on this service was that the intern on call at night had to do a complete work-up on every new admission, which included a history and physical examination and all the laboratory work, except for blood chemistries, which were done in the central hospital laboratory. We did spinal taps, spinal fluid smears, and cultures, when indicated, complete blood counts, sedimentation rates, sputum smears and cultures, and stool studies for parasites or occult blood. We were expected to have the complete work-up ready for presentation at morning rounds. It was not uncommon to be up all night, several nights each week, and all of us were in a chronic state of fatigue. I was so busy and so tired, that there was no time to be homesick, or to worry about the war, or wonder what my role would be when I finally entered active service.

In an attempt to give the house officers who were going into the military service some practical experience that might be helpful, we were assigned two weeks in the emergency room where we treated lacerations, bruises, and some fractures, but no major injuries. Those were handled by the surgical residents and interns. Our training did not prepare us to do surgery of any magnitude, nor was this internship designed to give us that type of training. We were concerned about this deficiency in our war preparation, but assumed we would be stationed at large hospitals with specialty services, or that we may be assigned to do physical examinations in recruiting and induction stations, where surgical know-how would be unnecessary. I'm glad I didn't know then what my navy assignment was going to be.

In 1973, the Harvard Medical Service and the Thorndike Memorial Laboratory, for various complex political reasons unknown to me, were phased out of the Boston City Hospital. Boston University became the only surviving service at the hospital. Harvard and Tufts withdrew to their parent centers, and the Thorndike Laboratory moved to Beth Israel Hospital. Thus ended a great and wonderful medical service on which I was privileged to serve, if ever so briefly, during its glory years. Dr. Cecil Watson was indeed correct when he told me, "It would be the experience of a lifetime."

My tenure was completed at the Boston City Hospital on December 31, 1943, after which I returned to Minneapolis for a delightful five-day respite with family and friends. I then reported for active duty to the United States Naval Hospital in Newport, Rhode Island, on January 10, 1944. This marked the beginning of my tour of duty in the U.S. Navy and the reason for writing these memoirs.

During the five-year period of medical school and internship, 1939 to 1944, I was totally engrossed, challenged, and fascinated by the wonders of medicine. The monumental struggle going on between belligerents in both the European and the Pacific theaters of war, amply covered by newspapers, magazines, and Movie Tone or Pathe News in the cinema (there being no television) did not often penetrate my consciousness. War news could not be avoided entirely, of course, because it dominated all the news media. Headlines shouted the gains or losses as the battles reached ever greater crescendos, unprecedented in all history for the magnitude of its destructive power.

PART ONE

....

THE WAR
IN EUROPE

THE PLOT TO ASSASSINATE HITLER

....

IN 1938, GERMANY FLOUTED THE MUNICH PACT. BY EXPLOITING ALLIED weakness, and by threats, blackmail, and intimidation, Germany occupied the Rhineland, Austria, the German-speaking Sudetenland, and the rest of Czechoslovakia at virtually no cost to itself.

In his fascinating book *The Oster Conspiracy of 1938: The Unknown Story of the Military Plot to Kill Hitler and Avoid World War II*, Terry Parsinnen, history professor at the University of Tampa, in Florida, tells about how very close the world came to avoiding WWII altogether. His facts came from voluminous records collected by the late distinguished professor of history at the University of Minnesota, Harold Deutsch, and stored at the U. S. Army Military Institute in Carlisle, Pennsylvania. These papers (over 20 boxes) were based on interviews Deutsch had with the few surviving conspirators or their relatives and from the sparse written material that he managed to uncover. Deutsch had authored two books covering the turbulent years in Germany before 1940 and had intended to write a book about the conspiracy of 1938. Unfortunately Deutsch died in 1995 before he could start.

A few historians have dealt with this event, including William L. Shirer, J.W. Wheeler-Bennett, and Theodore S. Hamerow. For the most part they downplay the conspiracy, characterizing its members as "indecisive, ineffectual or just plain cowardly." They, however, did not have the advantage that Parsinnen did: access to the richest source of information from this period, the Deutsch files.

The conspirators were a large group of disaffected Germans who hated Hitler and his black-shirted Schutzstaffel (SS) on moral, philosophical, religious, and military-policy grounds. Many of them believed Hitler was psychopathic if not psychotic. They included such important leaders as the commander in chief of the army, Colonel General Walter von Brauchitsch, the chief of the Army General Staff, Franz Halder, the commander of Germany's West Wall, General Wilhelm Adam, the head of the Department of the Interior, Hans-Bernd Gisevius, the first and second in command of the Abwehr (Military Intelligence), Admiral Wilhelm Canaris, chief, and Lieutenant Colonel Hans Oster (who was also the principal organizer of the conspirators), the police president of Berlin, Wolf Graf von Helldorf, Embassy officials, Erich and Theo Kordt, the former Minister of Finance and head of the German Reichsbank, Hjalmar Schacht, the secretary of the Foreign Ministry, Ernst von Weizsacker, and many others of high rank and importance. They had the power and planning to carry out a successful coup if the right circumstances developed.

Oster and many of the other conspirators watched with mounting concern Hitler's brazen occupation of the Rhineland and particularly the brutal acquisition of Austria in March, 1938. Contrary to Nazi propaganda, the *anschluss* in Austria was far from bloodless. Thirty-five thousand Austrians were executed at Mauthausen and 76,000 were sent to the infamous Dachau concentration camp, including Austrian Chancellor Schuschnigg. Hitler's threats to invade Czechoslovakia if the Sudetenland wasn't ceded to Germany by October 1, 1938, alarmed the dissidents. They knew that France had a mutual defense treaty with Czechoslovakia that could spark a European war, particularly if Britain backed France. Hitler accompanied his fiery rhetoric and patriotic fervor with showy military marches down the main streets of Berlin. To his disgust, the general population was turned off by these displays, staying indoors and providing no approbation. Hitler complained to Ribbentrop, "How can I fight a war with these kinds of people?" They liked what Hitler had done for their economy, but they hated even the thought of war, still a painful memory to most German adults.

During the tense month of September, 1938, the conspirators hoped for an ultimatum from Britain to Nazi Germany threatening war if Hitler invaded Czechoslovakia. General Franz Halder, chief of the Army General Staff, an extremely important member of the conspiracy, stressed the importance of Britain and France standing firm against Hitler's threatened invasion. This would assure the support of the German population and any wavering members of the armed forces.

Through clandestine diplomatic channels, Britain's Prime Minister, Neville Chamberlain and Foreign Secretary, Edward Halifax, were apprised of this position and its import, but they didn't comprehend it, or didn't want to act on it. Unfortunately, Chamberlain's past experience in government did not include foreign affairs. He had served as minister of health and chancellor of the exchequer and was imbued with the general public's dream of "no war at any cost." He believed that taking a firm stand now would lead to a major war, which was anathema to most British citizens. He felt he could personally defuse the entire situation by a one-on-one diplomatic mission to Germany to confer with Hitler personally. This would be his first experience with air travel, which heightened the drama. It was also a great boost to his ego to consider that he could be the man that saved the peace, not only for Europe, but for the entire world. What he didn't grasp was that the only way to avoid a world war was to eliminate Hitler and the Nazi party. Ironically, the leaders in Britain who knew the truth and were willing to stand up to Hitler with force of arms were on the sideline: Winston Churchill and Anthony Eden. Had Churchill been in power at the time, Britain would have stood up to Hitler, the German conspirators would have launched their coup, and in all likelihood Hitler would have been assassinated and the Nazi party decimated.

During this chaotic period there were three meetings between Chamberlain and Hitler: the first at Hitler's home, Berghof, at Berchtesgaden on September 15, 1938; the second at the resort town of Bad Godesburg, on September 22; the third and most infamous meeting, in Munich on September 29, with Mussolini and French Premier Daladier also in attendance. Czechoslovakia, part of whose country was being ceded to Germany at this meeting, was not invited to send top representatives. At each of these meetings Chamberlain yielded a little more to Hitler's demands until at Munich he literally gave Hitler everything he wanted. The only concession by Hitler was to delay the move into Sudetenland from October first to the tenth. Chamberlain commented during the course of the deliberations that he really didn't much care if the Sudeten Germans lived in Czechoslovakia or Germany, which opened the door for Hitler. He now knew there would be no ultimatum from France or Britain.

Great pressure was placed on Edvard Benes, president of Czechoslovakia, to cede the Sudeten territory to Germany. He at first refused, but under continuing pressure, he yielded, hoping Hitler would be satisfied with the Sudetenland. Benes had over 35 well armed divisions plus the excellent Skoda munition's plant, but he needed the support of France and Britain, which never materialized.

Chamberlain badly misread Hitler's psychopathic mind, making such statements as "Herr Hitler's objectives are strictly limited" and "Herr Hitler would be better than his word." For his concessions to Hitler, all Chamberlain got in return was a document, the substance of which was an insipid statement to the effect that Germany and Britain would never go to war against each other. Based on that vapid resolution, Chamberlain returned to London in triumph declaring, "My good friends, this is the second time in our history that there has come back from Germany to Downing Street, peace with honour. I believe it is peace in our time."

During this fateful September of 1938 the conspirators were poised to strike and desperately awaited the British-French ultimatum which never came. Hitler moved his army into the Sudetenland and then into the rest of Czechoslovakia. German forces triumphantly entered Prague in March, 1939, against ineffectual resistance. It was only after the German army attacked Poland in September, 1939, that Chamberlain and the British parliament realized Hitler had designs on the whole of Europe, including Britain. England and France then declared war on Germany and World War II was launched. Chamberlain had lost the confidence not only of Parliament but also of the public as well. He resigned in May of 1940 and died not long after. Churchill was voted into power and the monumental struggle which claimed millions of lives and untold suffering began its six-year run of hell on earth.

Had Britain issued an ultimatum and declared war on Germany for attacking Czechoslovakia, this would, according to Parsinnen, "have triggered the coup that had been so meticulously prepared by Oster and his fellow conspirators. If Hitler had been killed and the Nazis deposed, the coup would have brought into power men dedicated to restoring moral order to Germany and peace to Europe. World War II would never have taken place, fifty million people would not have lost their lives, and the shape of the twentieth century would have been vastly different."

Erich Kordt wrote, "The Munich Conference prevented the coup d'état in Berlin." Gisevius was even more blunt: "Chamberlain saved Hitler."

In the spring of 1939, the Allies tried vainly to form a mutual alliance with Russia. Maxim Litvinov, Russia's pro-western foreign secretary, attempted to forge a ten-year pact with France and England, but he was summarily replaced with hard-liner Vyacheslav Molotov (the "Hammer"), who not only scuttled the Allied Pact, but also began secret negotiations with Germany to sign a non-aggression pact. On August 23, 1939, the world was stunned to learn of this totally unexpected and unholy alliance. With Russia's cooperation, Hitler was now free to invade Poland, and then to direct his entire force against Western Europe. To complete Hitler's perfidy, in due time, Russia would become another of Germany's victims. Hitler rightly assumed that Stalin was as greedy and as unprincipled as he.

With this new unsavory partnership, it became apparent to the Allied Powers and especially to the Poles, that Poland was about to become Germany's next victim. Russia's cooperation with Germany was assured by the promise of the eastern half of Poland, the Baltic States, and Bessarabia. Finland would also be "fair game" if Russia was so inclined.

THE INVASION
OF POLAND

....

O N SEPTEMBER 1, 1939, THE GERMAN INFANTRY, ON TRUMPED-UP
charges against the Poles, stormed across the Polish border behind *Panzer*
tanks and *Stuka* dive bombers. The attack introduced the Poles and the rest of
the world to a new form of warfare, the *Blitzkrieg* (lightening war), with its devastating, destructive power. Two days later, a numbed and disbelieving England
and France, fulfilling their mutual protection pact with Poland, declared war
on Germany, and World War II officially began. Long-delayed military preparations, resulting from misguided disarmament policies, both in England and
France now confronted them with the chilling prospect of having to face this
new military juggernaut that was sweeping across Poland. From all appearances
it would soon turn its fury on the Low Countries (Belgium and the Netherlands)
and then on France and Britain. Except for the superior strength of the British
navy, the disparity between the German and Allied readiness was painfully
apparent. (MAP 1)

One very important additional military advantage Germany had over the
Allied forces was the practical war experience it had gained during the bloody
Spanish Civil War (1936–1939) on the side of Francisco Franco's Fascist regime.
Here Germany developed the technique of the *Blitzkrieg*, coordinating tanks,
dive bombers, and paratroops in rapid, demoralizing frontal assaults or pincer
attacks. Such attacks could quickly surround an entire enemy division, strike its
flanks, or even attack from the rear. German officers were more interested in the
process of that war than in its outcome. Franco ultimately won in May of 1939,
but at a tremendous cost to Spain: 600,000 war dead and 400,000 deaths from
privation, disease, and exposure.

Several factors resulted in Poland's crushing defeat in just over one month. First, Germany had almost total control of the air and was able to determine exactly where Poland's armed forces and logistical support were located, yet Poland had practically no knowledge of German troop movements. Second, the Germans utilized a totally novel approach that did not engage the Polish armies in frontal attacks, but instead destroyed rail lines, supply depots, and other logistical support behind the lines. They then surrounded the Polish armies in huge rapidly advancing pincer movements and confronted them with the miserable option of surrender or total annihilation. Probably the most important factor, however, was Russia's move into East Poland, which eliminated the Pole's planned option of retreating, and then regrouping in the eastern Pripet marshes. Another great disadvantage that hampered Poland's defense was the long delay, 36 hours or more, before marshalling any of their forces in late August, at the urging of France and England. Ostensibly the delay was to remove any excuse Germany might claim for their attack. Germany, of course, provided its own justification by capturing a few Poles at the border, clothing them in German uniforms, shooting them, and then blaming the Poles for unprovoked murder!

The German paratroop force, the *Condor Legion*, had developed its assault technique in the Spanish Civil War. The force helped attack the western forts of Poland near the German border, principally the fort city of Kaltowicz. Actually, they weren't needed because that whole area was enveloped by the *Blitzkrieg* advance.

The German occupation of Poland proved as horrible as the relentless pounding of the initial invasion. There were concentration camps and firing squads for political prisoners and death camps for Jews. There were 694,000 Polish prisoners of war in German camps, and 217,000 in camps of the Russians. The number of dead, wounded, and missing Poles will never be known. Germany counted only 10,572 dead, 30,322 wounded, and 3,409 missing in action. Russian losses were minimal.

Although Poland did not delay the Nazi war machine for long, nor inflict any serious damage to its army or air force, the Poles made one tremendous contribution to the ultimate victory of the Allies: they cracked the German radio code, *Enigma*, and shared this vital secret with Britain and France which dubbed it *Ultra Secret* or *Ultra* for short. The Allies used this knowledge to their great advantage throughout the war. The Nazis were so confident of the infallibility of their code, they could not conceive that any of their less bright enemies would ever break it.

From the fall of Poland in October, 1939, until April of 1940, there was a relatively quiet period on the western front. This was the "phony" war. During this time Hitler floated peace feelers to France and England, encouraging them to recognize the new border realities of Poland and its new political regime. He wanted an armistice with Britain and France now to eliminate the risk and burden of having to fight a war on two fronts when he launched his planned assault on Russia, which was his highest priority. These overtures were summarily rejected by the Allied powers which had finally awakened to Hitler's duplicitous nature.

Russo-Finnish and Scandinavian Wars

....

To no one's surprise, Russia attacked Finland on specious charges involving a border dispute on November 30, 1939. They struck with superior force but were repulsed by courageous, well-trained Finnish troops in guerrilla-type actions for a remarkable length of time. Finally, out-manned and out-gunned, Finland surrendered on March 12, 1940. What Russia had expected to accomplish easily as a two to three week military exercise, took over three months of bloody, costly fighting to achieve. Finland sustained a loss of 25,000 soldiers compared to 200,000 lost by Russia. Finland's heroic defense was heralded by free countries all over the world.

On April 9, 1940, Germany ended the phony war with a bang, invading Norway at six sites: Narvik in the north, Kristiansand in the south, and Stavanger, Bergen, Oslo, and Trondheim in between. The British navy exacted a huge toll against German surface ships on the North Sea coastal waters and fjords. British land forces could not dislodge the more powerful and better-situated German Army, so finally evacuated, thereby ceding Norway to Germany. Denmark fell to the Nazis in less than 48 hours. (Map 2)

Sweden's strict neutrality was not violated by Germany because the Swedes provided high-grade iron ore and other material for Germany's war machine. The Swedes were criticized by many for aiding Germany, but they didn't have much choice. As long as they cooperated with Germany, Sweden would not be attacked.

The German invasion of Norway was facilitated by a Norwegian naziphile, Vidkun Quisling. The betrayal of his country has made the word "quisling" synonymous with "traitor." Quisling, who was repudiated by King Haakon of Norway, tried to nazify the church, schools, and Norwegian youth. He persecuted the Jews, sending at least 1,000 to their deaths in concentration camps. Despite being hated by most Norwegians, under the protection of the occupying Germans, he held office until Norway was liberated in 1945, when he was captured by Allied forces, found guilty of treason, and executed on October 24, 1945.

Control of Norway and Denmark guaranteed the flow of war materiel from Sweden to Germany the year around, and the Nazis were delighted to add these countries to the Third Reich. After the "great Nazi victory," Sweden, of course, would be "invited" (forcibly if necessary) to join the Reich.

The Allies received bad press in the free world for their poor showing in Norway, but Germany earned much greater condemnation, especially in the United States, for its brutal, unprovoked assault on the Norwegians. The strict neutrality position of many Americans, including members of Congress, began to shift toward providing some material help to the Allies, at least on a cash and carry basis.

President F.D. Roosevelt recognized the Axis' intentions to conquer all of Europe and the Axis' great military superiority over the European Allies. Although the United States was a neutral power and the majority of the people and of the Congress preferred to stay out of the war, F.D.R. believed the United States would have to strengthen the besieged and faltering Allies.

In January, 1941, after a fishing trip in the Caribbean, Roosevelt came up with the brilliant concept of "Lend-Lease." The program permitted the Allied countries to obtain military supplies from the United States without having to pay for them. This included 50 WWI-era U.S. destroyers. Though this bill was fiercely debated in the U.S. Legislature, it passed in March, 1941. With its passage the United States became the principal arsenal to the Allies. Strict neutrality had to be breached to deliver military supplies: guns, ships, and tanks. The risk of our becoming actively involved in the war increased with every passing day.

To provide the maximum support to Britain and its courageous Prime Minister, Roosevelt arranged a meeting with Churchill at Argentia Bay, Newfoundland, August 9 to 12, 1941. The American President travelled there on the cruiser, *Augusta,* and the Prime Minister on the battleship, *Prince of Wales.*

They got along famously, and out of this meeting was developed the Atlantic Charter, which set forth certain fundamental tenets for the post-war world that were later incorporated in the Declaration of the United Nations. In addition, Churchill was able to reiterate his position that Britain would fight the war alone against the Nazis if the United States would provide the weapons. Little did they know that in less than four months the United States would become an active belligerent in the growing war.

Western European Attack—Dunkirk

....

T HE SCANDINAVIAN OPERATION, HOWEVER IMPORTANT, WAS MERELY THE prelude to the main event. The long delayed, all-out Nazi attack on the West was launched with spectacular success, May 10, 1940, one month after the invasion of Norway. At 0530, German parachute troops landed on the bridges of Rotterdam, Dordrecht, and Moerdijk, Holland, as well as on the fortress of Eben Emael in Belgium. From May 10 to 27, the German troops wheeled through Holland, Belgium, Luxembourg, and then west to France, toward Calais and the North Sea coast. Belgium's strict neutrality, which precluded stationing British troops in that country in the hope that this time they wouldn't be invaded by Germany, proved to be fruitless, and compromised any resistance Belgium might have mustered against the invading Germans.

Germany's success against the Allies was attributed not only to superior force, but to a brilliant strategy. German forces penetrated the Ardennes Forest between Sedan and Dinant in eastern France through a 50-mile gap between the Allied armies. The French command considered the area to be virtually impenetrable, so lightly defended it. This was, in effect, an end run around the Maginot Line, permitting Germany to march up eastern France to the sea almost unopposed.

On May 10, 1940, Prime Minister Chamberlain, the "appeaser," was replaced in office by the "warmonger," Winston Churchill. Chamberlain died six months later, a broken man.

A huge contingent of over 385,000 British, French, and Belgian soldiers were forced to retreat before the driving German Panzer divisions all the way to the harbor of the French coastal city, Dunkirk. Courageous rear-guard delaying action by the Allies and an inexplicable halt of the German invaders prevented Germany from decimating the entire Allied Army. Apparently the Germans needed a break from their mad dash west to service their tanks and rest the troops. They had the Allies surrounded, and with their superiority in the air, they could deal with the trapped armies almost at leisure. To their amazement and chagrin, between May 27 and June 4, 1940, 338,226 men, including approximately 120,000 French and Belgian troops, were evacuated from Dunkirk in one of the most daring and courageous escapes in recorded history. The trapped soldiers were miraculously spared certain death or imprisonment by the unprecedented participation of every available ship, private yacht, and fishing boat in Britain, a mass evacuation numbering thousands of soldiers. During this harrowing period, 200 British ships and 177 aircraft were lost. To provide as much space as possible on the ships for the soldiers, the Allies left behind 2,000 guns, 60,000 trucks, 76,000 tons of ammunition, and 600,000 tons of fuel and supplies. The British Isles were left practically unarmed. Though the loss of war materiel was great, the bulk of the British Army was saved. In a speech to the House of Commons on June 4, 1940, Churchill made it clear that before the British Isles fall to the enemy, the war would be carried on from all the countries of the Empire: "We shall fight on the beaches, we shall fight in the fields, we will never surrender!"

BATTLE FOR FRANCE

....

O N JUNE 5, 1940, THE DAY AFTER THE LAST ALLIED TROOPS WERE evacuated from Dunkirk, the battle for France began in earnest. The Nazi *Blitzkrieg* directed its fury southwest to advance rapidly into central France without serious opposition. By June 11, Rheims fell to the invading army, and Paris was declared an open city to prevent its total destruction. By June 14, 1940, Paris was occupied by German forces, and the French government moved from Tours to Bordeaux. By June 21, the battle for France was over, with Germany taking three-fifths of the country, and the remaining portion allotted to the existing French government, with Marshal Henri Philippe Pétain, WWI hero of Verdun, as its premier. The only reason Hitler did not occupy all of France was that he wanted to retain, on paper at least, a "sovereign" France which he concluded was the best way to prevent Britain from taking over the French Colonial Empire.

By June 25, 1940, all hostilities on French soil ceased and the armistice was signed. The terms of the Franco-German armistice were harsh. The cost of the German occupation would be borne by France, the French Army would be reduced to 100,000 men, and prisoners of war would not be released. (MAP 3)

During the brief battle for France there were 92,000 French soldiers killed, 250,000 wounded, and 1,500,000 taken prisoner. Britain's losses were 3,500 soldiers killed and 14,000 wounded; Belgium suffered 7,500 killed and 16,000 wounded; Holland, 2,900 dead and 7,000 wounded. Compared to Allied losses, Germany had relatively few: 27,000 killed, 111,000 wounded, and 18,000 missing.

The French government moved from Bordeaux to Vichy. It was soon called the Vichy government of "Vichy France," in actuality a mere puppet government of Germany. The chief collaborators who believed they would have a better chance directing the destiny of France if they cooperated with the Nazis, were Pétain, Admiral Jean François Darlan, chief of the French navy, and Pierre Laval, the most hated of all the turncoats. They were convinced that Germany would easily defeat the Allies.

When Vichy France requested release from the Franco-British mutual defense pact, Churchill agreed, on condition that the French fleet not fall into the hands of the Germans, and either sail to British or neutral ports, or be scuttled.

An unfortunate incident occurred on July 3, 1940, shortly after the dissolution of the mutual defense pact. Fearing that vital French ships moored in the harbor of Mers-el-Kebir, Algeria, adjacent to Oran, would fall into German hands, the British launched a naval operation, *Catapult,* to either neutralize these ships, or destroy as many as possible. Due to a communication mix-up, the deadline for the French admiral's response was not met (although his intention was to comply), so the British ships opened fire on the French fleet, severely damaging four ships and killing 1,300 French sailors. Several ships, including an aircraft carrier, managed to run the British blockade and escaped.

Needless to say, French reaction to this incident was extremely hostile, and for a time it appeared that France might declare war on Britain. Fortunately, this anger subsided in the realization that now only Britain stood against Germany's conquest of all of Europe and was France's only hope for salvation from Nazi tyranny. Crippling or destroying the French fleet before it fell to Germany was imperative to preserve Britain's naval superiority and to prevent an imminent German invasion of Britain. In answer to the severe criticism Britain received for destroying French ships, including the condemnation of General Charles de Gaulle, leader of the *Free France Organization,* then exiled in London, Churchill responded in a speech to the House of Commons on July 4, 1940: "I leave the judgment of our actions with confidence to Parliament; I leave it to the nation; I leave it to the world and to history."

Battle for Britain

....

WITH THE DEFEAT OF FRANCE, HITLER TURNED HIS ATTENTION TO THE Battle for Britain. The planned German invasion of Britain, *Operation Sea Lion,* would be launched in waves from multiple staging sites in France, to a broad expanse of England's coast. Although the German high command was leery about the success of such a venture, their fears were allayed by Herman Göring's guarantee of the destruction of the Royal Air Force (R.A.F.) within four weeks and complete German domination of the air over Britain and the English Channel.

Accordingly, *Operation Sea Lion* was delayed to late September to permit prior destruction of the Royal Air Force. On August 11, the battle for Britain began with Göring's categorical order to the Luftwaffe: "Crush the British Air Force by every means available."

Waves of German fighter planes and bombers attacked Channel coastal targets in daytime raids. Over 200 planes struck radar stations in Portland and Weymouth on the south coast of England. Britain could launch only about 1,100 planes, (740 fighter planes and 350 bombers) compared to 2,669 German aircraft, mostly bombers. However, Britain enjoyed the definite superiority of the British fighter plane, especially the *Spitfire,* over the German bombers. For example, the German *Stuka* bomber had a maximum speed of 190 m.p.h. and a ceiling of 11,000 feet. The *Spitfire* could reach speeds of 375 m.p.h. with a ceiling of 33,000 feet and was far more maneuverable. On this first day of bomber raids, the Luftwaffe lost 45 planes to the R.A.F.'s 13 planes and seven pilots.

In addition to *Ultra,* radar was another great advantage the British Air Force had over the Luftwaffe. This permitted them to "see" enemy planes at night and determine the size and location of bombing attacks. The Germans knocked out some of these radar stations, but radar continued to be operational to varying degrees throughout the war.

Failure of the Luftwaffe to destroy the R.A.F. and gain total air control resulted in Hitler postponing the invasion of Britain until the spring of 1941. The skill and courage of the R.A.F. prompted Churchill to remark, "Never in the field of human conflict was so much owed by so many to so few."

The Battle for Britain then became one of heavy bombing raids, at first over principal military targets in daylight raids, but as Germany's air losses mounted, mostly as night raids over cities, with indiscriminate targets, including residential areas, churches, hospitals and even Buckingham Palace. The city of Coventry, including the magnificent Coventry Cathedral, was almost totally demolished the night of November 14, 1940. Although Britain knew ahead of time that Coventry was going to be bombed, it did not want to respond too soon for fear that Germany would then know it had broken their code.

The object of the German attack became one of pounding Britain so relentlessly that a demoralized British people would sue for peace. Meanwhile, during the latter half of 1940, Britain began bombing attacks on German cities including Berlin, Kiel, and Cologne. Hitler was furious at Britain's bombing of German cities and vowed, "If they bomb our cities we will simply erase theirs!"

Despite the extensive destruction of her cities and the loss of thousands of lives, British resolve never wavered in its determination to continue the battle against Germany.

Later in the war, Dresden's total destruction in February of 1945 by both British and U.S. bombers was United Kingdom's revenge for Coventry—and for London, Plymouth, and Southampton as well. This abhorrent debacle was totally unnecessary militarily. The war was almost over, the Allies had total control of the air, and they were rapidly advancing on the ground. From 30,000 to 60,000 civilians were killed and priceless historic monuments were totally destroyed. Such are the horrible vagaries and tragedies of war. "They did it to us so we are justified in doing it to them." What can you say?

A change in Hitler's overall strategy became apparent with his signing of Directive No. 20, which outlined his plans for the invasion of Russia. Hitler now felt that Britain was close to being knocked out of the war, and it would soon be safe to begin his major offensive east, into Russia, to fulfill the most important aspect of his war agenda. In his book, *Mein Kampf,* Hitler declared a policy priority: the acquisition of most or all of Russia for the future growth of the great Aryan people.

Another important factor leading to Hitler's decision to attack Russia early was to make use of the huge army he had crowding the eastern coastal areas of the English Channel. The alternative was to keep these troops stationed in western France all winter and spring, hoping for suitable conditions to launch *Operation Sea Lion* in early summer.

The Luftwaffe had failed to destroy the R.A.F., and British surface naval strength was far superior to that of Germany, making a Channel crossing too hazardous. Furthermore, Hitler was convinced that Germany would defeat Russia in a matter of a few months. Germany would then turn its full attention back to Britain for a quick victory there as well.

RUDOLPH HESS

On May 10, 1941, shortly before Germany invaded Russia, a bizarre incident occurred that caught the attention of the world. Forty-seven-year-old Rudolph Hess, the number-three man in the German hierarchy behind Hitler and Göring, on his own initiative and without the knowledge or permission of Hitler, flew an unarmed plane to Scotland to single-handedly broker a peace between England and Germany. He had met the Duke of Hamilton at the 1936 World Olympics in Berlin, and sensed that he was favorably disposed toward the Nazi movement and might now serve as a contact with influential members of the British Parliament. The deal he planned to present was that Germany would guarantee not to invade the British Isles or any part of the British Empire, in exchange for which Britain would promise not to interfere with Germany's impending war on Bolshevism. Britain would also have to agree to eliminate Churchill from leadership.

Unfortunately for Hess, he broke his ankle parachuting from his plane, was apprehended by a Scottish farmer wielding a pitchfork, and never did see the Duke of Hamilton. This escapade provided great propaganda for the British

War Office that needed all the help it could get during those very bleak times. The War Office heralded the episode as proof that the top German command was beginning to crack.

Hitler was furious, and wrote off the entire event in the German press as the action of a hallucinating madman. Rudolph Hess was found guilty at the war crime trials in Nuremberg and spent the rest of his life imprisoned in Spandau, Germany. He died in 1986.

NORTH AFRICA AND THE MEDITERRANEAN

....

WITH THE IMMINENT FALL OF FRANCE, AND THE BATTLE FOR BRITAIN about to begin, on June 10, 1940, Mussolini, sensing a great opportunity to extend Italy's holdings in North Africa to include Egypt and the Suez canal, declared war on the Allied countries. Italy had held Libya since 1911, and with the fall of France, Tunisia, Algeria, and French Morocco would be essentially neutralized. Italy had already conquered Ethiopia in a rogue attack in 1936, and since then had extended its holdings to the Sudan and British Somaliland. Eritrea and Italian Somaliland were already in Italy's column.

The stage was now set for Italy to launch a giant pincer attack against the British garrison in Egypt. Existing troops would march northward up the Nile valley from the horn of Africa, with a second army marching east from a landing in Libya to Cairo. Destruction of the British Army in Egypt and control of the Suez Canal would make Mussolini's fondest dream come true: the Mediterranean would become *Mare Nostrum* (Our Sea).

Thus motivated, on June 28, 1940, Mussolini sent 250,000 troops to Libya for the move east to crush the vastly outnumbered British forces lodged in Egypt. Unfortunately for his cause, the Italian commander, Graziani, delayed any movement out of Libya until September 13, 1940, when he led his troops 60 miles into Egypt, where they seized the small town of Sidi Barini with much fanfare and jubilant media coverage back home. Here the fatal stalling tactics continued while the Italian Army developed an elaborate defensive fortress with all the comforts of home.

Meanwhile, the British Army, led by Field-Marshal Sir Archibald Wavell, far smaller but much better equipped and seasoned to desert warfare, discovered a 15-mile gap in the Italian defenses. On December 15, 1940, British troops exploited the gap with stunning success. During the two-month campaign which followed, British Commonwealth forces drove the Italians west to Benghazi, Libya, capturing the Italian stronghold of Tobruk on the way. Over 120,000 Italian prisoners plus 400 tanks and more than 1,200 guns were captured. When asked how many Italians he had captured, one battalion commander responded, "Five acres of officers, and 200 acres of other ranks."

With the remainder of the Italian troops retreating pell-mell towards Tripoli at the western end of Libya, Hitler became alarmed that the possible defeat of Italy would expose Germany's southern flank. Hitler reluctantly dispatched troops, tanks, and planes to Africa, with Erwin Rommel to head the *Afrika Korps*.

Rommel, 49 years old, had become one of Hitler's favorite officers, following his success in leading the 7th *Panzer Division* to many victories in France. Some of his exploits bordered on the miraculous, with flanking attacks of 150 miles in a day around enemy emplacements, then striking from the rear. These unexpected rear guard appearances awed the French soldiers and earned the 7th *Panzer* group the name *Phantom Division*. Hitler particularly liked Rommel's unconventional style which generated the deep respect of his troops, and inspired them to extend themselves to the very limit of their endurance. (Map 4)

Following the landing of the *Afrika Korps* in Tripoli, on February 14, 1941, Rommel quickly organized his forces and after briefly scouting enemy positions, began an immediate march eastward across the desert. This drive moved well, encountering little enemy resistance. What Rommel didn't realize was that on February 11, 1941, just before his arrival in Africa, the British had diverted a large number of troops from North Africa to fight the Axis invasion of Greece. Mussolini, after taking defenseless Albania, wanted to conquer Greece on his own, without notifying Hitler. He deliberately snubbed Hitler in this adventure, because Hitler had taken the Roumanian oil fields on October 11, 1940, without informing Mussolini. Mussolini wanted to get even. On October 28, 1940, Italy invaded Greece from Albania. Unfortunately for Mussolini, Greek resistance proved too great, and after several months of fighting, the Italian invaders were thrown out of Greece. Only Hitler's later intervention saved the day for Italy.

Yugoslavia infuriated Hitler by sustaining an anti-German coup d'état which brought them immediate and bloody retribution. Both Yugoslavia and Greece were smashed to submission in less than a month, revealing the stark contrast in military strength between Germany and Italy. This fiasco, however, came at the wrong time for Hitler's time table since it necessitated diverting troops and heavy equipment into Yugoslavia and Greece in April 1941, which delayed the start of Germany's invasion of Russia, *Operation Barbarossa,* from May 1 to June 22, 1941.

The course of the war in North Africa raged back and forth and back again across the desert, with changes in fortune between belligerents occurring at frequent but unexpected intervals. Both sides had excellent generalship, but Rommel, most of the time, was forced to do with much less than his British counterparts, and he exhibited amazing creativity and daring to compensate for this deficiency. If the North African War were the World Series, Rommel would most likely have won the M.V.P. award for desert generalship, even though he lost the war. British General Bernard Montgomery was also a great leader and tactician, but he refused to initiate an attack until he had a full complement of well-equipped fighting troops and reserves.

The success of all operations depended upon providing logistical support to often greatly extended battle lines. When adequately supplied, either side was capable of making great gains. Ultimately the Allies won because they were able to out-supply and out-man the Axis. Another important factor in the Allied victory in North Africa was the United States' debut into the European Theater of War on December 11, 1941, shortly after Pearl Harbor. The United States provided ever-increasing war materiel to the British military forces.

On June 21, 1942, Rommel recaptured Tobruk, where he gained needed supplies. He continued east to El Alamein, where he was stopped by determined and better-equipped British troops. Rommel's lines were again stretched thin, and too many Axis convoy ships were being sunk to permit further advance.

By contrast, Montgomery's army was up to full strength with large numbers of new tanks, some of them American *Sherman* tanks, heavy weapons, and air cover.

Soon the great Allied pendulum began swinging west again, and Rommel's forces were defeated in the great battle of El Alamein. They were then driven out of Tobruk all the way back to Tunisia, where they dug in and were quite well, though only intermittently, supplied.

On November 8, 1942, combined British and American troops, under the command of General Dwight D. Eisenhower, launched *Operation Torch*, a massive invasion into west North Africa, the first significant American involvement in the European war with Major General George S. Patton leading the American forces on the ground. With landings in Morocco, on the Atlantic side of Gibraltar, and two in Algeria, on the Mediterranean side, this three-pronged invasion was designed to crush the Axis Army in Tunisia between the advancing Montgomery forces, driving west and the invading *Operation Torch* armies, grinding east.

Fortunately for the Allied cause, Admiral Jean Darlan, the French collaborationist mentioned earlier, was in Algeria visiting his polio-stricken son. Allied leaders sought Darlan's help in reducing French-African resistance to the Allied invaders, especially in the coastal cities. Since Hitler had violated the French-German treaty earlier by occupying Vichy France, Darlan had become disenchanted with the Nazis. He agreed to use his influence to halt French resistance to the Allied landings. Indeed his intervention helped the Allied cause immensely, but because he was a traitor to both sides, he became a liability to the Allies, and they didn't know exactly how to handle the situation. De Gaulle was furious at this duplicity, and the Allied top brass were taking heat from all sides. Fortuitously for everyone except Darlan, he was assassinated by a dissident French student monarchist, Bonnier de Chapelle, on Christmas Eve, 1942. Darlan had served a very useful purpose in effecting a cease-fire on the part of most of the French colonialists and "bowed out" at just the right time. Allied condolences were tempered privately with great relief. Whether Chapelle acted independently, was an agent for William J. (Wild Bill) Donovan, founder and Chief of the U.S. Office of Strategic Services (OSS), forerunner of the CIA, or was "handled" by Sir Stewart Menzies, Chief of the British Secret Service (SOE), will perhaps never be known. Both Donovan and Menzies were in North Africa at the time of the assassination, and both reviled Darlan.

A few additional facts regarding W.J. Donovan, are appropriate here. A classmate of F.D.R. at Columbia Law School in 1907, Donovan became an advisor to the President during the years leading up to and during WWII. Roosevelt valued his advice and credited him with being his eyes, ears, and legs in the hot spots of the world. In 1938 and 1939, he had lengthy visits with Hitler, Stalin, and Mussolini. Donovan drew conclusions regarding their military intentions that flatly opposed the conclusions of Chamberlain, Charles Lindbergh, or Joseph Kennedy.

Donovan's primary contribution to the Allied victory was his complete change of the style and conduct of war intelligence and unconventional warfare. Although Secretary of War Henry L. Stimson declared "Gentlemen do not read other people's mail," Donovan held a radical modus operandi: in war, "anything goes." He used "disinformation," psychological warfare, sabotage, assassination, rescue missions, and deception as attack weapons.

His courageous and brilliant service during both WWI and WWII earned him the four highest medals attainable in the United States: the Distinguished Service Medal, the Distinguished Service Cross, the Congressional Medal of Honor, and the National Service Medal. No American has received as many sterling awards. He also received medals from fifteen other countries.

His unusual, occasionally bizarre, methods created a number of detractors and enemies within the U.S. Government, including J. Edgar Hoover, Harry Hopkins, Secretary Stimson, and for a time, President Truman.

Following Darlan's death, General Henri Giraud, Chief of the French 9th Army, who had escaped a Nazi prison camp in 1942, was appointed High Commissioner of all of French North Africa by the Allied Chiefs of staff. Roosevelt, who disliked de Gaulle intensely, approved Giraud's selection. De Gaulle, however, raised such a ruckus, that Giraud was eventually eased out in de Gaulle's favor.

The key to the Allied final North African victory over the Axis in May, 1943, was control of the Mediterranean sea lanes. By retaining the strategic island of Malta (the "bone in Italy's throat," and the "unsinkable aircraft carrier" of Britain), despite horrific bombing attacks, the Allies managed to maintain control over the two most important access points to the Mediterranean: the Strait of Gibraltar, west, and the Suez Canal, east, and thus cripple the Italian Navy. If Hitler had convinced Spain's dictator Franco to join the Axis to dislodge Britain from Gibraltar, or if Rommel had captured the Suez Canal, or if Mussolini's planned invasion of Malta had not been canceled and the invasion force diverted to augment Rommel's drive east, the Axis would likely have won the Desert War. WWII would probably have lasted much longer, resolved with a brokered armistice instead of an unconditional surrender.

THE CASABLANCA CONFERENCE

During the fighting in North Africa, Churchill and Roosevelt met for ten days in Casablanca, Morocco, in late January, 1943. Stalin claimed he was too busy directing the war against Germany to attend. Despite Stalin's pressure on the United States and Britain to launch a cross-Channel attack into France in 1943, the Western Allies determined that this would be impossible until some time in 1944. To placate Stalin, at least to some extent, they did agree to invade Sicily, Italy, and then Southern France immediately after what appeared to be an imminent victory in North Africa. In actuality, the Allied attack in North Africa was a great boon to Stalin because it diverted vital German troops, supplies, and airplanes to Africa and away from the desperate battle for Stalingrad.

It was at the Casablanca Conference that Roosevelt announced to the world that the Allies would continue the war against the Axis until they achieved an "unconditional surrender." Churchill took exception to this position, or at least to announcing it, because he believed it would serve only to increase Axis resistance and thereby lengthen the war. He did not, however, favor an armistice.

The Axis Army in Tunisia was partially re-supplied by Germany from Sicily for this final battle, but these efforts were inadequate. During several months of bloody fighting, Axis forces conducted desperate rear-guard actions designed to prevent the eastern, Montgomery-led 8th Army from joining the Allied forces from the west in Tunisia. During these final struggles, on February 19–20, 1943, a large American component of mostly inexperienced troops was attacked and beaten in the Kasserine Pass by Rommel. The news of this setback caused great concern throughout Allied countries, but the defeat only delayed and did not stop the now greatly superior Allied armies. The jaws of the giant Allied pincers finally closed around the remaining Axis troops in Tunisia. They surrendered to the Allies on May 13, 1943. Over 250,000 German and Italian soldiers were taken prisoner. Had Hitler or Mussolini granted Rommel's urgent request to evacuate his troops from Tunisia before they were overrun, all these soldiers would have been able to fight another day.

The final strongholds to fall were Tunis and Bizerte located across the narrow Strait of Sicily. Their fall set the stage for *Operation Husky,* the invasion of Sicily, and the beginning of the arduous battle for the mainland of Italy.

The Battle for Sicily and Italy

....

T HE ROUGH TERRAIN OF SICILY, WITH ITS PEAKS, VALLEYS AND NARROW mountain roads, sharply contrasted with the flat desert sands of most of North Africa. But the Allies adapted quickly to this new environment, conquering the island in just 39 days. Messina surrendered to General Patton's troops on August 17, 1943. Patton edged out Montgomery in their race to this east coast city. Unfortunately, almost all of the Axis soldiers (about 100,000) and equipment escaped across the Messina Strait to Italy.

During the battle for Sicily, great unrest arose in Italy. On July 25, 1943, Mussolini was deposed by his own Fascist Council, and Marshal Pietro Badoglio was appointed Prime Minister by King Victor Emmanuel III. Further evidence of the crumbling Italian resistance surfaced on August 31, 1943, when the Italian government requested an armistice with the Allies, to be announced at the time of the principal Allied landing on the Italian mainland.

In an incident publicized all over the world, General Patton, while visiting an army tent hospital in Sicily, used his glove to slap a sick soldier across his face. Patton called the man a disgrace to the United States and a coward because he had no obvious wounds or bandages. Patton mistook him for a malingerer, when in actuality, he was suffering from malaria and chronic dysentery. After a second similar and even more outrageous episode, Eisenhower reprimanded Patton severely and demanded he make a public apology to all concerned. Though Eisenhower temporarily relieved Patton of his command, he considered him too valuable an asset to have him permanently sacked or court-martialed.

The invasion of Italy began on September 3, 1943, with a decoy landing by Montgomery's Eighth Army on the Calabrian coast. The main event, *Operation*

Avalanche, occurred on September 5. Mark Clark's combined U.S. Fifth Army landed on the beaches of Salerno, located on the west coast, a little north of the decoy. On September 8, 1943, Eisenhower announced to the world the unconditional surrender of Italy, and its pledge to help eject the German aggressor from Italian soil. (MAP 5)

SALERNO

Operation Avalanche at Salerno came as no surprise to the ready Germans. They blasted it unmercifully with powerful shore batteries and *Luftwaffe* bombing runs. This was a truly "hot" beach and only after nine days of desperate fighting was the beachhead finally secured. This was the first large-scale opposed landing on the European continent, and it came within two miles of being pushed back into the sea. There were 3,500 American and 5,500 British casualties. The Allies were now in Europe to stay.

There was a sharp difference of opinion between Churchill and Roosevelt regarding the invasion of Italy. Churchill viewed it as a major invasion into the soft "underbelly of Europe." Roosevelt and General George C. Marshall saw it as a diversion to draw German troops away from the proposed cross-Channel invasion of Normandy. Both sides recognized its value in providing at least a partial response to Stalin's insistent demand for an immediate Second Front.

The Italian campaign strategy unfolded extemporaneously. It grew from initial plans to secure only the southern half of Italy. Later plans involved conquering the entire country. The surrender of Italy to the Allies was an important factor in this decision.

Churchill, fearing Russian seizure of the Balkans, wanted the Allies to continue north to occupy those countries as well. This strategy, however, was firmly rejected by the Americans. They wanted to launch the Second Front in Western Europe in May, 1944, in order to knock out Germany as soon as possible by a direct, overwhelming blow, which would then permit the United States to concentrate its forces in the Pacific against Japan. Stalin strongly opposed Western Allied occupation of the Balkans for the obvious reason that he wanted them.

To comprehend the magnitude of the problems facing the invading Allied armies, one must appreciate the geography of Italy and visualize a well armed German army securely lodged in multiple strongly defended bastions across the Italian peninsula.

The Apennine mountain range, like a giant spine, runs longitudinally down most of the 750-mile length of Italy, with jagged ridges, like ribs, that extend laterally for 80 to 120 miles. Its multiple cliffs, peaks, valleys, and rivers are difficult to cross at any time; they are close to impossible to cross during the winter and spring thaw, especially in the face of well entrenched enemy fire. Tanks are useless over this terrain. Northern Italy is protected by the Italian Alps, higher and more rugged than the Apennines. The only decent tank terrain that could benefit the Allies in their drive north was the Po Valley plain of Lombardy, north of Bologna, but a long, rugged distance from the Salerno beach head.

The inhospitable terrain of Italy, together with its cold, wet, and snowy winter weather, made the Italian campaign one of the longest and most difficult of the war, lasting almost two years. It is impossible to do justice to the problems and suffering experienced by the combatants involved in the Italian war in this brief account, but a quote from a closing paragraph in a Time-Life book, *Italian Campaign,* is apropos: "The campaign for Italy, a grinding bloody, inch by inch slog through mountains that seemed to go on forever, was finally coming to an end."

ANZIO

With the American Fifth Army moving up the Tyrrhenian coast on the west and the British Eighth Army moving up the Adriatic coast on the east, conquering Rome became the principal military and propaganda objective. To accomplish this end, a third amphibious landing, *Operation Shingle,* was launched on the west coast at Anzio, just below Rome, at about the same time the formidable mountain fortress, Monte Cassino, was attacked. The landings at Anzio were virtually unopposed, but the nine-day delay readying the troops for the drive north allowed German forces to move in and almost wipe out the Allied invaders. In contrast to Salerno, Anzio started easy, but ended tough.

MONTE CASSINO

The battle for Monte Cassino was one of the bloodiest of the war. Numerous frontal attacks by Allied forces involved hand-to-hand combat up the steep cliff sides.

Italy, the home of some of the greatest art treasures in the world, posed problems to all combatants who strove to minimize damage to these magnificent structures, yet accomplish their military objectives. One such Solomonaic conundrum for the Allies was what to do with the Benedictine Monastery atop Monte Cassino, 1,700 feet above the valley. This monastery had been founded by Saint Benedict in 529 CE was revered throughout the Christian world, but was now considered by the Allies to be a fortress for the German Army and the reason for their failure to capture Monte Casino.

Following much soul searching and argument, the decision was made to carpet-bomb the monastery, after a two-day warning, to allow for the evacuation of the monks and their associates. Unfortunately, through some communication error, 600 tons of bombs were dropped on the target one day early, killing many of the inhabitants. Ironically, it was later discovered that the Germans had assiduously kept their soldiers out of the monastery and worse, that the remaining walls and rubble afforded an excellent redoubt for the besieged Germans.

On May 18, 1944, an Allied assault by 46,000 Polish troops attacked Monte Cassino in waves and after heavy losses, wrested it from the German defenders, opening the way to Rome.

THE FALL OF ROME

Acquiring Monte Cassino created the opportunity for General Mark Clark to cut off and destroy or capture the bulk of the German Army as they retreated in disarray. Instead, much to the chagrin of the British officers, he elected to go straight for Rome to be the first to enter the city, which he did in early June. Clark defended his action as strategically sound, but was roundly criticized as being motivated by personal aggrandizement and for putting a strain on British-

American relations. The drive to Rome cost the Allies 40,000 casualties and the Germans 38,000.

Pisa fell to the Allies on September 5, 1944, but the drive north was temporarily halted by winter weather and German rear-guard defensive action. During spring of 1945, the Fifth and Eighth Allied armies united north of Bologna and drove the retreating German soldiers across the Lombardy plains where they surrendered by the thousands.

The Allied cause was greatly aided by the Italian partisan attacks on the Germans in Genoa, Turin, and Milan. For every German soldier killed by a partisan, the Germans would kill ten Italian partisans or other adult males. By the time the Allies reached these northern cities, the German garrisons had been taken over by the partisans. At the end of April, 1945, the battle for Italy was won, and the war in Europe was rapidly approaching its final stages.

MUSSOLINI'S DEMISE

One of the most interesting episodes associated with the Italian war was the arrest and imprisonment of Mussolini, followed by his "mission impossible" rescue from prison by Hitler.

Mussolini had been moved from prison to prison, and for maximum security, under heavy guard, was finally moved to the Hotel del Gran Sasso, a remote ski resort inn located on a 6,500-foot-high mountain plateau. After clever sleuthing, one of Hitler's top SS agents, Captain Otto Skorzeny, managed to land 100 soldiers via gliders and one small plane on the mountain plateau, subdue the guards, and fly off the mountain with the Duce. He was then transferred to a larger plane and flown to Munich, where he met his wife, and then to Rastenberg in East Prussia, to join Hitler on September 14, 1943.

Hitler then forced Mussolini to establish a new Fascist Republic in northern Italy with German supervision. All the members of the Grand Council who had voted against Mussolini were executed, including his own son-in-law, Ciano.

By this time, the people of Italy had come to hate and distrust Mussolini, and this disaffection grew as the Allies plodded north. In April, 1945, with the

Allies and the partisans moving north, Mussolini fled by truck, disguised as a German soldier, toward Austria. He was apprehended by a group of partisan soldiers who recognized him as the Duce by his expensive boots.

The following day, together with his mistress, Claretta Petacci, he was executed by machine-gun fire at point-blank range.

Their bodies were dumped in front of a garage in Milan's Piazzale Loreto and then hung upside down. Crowds that gathered spat on Mussolini and riddled his body with machine-gun and small-arms fire in vengeance for the loss of loved ones. Two years after his arrest, Mussolini once commented on his life, "From dust to power and from power back to dust."

Mussolini's ignominious demise stemmed from greed and love of power. He went from being a mediator trying to broker peace between the Allied countries and Germany at Munich in 1938, to joining the Nazis in 1940. By uniting with the Axis powers, he hoped to share in some of Hitler's growing acquisitions. A whole new colonial empire beckoned him. At the very least, he hoped to annex Southern France. He had no sense of what was morally right or wrong for Europe, but only what would benefit Italy and redound to his glory.

As a result of this egregious amoral position, he brought tremendous suffering, privation, and death to millions of his own people, and total economic collapse to his country.

BARBAROSSA— THE INVASION OF RUSSIA

....

O N JUNE 22, 1941, GERMANY LAUNCHED THE GREATEST MILITARY operation in history, code-named *Barbarossa* after the red-bearded twelfth-century German Emperor, Frederick I, who had waged a successful war against the Slavs. More than three million soldiers, (80 percent of the German Army), together with over 3,300 tanks, 600,000 other vehicles, 7,000 artillery pieces, 2,770 airplanes, and 625,000 horses were strategically ranged along the 1,350-mile western border of the Soviet Union, extending from the Baltic Sea, to the Black Sea. As the invasion progressed, the German front took on a funnel shape stretching the attack line to 2,000 miles.

Even more astonishing than the immensity of this invasion was the almost total absence of any effective defensive readiness by Russia. Despite many warnings from bona fide sources to Stalin of its imminence, including the exact date and time, the Soviets were ill-prepared. The movement of this huge military force from Western Europe to the Russian border, with many reconnaissance flights over Russia in the months preceding June 22, was also known to Stalin, but enigmatically ignored. In the absence of any explanation from Stalin himself, the prevailing theory for this strange failure to prepare holds that Stalin expected an ultimatum from Germany with new demands prior to any attack. This was the approach Hitler had used with his other acquisitions. These negotiations would have bought more time for military preparations. A few more months of stalling would have precluded a German invasion in 1941 because of the proximity of winter. By 1942, Russia would be much stronger, and Stalin had voiced serious consideration to invading Germany during that year to stamp out German Fascism, the arch-enemy of Communism. Another theory holds that Stalin considered the buildup of military strength in eastern Europe by the Nazis to be a ploy to deceive Great Britain into thinking the Germans were going to strike east when in actuality they were going to invade Britain. This misconception was supported by Hitler's false assurances to Stalin that he was moving troops east to protect them from British bombing.

Whatever his true rationale, Stalin apparently did not want to provoke Hitler and provide him with an excuse to attack Russia, so he steadfastly and blindly clung to the status quo. It was not until 0715 on June 22, 1941, almost four hours after the invasion had begun, that Stalin authorized the Russian Army to fight the invading hordes. This order was accompanied by the strange and irrelevant admonition that the Red Army was not to cross the boundary into Germany. An error of this magnitude would have resulted in impeaching, sacking, or shooting the leader at some point in most countries. But not in Russia, where Stalin firmly held all the levers of power and was not vulnerable to liquidation.

Another important factor in Russia's poor military preparedness was Stalin's political purges. These eliminated, through execution or imprisonment, 30,000 army and navy officers (90 percent of the generals and 80 percent of the colonels). Their duties were assumed by Communist functionaries (Commissars). The lack of expert military leadership was obvious in the poorly fought Russo-Finnish war when 200,000 Finish soldiers held off one million Russians for four months. One Finnish officer likened the Russian Army to a "badly conducted orchestra."

Hitler was well aware of Russia's weaknesses. When Hitler was confronted by his own generals with the risk of a two-front war, especially against a country the size of the Soviet Union, he responded, "Just kick in the door and the whole rotten structure will collapse."

He also pointed out that it really wasn't a two front war, because "England is beaten and only a little remains to be done."

Hitler expected to conquer Russia in eight to ten weeks. Based on this optimistic analysis, only 20 percent of the German Army was provided with winter gear. He predicted that most of the army would be back home before the onset of winter.

In the rosy glow of supreme optimism, confident of early victory, Germany struck at the appointed day and hour, 0330 on June 22, 1941, against an unwitting and fortuitously compliant enemy.

The attacking German Army was divided into three major forces. The first force, Army Group North, under the leadership of Field Marshal Wilhelm Ritter von Leeb, struck from East Prussia northeast to Leningrad, securing the Baltic Sea flank with help from Finland. The second battle group, Army Group Center led by Field Marshal Fedor von Bock, struck from East Prussia and Poland in two prongs designed to encircle most of the Red Army, capture Smolensk, Minsk and ultimately the grand prize, Moscow. The third branch, Army Group South led by Field Marshal Gerd von Runstedt, and helped by Roumania, attacked from Poland across Russia's richest food source, the Ukraine, to seize Kiev. This group would then assault the heavily industrialized basin of the Donet's River, then strike toward Stalingrad, the Crimean peninsula, Sevastopol, the Caucasus, the Baku oil fields, and on into the Middle East. Hitler expected the British Army to be defeated in North Africa and the Axis to take the Suez Canal to meet Army Group South in the Middle East, to seize control of the world's largest source of oil. Heinz Guderion, originator and master of *Panzer* warfare, was attached to Army Group South. The supreme commander of the entire Eastern Front was Field Marshal Walter von Brauchitsch.

The overall plan was to conquer only the well developed western quarter of the Soviet Union up to a line roughly from Archangel on the Barents Sea, in the north, to the Caspian Sea, just east of the Volga river, in the south. The Russian Army would be destroyed in giant pincer maneuvers that had proved so successful in Poland and France. The rest of the population would be neutralized through systematic extermination, starvation, or slavery. Whoever managed to escape into the vast hinterland east of the Ural mountains would be no threat to German-occupied western Russia. Hitler's dream of *lebensraum* for the Aryan race, expressed so vividly in *Mein Kampf,* was about to come true.

The initial drives of the German armies met with great success on dry roads and firm fields against a surprised and disorganized enemy. Rivers were crossed in record time. Whole divisions of the Red Army were encircled, killed, or captured. Hundreds of thousands of prisoners clogged roads as they were herded west by their captors. Special, watertight *Panzer* tanks with breathing tubes and periscopes were used to cross the Bug River, 13 feet underwater. Here was modern warfare functioning at its very best.

LENINGRAD

....

As Army Group North fought its way towards Leningrad, perhaps only a few soldiers realized this beautiful city, the "Venice of the North," had been built by Czar Peter the Great in the eighteenth century as a "window to the west." Located on the Karelian Isthmus, between the Gulf of Finland and Lake Lagoda, Leningrad, or St. Petersburg as it was known then, was built on one hundred small islands in the center of swamp land.

Leningrad was Russia's leading industrial center, and manufacturer of munitions, trucks, and ships. It was also a cultural center with opera, ballet, and theater. The Hermitage museum contains some of the greatest art in the world.

Following the Bolshevik Revolution, the name, St. Petersburg, was changed to Leningrad. Hitler hated Leningrad for being the birthplace of Communism and once remarked, "Leningrad is a poisonous nest that must vanish from the earth's surface."

To accomplish this end, 340,000 German troops with help from Finland surrounded the city. Hitler's professed plan was to "Render Leningrad uninhabitable so as to relieve us of the necessity of having to feed the population during the winter."

By September, the encirclement was complete. The Finnish troops occupied the northern approach to Leningrad and sealed it off. They had advanced rapidly on both sides of Lake Lagoda, but as soon as they had regained all the land lost to the Russians in the Russo-Finnish war, they stopped their advance and took defensive positions, much to Hitler's consternation. They dug in on the Karelian Isthmus, less than twenty miles from Leningrad, but would go no further despite German entreaties and pressure.

During this siege, Leningrad was bombed for nine hours a day, for several months. Almost one-half the population of three million died or were killed during the period from October 1, 1941, to April 1, 1942.

Food, water, and fuel became scarce. The daily bread ration for workers was nine ounces and for non-workers, half that amount. Food was made from sawdust, book-binding paste, hair oil, leather belts, cats, dogs, and rats. There were instances reported of cannibalism. By mid-winter, over 7,000 people died every day. The only access to the rest of Russia was east, across Lake Lagoda, along a narrow band that miraculously was kept open all year round for very limited supplies. Without this access, the entire population would have succumbed. The siege lasted 900 days but was finally lifted by the burgeoning Red Army in 1943.

Smolensk, Minsk, and Kiev fell to the *Wehrmacht*. By November, 1941, Army Group Center had reached the western suburbs of Moscow, less than fourteen miles from the city limits.

With the fall of Kiev on September 19, 1941, the Russian Army suffered its largest single battle defeat in history. Over one million Russian soldiers were killed, captured, or wounded, and huge numbers of tanks, military vehicles, and artillery pieces were impounded. The extent of these losses was attributed in large part to Stalin's edict that there would be no surrender and no retreat. The order, "Stand fast and die," was one that both Hitler and Stalin used to the consternation of their generals and the unnecessary sacrifice of their soldiers.

RASPUTITZA—GENERAL MUD

By November, 1941, the Red Army, fighting desperately for its life and for "Mother Russia," stiffened its resistance and slowed down the Northern and Central armies to a virtual halt. Heavy autumn rains converted roads and fields to quagmires of sticky mud, miring tanks, trucks, and horses and literally sucking the boots off the enemy's feet. Late fall rains and spring thaws, termed "Rasputitza" or "General Mud," were the scourge of military advance, and would often delay any significant progress for a month or more. This several-week episode of being stuck in the mud provided Stalin time to get fresh Siberian troops from the Japanese front to augment his army.

At this point, the German generals requested that they be given permission to hunker down along a defensible winter line, to obtain winter clothing and equipment, and to gather strength for an all-out assault in later winter or early spring. This would have been the wise thing to do under the existing field conditions, but Hitler, who assumed the role of Supreme Military Commander, denied this request and demanded that the army continue its advance on Moscow. This was only one of many serious military blunders committed by Hitler in overriding superior tactical decisions of his field marshals and generals. Such decisions were responsible for the growing disaffection of Hitler's professional military staff with his leadership. Hitler was driven by the desire to deliver the knockout blow to Russia before it could reorganize and counterattack. More than thirty-five generals were sacked by Hitler for questioning his directive to "hold fast" in hopeless circumstances. In many of these situations Hitler took over operations of that particular army group himself, in addition to his duties as Supreme Commander.

KING WINTER

During this late fall and early winter standoff, Red Army General Georgi Zhukov was switched from directing the Leningrad defense to leading a huge army that had now grown to 100 divisions. He was assigned by Stalin to mount a counterassault against the vulnerable German lines stalled before Moscow.

On December 6, 1941, Russia's mightiest defender, King Winter, roared onto the Russian stage, indiscriminately enveloping all of the players with driving blizzards and sub-zero temperatures in one of his most bitter performances. The King froze the entire company in place like some gigantic diorama. King Charles XII of Sweden in the eighteenth century and Napoleon Bonaparte in the nineteenth had fallen before this most inhospitable and unyielding Russian defender.

Although King Winter played no favorites, there was a vast difference in preparation between belligerents for his dramatic and paralyzing entrance. Whereas the Russian soldiers were snugly outfitted for this worst of winters with warm clothing and insulated boots, as well as winterized tanks, trucks, and artillery, 80 percent of the German soldiers were dressed in summer gear, augmented where possible with cardboard, rags, and stolen clothing. The mechanized equipment and automatic weapons were no better protected than the men, and most of them froze up and functioned only erratically. Thousands of German soldiers were disabled with frostbite or froze to death. A deep sense of foreboding and depression gripped the German Army Central as it prepared to make its next advance.

With the German Army staggering under the punch of the first winter blizzard, Zhukov's well equipped 100 divisions, motivated by anger, hate, and patriotic fervor, annihilated large sections of the German Army Group Central. The victories forced a German retreat and saved Moscow.

While German Army Group North desperately fought to subdue Leningrad, and Army Group Central was being routed by Zhukov, Hitler ordered Army Group South to take the offensive for the honor of the Reich and to capture Rostov, Sevastopol, Stalingrad, and the Caucasus. His generals tried to explain that this task was close to impossible with the forces available. Hitler was again adamant that generals Rundstedt, Manstein, and Paulus launch the spring offensive as soon as possible. During the spring and summer of 1942 these generals led brilliant and punishing attacks against the assigned targets and almost succeeded in accomplishing all their objectives. Unfortunately for Hitler, the high attrition associated with these ambitious and bloody projects further weakened the German Army's core strength and forced it to retreat. The bulk of the German Army would have been totally destroyed at this time except for superb generalship, especially that of Field Marshal von Manstein.

STALINGRAD

....

THE BATTLE OF STALINGRAD WHICH BEGAN IN THE LATE SUMMER OF 1942 dragged on until January of 1943. The battle was terribly costly for both combatants, especially the Germans. The defenders of the city did not succumb to daily *Luftwaffe* bombing raids or heavy artillery fire, as had been expected. Instead, every single block of the city had to be won by hand-to-hand combat in bombed out houses, stores, cellars, sewers, and factories. In a brutal, take-no-prisoners advance, the Germans gradually dislodged the entrenched, frantically fighting Russians from the central city. Still, the Russians desperately clung to the twelve mile northern strip of industrial Stalingrad along the Volga River. By autumn and early winter, the vastly larger and better-equipped Soviet army recaptured the entire city and destroyed or captured most of Paulus' army. With the obvious mismatch of forces, Paulus urgently sought permission for a strategic withdrawal. Here again, Hitler's "hold fast" policy proved disastrous, and wasted an army of 300,000.

The Stalingrad debacle marked the end of the *Wehrmacht's* advance into Russia and the beginning of the long bloody retreat over previously won ground. There were a few brilliant counterattacks against Russian targets, but the disparity between the size and strength of the two combatants became so great that by 1943 the Russian Army dominated the entire Eastern Front.

The inexorable march west by the Russian Army slowed momentarily at heavily defended natural obstructions and at a few cities that were designated by Hitler as "hold to the death" forts, but the Red Tide never stopped except to crush an occasional counterattack or to re-group and re-supply.

Kursk

....

I N AN EFFORT TO DESTROY A LARGE CENTRAL PORTION OF THE RUSSIAN line, Hitler designed a counterattack at Kursk, a small Russian town. Kursk itself was significant only because it was situated at the center of a westward bulge of the Russian Army. This part of the army could be pinched off by massive drives from the north at Orel and the south at Belgorod. A huge chunk of the Soviet Army would be entrapped when the north German troops met those from the south in Kursk. Called *Operation Citadel,* Hitler hoped and expected that this bold maneuver would not only halt the Russian advance, but would open a huge hole that would permit a new German offensive.

Unfortunately for Germany, a Russian spy, code-named *Lucy,* had access to Germany's top military plans on a day-to-day basis and passed this information directly to *Stavka,* the Soviet top command. *Lucy* was Rudolph Rossler, a disenchanted anti-Nazi German veteran of World War I, who had moved to Switzerland in 1934. In actuality, *Lucy* was fed timely information from British Intelligence, courtesy of *Ultra* through another intermediary, keeping from *Stavka* the fact that the Western Allies had cracked the German code, *Enigma.* With this information Russia knew the exact time and date of *Operation Citadel* as well as the size and location of the forces involved.

On July 5, 1943, when the Kursk fronts exploded, the Russian Army was ready. They had time to dig trenches, sow mine fields, and move up huge, well equipped army units that knew every detail of the attack.

The German Army launched a tremendous assault that under normal circumstances would most likely have been successful. At its climax, over 3,000 tanks were fighting at point-blank range in the largest tank battle of the war. After ten days of desperate battle, the sheer weight of the inexhaustible Russian Army prevailed, and *Operation Barbarossa*'s fate was sealed.

In another counterattack for the city of Kharkov, the Germans succeeded briefly but the Russians drove them out in a few months for the second and last time. The unfortunate city of Kharkov had suffered four major assaults, two by the Germans and two by the Russians.

Part of Hitler's optimism for the success of *Operation Citadel* was the great hope he placed on three new German tanks, the *Tiger,* the *Panther,* and the *Ferdinand.* The *Tiger* was superior to any Russian tank, but it couldn't be produced fast enough to have any significant impact. The *Panther* was also an excellent tank, but it suffered from an unbelievably stupid design flaw: the fuel tanks on the rear were exposed with no surrounding armor and when hit would explode, burst into flame, and destroy the tank. This was later corrected. The *Ferdinand,* named for Ferdinand Porsche, Hitler's hero and designer of the Volkswagen and the Porsche sports car, was a total failure. The *Ferdinand,* heavily armored with double-thickness steel plates, carried a huge tank-killing cannon, which, oddly enough, had a turret that could move only 14 degrees laterally. There were no machine guns to protect its flanks or rear, making it vulnerable to close-range, hand-thrown explosives, which would tear up its tracks, bring it to a halt and lead to its quick destruction. At Kursk this hopeless giant proved to be a fiasco and was far more lethal to its six-man crew than to enemy tanks. The costly defeat at Stalingrad, the failures at Kursk and Kharkov, and the loss of North Africa were blows from which Germany never recovered.

In the first year of battle of the invasion of Russia, the Germans lost one and one-half million men and didn't have anywhere near that number of replacements. In addition to war casualties, the eastern *Wehrmacht* was weakened by troop transfers to problem fronts: North Africa, Italy, and the Western Front in anticipation of an Allied invasion. By contrast, the Russian Army continued to grow despite huge losses. German General Haider complained in his diary, "At the outset we reckoned with 200 divisions. Now we have already counted 360. If we smash a dozen of them, the Russians simply put up another dozen." The Russians could afford to lose five soldiers to every one lost by the Germans and stay even. The German High Command didn't know that Russia had a pool of five and one-half million ready reservists who had enlisted at the time of the invasion and over twelve million additional eligible males to draw from as needed.

Dwindling German manpower was bad enough, but the logistics of replacing destroyed military equipment and supplies to the front line soldiers over distances often exceeding five hundred miles, crossed only by inadequate roads and mismatched railroad tracks, posed an even greater problem for the *Wehrmacht.* All the wider gauged Russian tracks had to be replaced with narrower German ones before anything could be moved into Russia by rail, the most effective means for resupply. All this massive transport had to be carried out across territory that harbored large numbers of hostile partisan gangs that disrupted the flow of these vital materials where and whenever possible. Airlifts to isolated and surrounded units were never adequate to fill the insatiable needs of the fighting army.

During the first year or so of the German attack, Russian supply lines were comparatively short and factories east of the Ural Mountains began producing tanks, planes, and guns in ever-increasing numbers and of a higher quality than that of Germany. The Russians had also developed a weapon of mass murder, the multiple rocket artillery called *Katyusha* or *Little Kate* which was fired from a truck with special mounted rails. With a range of four miles it could shower shrapnel on impact. It had an eerie whining howl that terrified German infantry and even front line Russian soldiers. *Little Kate* became known as *Stalin's Organ*.

In addition to their own increased production between October, 1941, and April, 1944, Russia received a huge boost from the United States: nine and one-half million tons of war materiel, including 8,800 aircraft, 5,500 tanks and armored cars, 19,000 railway trucks, and 160,000 other vehicles.

Germany's better trained and experienced tank personnel and vastly superior tactical maneuvering compensated to some extent for its smaller number and inferior quality tanks.

In addition to his many military blunders, Hitler's paranoia against all races except "Aryan," particularly Jews and Slavs, hastened his ultimate defeat. Had he capitalized on the widespread Russian hatred and fear of Stalin and the Communists, especially in the Ukraine, he might have sparked an anti-Communist revolution that could have greatly advanced his cause, and may even have changed the war's outcome. At first, the *Wehrmacht* was welcomed enthusiastically by the Ukrainians as the great deliverer from Stalin's oppression. Yet as the SS *Einsatzgruppen* troops began their horrible persecutions, disillusionment gripped the population and Germany was recognized as the greater of two evils. Hitler's war of extermination against ideological and racial enemies unified all Russian peoples against this most despicable enemy more completely than any amount of Stalinist propaganda could have. Large numbers of partisan units were spawned that bedeviled German supply lines throughout the war and played an important role in Germany's defeat.

By spring of 1944, the German Army had been thrown out of the Crimea and Sevastopol in the south, and was forced west to the Baltic states in the north. In the central province of Belorussia, the German line bulged eastward, not far from the point it had reached in 1941. The occupation of this much Russian territory in 1944 by Germany was not due so much to German strength, but rather to the concentration of Russian forces on either side of Belorussia. The Army Group Center's turn was about to come.

As Russia coordinated its massive forces for this monumental blow against Army Group Center, Hitler committed one of his worst strategic blunders. He assumed that Stalin's lust for the Balkans would cause him to deploy most of his forces into Roumania, Bulgaria, and Hungary. To counter this thrust, Hitler transferred south from Army Group Center 15 percent of his divisions, 33 percent of his heavy artillery, 50 percent of his tank destroyers, and 88 percent of his tanks. This reduced Army Group Center's strength from one million men to four hundred thousand along a 450-mile front.

Against this attenuated German line, Zhukov and Vosilevsky, during May and June, had assembled an army of 2.5 million men, 5,200 tanks and self-propelled guns, 7,000 fighter planes and bombers, and more than 31,000 field guns. In addition, one hundred trainloads of ammunition, food, and fuel arrived daily in the front areas. When Hitler was informed of this marked increase in Russian activity, he dismissed it as Russian deception, a feint to the center prior to the main strike against the Balkans. Seizing the Balkans would deprive the Axis of its main Roumanian oil supply as well as open the road to Austria and southern Germany.

After the Teheran Conference in November, 1943, Stalin suspected that the Western Allies were preparing to move into the Balkans ahead of the Russians. But with the Normandy invasion planned for June, 1944, he knew they would not divert troops to this area for at least five months or more. This would permit the Red Army to strike the Belorussian German line now and the Balkan front shortly thereafter. Hitler knew nothing of this rationale and thus doomed another huge portion of the German Army. Not only were the Germans shorthanded along the front lines, they were further weakened by Hitler's decision to commit eight of his best divisions to four cities that he had designated as "hold fast" fortresses.

OPERATION BAGRATION

....

EARLY IN THE MORNING OF JUNE 22, 1944, EXACTLY THREE YEARS AFTER the German invasion of Russia, in a flaunt to the Germans, the Russian Army struck back in *Operation Bagration*. This operation was named for a warrior prince who fought Napoleon. With overwhelming superiority, the Russian Army moved rapidly westward destroying large segments of the German forward lines and simply bypassing the fortress cities to mop them up at leisure later. The Germans tried to break out to the west but the giant Russian pincers around the Belorussian bulge prevented any significant escape and the majority of Army Group Center was destroyed. A German officer who escaped later described the horrible circumstances. "No one knew what was going on. There were Russians behind us, to the right and to the left. Rumor had it that men who lost touch were abandoned by headquarters. We were told we were in the midst of Russian positions. We wanted to break out. We fired. My God, but it was useless. It was like firing at the ocean waves with the tide coming in."

General Teryomov reported the slaughter from the Russian position. "Our guns opened fire from a range of 700 meters and machine guns joined in from 400 meters. The Nazis continued to advance. Shells exploded in their midst and machine gun fire mowed them down. Still they came forward, stepping over bodies of their own men. They came on blindly. There was nothing heroic in it. There was in the movement of this enormous mass of men, more of the mulish stubbornness of the herd, than of fighting men intent on forcing their will on the enemy at all costs."

By July 11 the battle was over. Twenty-eight German divisions—300,000 to 350,000 men—had been killed or captured. A 250-mile hole had been torn out of Army Group Center's line. The Russian soldiers, learning of German atrocities in Belorussia, where more than a million of the population had been killed during the German occupation, felt vindicated for their wholesale unrestricted slaughter of so many Germans.

With the central front secured, in late summer, 1944, ten Russian armies on a 250-mile front charged into Roumania and then fanned out into Bulgaria, Yugoslavia, and Hungary. An even larger force had marched into Poland. An army of 6.5 million men was now on the march westward, grimly bent on the destruction of Germany. As one soldier succinctly put it, "Our fury and thirst for revenge are more intense than ever." The price for Hitler's *lebensraum* had skyrocketed out of sight and payback time was just beginning. German soldiers, surrounded in fields, were crushed by tanks. Any that escaped were slashed to death by sword-swinging cavalry or mowed down by machine-gun fire. There were few prisoners. Soldiers who surrendered were usually shot. (MAP 6)

Poland Revisited: Warsaw Uprising

....

T HE RUSSIAN DRIVE THROUGH POLAND INTO GERMANY COULD HAVE BEEN
accomplished in a short time, except for Stalin's political agenda for
conquered Poland. He wanted his hand-picked Soviet-oriented Poles, The
Polish Committee of National Liberation, also known as the Lublin Committee
(for the Polish city of Lublin) to take over the post-war administration of the
country. Otherwise, he feared that the democratic insurgents, The Home Army,
with headquarters in London, under the direction of Prime Minister Stanislag
Mikolajcryk, would govern. The Home Army, under General Bar, headquartered in Warsaw, was made up of approximately 380,000 members, scattered
throughout Poland with 40,000 underground in Warsaw.

Stalin wanted total control of Poland following the war. He particularly
wanted to retain the Polish eastern border, which Russia had established after
the German-Russian invasion of 1940 that ceded to Russia 40,000 square miles
of Polish territory. The Home Army, on the other hand, had as its basic tenet
the restoration of the prewar Polish border. For this reason it served Stalin's
purposes to destroy The Home Army but without raising the ire of his Western
Allies. He needed the Germans to do the dirty work.

Implementing this cynical plan, the Soviet Army stopped a few miles east of
Warsaw, ostensibly to regroup and re-supply. Leaflets were dropped in Warsaw
by Russia exhorting the underground Home Army to rise up and strike the
hated Germans with the implied assurance that Russia would provide logistical
support if needed.

To boost their national pride, The Home Army wanted to liberate Warsaw
from the Nazis themselves, before Russian troops entered the city. Accordingly,

they stormed out of hiding and attacked the Germans, but unfortunately with inadequate arms and backup supplies.

Stalin's malevolent scheme of pitting one enemy against the other, to their mutual destruction, worked perfectly. Russia supplied neither food nor arms, and when Britain and the United States requested permission to refuel their transport planes behind Russian lines so they could parachute supplies to the hapless Poles, they were denied by Stalin.

When the insurgents had reached the limit of their endurance, they pled with Stalin to send in Soviet troops to come to their rescue, but Stalin ignored all entreaties, including those of Roosevelt and Churchill.

With no appreciable support, The Home Army finally surrendered. They were unaware that Himmler had ordered the German Army to kill every man, woman, and child in Warsaw and then level the city. Contrary to Himmler's order, in a rare moment of mercy, SS General Erich von dem Bach-Zelewski took prisoner 15,000 Home Army soldiers, including 2,000 women and 550 children, rather than kill them. He then allowed most civilians to evacuate the city before it was looted and totally destroyed. The Warsaw Uprising resulted in the deaths of at least 180,000 civilians and 18,000 Home Army fighters. Twice that number were wounded. The dead piled up in the streets and the stench was overwhelming. There weren't enough coffins, and the dead were buried wherever a patch of earth could be found between the rubble.

One young woman wearing a Communist armband, after placing a flower beside the face of a dead loved one, faced the Soviet Army ensconced on the other side of the Vistula River and screamed, "You sons-of-bitches, you haven't come!"

When all was quiet, after the "Gingham dog and the calico cat" had "eaten each other up," the Soviet Army finally lumbered into Warsaw, a dead city, in mid-January 1945. Stalin, the master poker player, had won another hand.

THE NORMANDY INVASION

STALIN HARBORED DEEP RESENTMENT TOWARDS HIS TWO WESTERN Allies, England in particular, for not launching a second front in France in 1942. He informed Churchill at the latter's visit to Moscow in August, 1942, that the British were not only unfair but cowardly as well, for allowing Russia to carry the entire war against Germany and sustain all the manpower losses. Churchill opined to his own staff later, that it was Russia that had been attacked by Germany and that they were fighting for their own survival. "The Soviet Government had the impression that they were conferring a great favor on us by fighting in their own country for their own lives. The more they fought, the heavier our debt became. This was not a balanced view." Stalin always gave Churchill a bad time, and seldom, if ever, extended any appreciation to him for all the material support Russia received from its Allied partners, or for the indirect help Russia realized from the British war effort in North Africa.

Stalin aside, the Western Powers had reasons of their own for a Second Front on the continent, the only question being when and where. They were worried that a desperate Hitler, during his retreat west, may try to negotiate another unholy alliance with Stalin that would contrive to divide and conquer the entire European Continent, and then together crush England.

Moreover, without a Second Front, Russia could end up occupying not only Berlin, but all of Western Europe including Germany, France, and the Low Countries. This would create a very awkward and compromised negotiating position for the Western Allies at war's end.

Perhaps the most cogent rationale for a Second Front, however, was U.S. Chief of Staff, General George C. Marshall's convincing argument: the quickest way to defeat Germany and end the war in Europe was to invade France from directly across the English Channel. The Allies would then be free to direct their total undivided power against Japan. Although Churchill favored Southern France as the target for invasion, Marshall's plan prevailed.

With a direct attack across the Channel, the Rhine-Ruhr Valley, the heart of Germany's industrial war production, would be only 750 kilometers from England, and Berlin only 250 kilometers further east. Both of these targets were over 2,000 kilometers west of the Russian front line.

The main obstacle frustrating the direct route to France was the English Channel, which had stopped many a potential conqueror in the past and had saved England from a German invasion in 1941. The twenty- to ninety-mile Channel crossing would be the shortest but the most difficult and dangerous distance that the Allies would have to traverse on their drive to Berlin. It was the monumental problem of building enough amphibious ships to transport 200,000 to 300,000 troops plus tanks, trucks, and artillery across the Channel on D-Day that prevented a Second Front in 1943. This need pushed ship production to the absolute maximum to meet the June, 1944, deadline.

One other important accomplishment of the Casablanca Conference of January, 1943, not mentioned earlier was the appointment of an extremely well qualified English Army officer, Lieutenant General F. E. Morgan, to undertake the huge task of planning the assault on the Continent by June of 1944. He was to be the Chief of Staff to the soon-to-be-designated Supreme Allied Commander to be selected later in the year. Morgan's acronym was COSSAC.

His task was complicated by the fact that many of the high military brass assigned to COSSAC didn't believe a cross-Channel attack on Europe was feasible. It was only after Vice Admiral Lord Louis Mountbatten convened a meeting in June, 1943, away from London in a small Scottish town, Largs, that a breakthrough in attitude occurred and an almost complete unanimity in favor of a cross-Channel invasion was reached. One attendee remarked, "In the end there was not only unanimity but enthusiasm." The plan to invade not against port cities in France, but instead along the beaches of Normandy converted the opposition. Critics were further placated by the plan to tow across the Channel prefabricated harbors made up of hollow concrete blocks and concrete-filled sunken ships. Called *Mulberries,* these artificial harbors would protect against the weather and be capable of receiving full-sized transport vessels for massive delivery of troops and equipment.

A progress report of the invasion plan, now code-named *Overlord,* was reported to Churchill, Roosevelt, and top military commanders at Quebec in August, 1943. The primary disagreement between the British and the American contingents related to the timing of the cross-Channel invasion. The Americans gave highest priority to launching the attack as soon as possible, whereas the British favored a war of attrition up the Italian Peninsula into Southern France and the Balkans with a somewhat later cross-Channel invasion. The Americans finally agreed to go along with the conquering of Rome, since Italy had recently surrendered. They also agreed to launch a diversionary attack against Southern France simultaneous with the cross-Channel invasion. Termed *Anvil,* the primary purpose of this southern strike was to draw the Nazi's attention away from the invasion of the western coast of France.

The loss of three U.S. LST's to German E-boats (torpedo boats) in a disastrous training exercise, *Tiger,* at Slapton Sands, England, on April 28, 1944, however, forced delay of *Anvil* to July 10, 1944, and the code name was changed to *Dragoon.*

The third conference, the Cairo Conference, was held in early November, 1943, in Cairo, Egypt, attended by Roosevelt, Churchill, and China's General Chiang Kai-shek. Here it was decided that at war's end, Japan would be stripped of its entire colonial empire, even its oldest ones, and China would be elevated to full Great Power status.

TEHERAN CONFERENCE

At the fourth and perhaps most important conference of the year, convened in Teheran, Iran in late November, 1943, all three major Allied Powers attended and Roosevelt met Stalin for the first time. Stalin was assured that a cross-Channel invasion of France would be definitely launched by June, 1944, and that this would be followed shortly by an invasion of Southern France from bases in Italy. Although Stalin, dubious about his Allies' intentions because no Supreme Commander had as yet been appointed, agreed to step up Russia's offensive in conjunction with the cross-Channel assault, and promised to enter the war against Japan after Germany's defeat.

Stalin left the Teheran Conference a happy man because not only had he been guaranteed a Second Front, but also a part of Poland east of the Curzon Line. This fact was to be kept quiet until after the 1944 presidential election, there being over one million Polish-American votes that would be lost for Roosevelt were this concession publicized.

Because the United States was providing the preponderance of troops and equipment for *Overlord,* it was agreed that the Supreme Commander should be an American. In making this appointment, Roosevelt wavered between General George C. Marshall and General Dwight D. Eisenhower. After agonizing analysis, in the end, he chose Eisenhower mostly because of his excellent record in directing the invasions of North Africa, Sicily, and Italy.

"Ike" had exhibited unusual leadership qualities in these actions, particularly in his ability to achieve cooperation from all branches of the service of both England and the United States. Even though there were intense rivalries and flat-out animosities between some of the commanding officers of both countries, Ike was able to instill a team-work mentality and cooperative attitude in most of the leaders. His optimism and cheerfulness were also important strengths. He could lift the spirits of the most dour participant. On one occasion he wrote that no matter how bad things got he had to, "Preserve optimism" in himself and his command. "Without confidence, enthusiasm and optimism, victory is scarcely obtainable. Any pessimism and discouragement I might ever feel would be reserved for my pillow." Under the most daunting circumstances he never gave up hope.

Eisenhower, an excellent military strategist, was also firm in his decisions when he believed he was right. Another reason Roosevelt picked Eisenhower over Marshall was because he once stated that he wouldn't be able to sleep at night with Marshall out of the country.

During the ensuing weeks, the ablest commanders from both countries were recruited to make up the top command structure of the Supreme Headquarters Allied Expeditionary Force (SHAEF). Chief of Staff under Eisenhower was the competent American General, Walter Bedell-Smith. A tough administrator and a superb diplomat, Bedell-Smith shielded Eisenhower from countless details and unpleasant confrontations. On one occasion, referring to an unwanted request of SHAEF, Eisenhower instructed Bedell-Smith to "Tell them to go to hell, but put it so they won't be offended."

Eisenhower appointed Air Chief Marshal Sir Arthur Tedder to the position of Deputy Supreme Commander in Chief. He had worked with him in the Mediterranean Theater and had grown to trust and like him very much.

He appointed Admiral Sir Bertram Ramsay, who had planned the North African invasion and the evacuation of British troops at Dunkirk, to Naval Commander, responsible for the awesome task of getting the armies across the Channel. This time he would be planning an attack instead of a retreat. Eisenhower then designated Britain's Marshal Leigh Mallory to be Chief of the Allied Tactical Air Force, and appointed the brilliant, though often controversial, General Sir Bernard Montgomery, as Ground Commander of the Allied Armies. For Chief of the American First Army he selected the extremely well liked and superbly qualified American, General Omar Bradley.

SHAEF headquarters was set up in a western suburb of London, Bushey Park, code named *Wide Wing*, in January, 1944. By March this complex had grown to include six divisions. Operations and Planning was the largest. The others were Intelligence, Civil Affairs (setting up political control in liberated counties), Supply, Psychological Warfare, and Engineering. There were specialists in every field, including medicine, numbering up to 750 officers and 6,000 other employees. With the myriad of logistical considerations, it was amazing how well this organization functioned without benefit of the computer.

As SHAEF was settling into its offices in Bushey Park, military personnel from *all* branches of the Armed Services were being mobilized and trained for the impending European invasion.

Operation Overlord — The Battle Plan

In January, 1944, SHAEF was hammering out the immense and complex battle plan to deliver in one day across the Channel to France an army of 250,000 to 300,000 soldiers and their necessary equipment, armaments, and supplies. They would have to break through the deadly beach obstacles, run the gauntlet of fire from German guns, and secure the area around the beachheads to permit a continuing flow of troops, tanks, and artillery into France and then on to Berlin.

There were hundreds of meetings and much disagreement regarding the location and timing of the invasion, the size of the forces to be used, and particularly rancorous arguments about whether parachute and glider troops should be used prior to the sea-borne landings.

The most serious disagreement, and one that almost caused Eisenhower to resign as Supreme Commander, was over the control of the American and British Bomber Commands. These two separate units under Sir Arthur Harris of the R.A.F. Bomber Command, and General Carl Spaatz of the U.S. Eighth Air Force, respectively, were independent and free of SHAEF command. They determined their own bombing strategy, which was, essentially, to bomb strategic targets within Germany. Harris wanted to bring about German capitulation through terror-bombing of its cities at night, and Spaatz elected to destroy industrial centers, synthetic fuel plants, and oil depots. Both thought they could bring about Germany's defeat without a Second Front. Eisenhower, on the other hand, wanted the Bomber Command to bomb railway and transportation centers for some miles back of the beach-head areas to slow German response time to the invasion. He mainly insisted on having temporary control of the bomber units during the invasion period to better coordinate the entire *Operation Overlord*. Both Harris and Spaatz considered *Operation Overlord* an unnecessary exercise which made Eisenhower's position difficult. Fortunately, all of the high command, including Churchill and Roosevelt, backed Eisenhower and his transportation bombing plan. They also yielded to his demand to have the two bomber units placed under SHAEF Command.

Eisenhower's greatest strength was his ability to mediate these many divisive arguments among a group of strong willed prima donnas. The pressures were so enormous that at one time he wrote his wife, Mamie, that if she had an exact diary account of his past week, "You'd get some idea of what a flea on a hot griddle really does." The pressures were such that he began smoking up to four packs of cigarettes a day. Through all these arguments and hard feelings, Ike maintained an aura of optimism and cheerfulness that won over his most ardent opponents. He was indeed the right man for the job.

After much discussion and many arguments, the location for the invasion was finally settled upon: the sixty-five-mile stretch of Normandy beach from the Orne River on the east to the Cotentin Peninsula on the west. The British-Canadian Second Army under Dempsey would be responsible for the eastern half of the shore line, and the U.S. First Army under General Bradley, the western. The British-Canadian sector was divided into three assault beaches named from east to west, Sword, Juno and Gold. The two beaches in the American sector were called Omaha and Utah. The original plan of deploying a total of three army divisions for the D-Day assault was increased to six.

The combined Western Allied armies, collectively called the Twenty-first Army Group, were under the command of British General, Bernard Montgomery. It included the United State's First, Fourth, and Twenty-ninth Infantry Divisions, the British Fiftieth, and Third Divisions and the Canadian Second Division.

The British Sixth Airborne Division would land just to the east and back of Sword beach between the Orne and the Dives rivers to protect the east flank of the British assault forces, and the United States' Airborne Divisions, the 82nd and 101st would land just to the west of and behind Utah and Omaha beaches to protect the west flank.

There were many highly trained specialized forces, all of them volunteer units, such as the U.S. Second and Fifth Ranger Battalions, which were considered by many to be suicide squads. Among other dangerous duties, they were assigned the extremely hazardous job of climbing the sheer 95 foot cliff wall of Pointe-de-Hoc and destroying the German gun emplacements by direct assault.

The duty of the Seabees (Construction Battalions) and the Engineer Special Brigade was to demolish beach obstacles, blow up mines, guide incoming craft through cleared channels, establish supply dumps, and act as beach-masters. Generally, the Seabees worked to neutralize the outermost obstacles that were deeper under water and the ESB units worked farther inland. The mortality in some of these groups reached 85 percent.

There were also British Commando Battalions with responsibilities similar to the U.S. Rangers: Barrage Balloon Battalions, Midget Submarine Units, and many others not discussed here that were essential to the success of *Operation Overlord*.

It is mind-boggling to consider the complexities of creating, staffing, coordinating, and supplying these vast numbers of military organizations and their constituent personnel. Add to that the immense problem of building enough landing craft, transport ships, planes, and mobile armaments in time for the

D-Day deadline, and one realizes that the successful launching of *Operation Overlord* was little short of a miracle.

Having determined the location of the invasion and the size of the army, the next decision was to select the optimal time for the invasion. The only possible dates in late spring when the moon and the tides were right were the first three days of May, or during the first and third weeks of June. The conditions thought to be necessary for the invasion were a partially full moon, without too many clouds for the paratroopers who would be dropped around midnight, a low tide just before dawn for the Seabees and the engineers to destroy beach obstacles, and a rising tide just after dawn for the assault troops so the landing craft could more easily float off the beach *after* discharging their troops.

Because preparations were not far enough along for a May assault, the first week in June was selected to be the best possible time, and June 5 was picked for D-Day. The third week in June would be the fall-back if a Channel storm struck on D-Day. Delaying the invasion two weeks, however, could prove disastrous with the difficulty of maintaining secrecy and of keeping so many troops sealed for that long. SHAEF could control time and place, but it could do nothing about the weather, except to hope and pray and keep a careful watch.

Although there were differences of opinion and arguments regarding the time and place of the invasion, the size of the initial invading force, and the function of the bomber commands, there was complete unanimity about the need for air supremacy, absolute secrecy, and for a deceptive battle plan that would confuse the German High Command.

The Germans knew there would be an invasion some time in the spring or summer of 1944, but they didn't know the exact date or location. For this reason Hitler ordered that the entire 2,500 mile coast from North Cape to the Bay of Biscay be developed into an impregnable fortress where any attempted landing could be crushed and thrown back into the sea.

Field Marshal Gerd Von Rundstedt was the Commander in Chief of all German Western armies, and Rommel, in November 1943, was appointed Commander in Chief of Army Group B, comprised of the Fifteenth Army at Pas-de-Calais and the Seventh Army stationed in Normandy and Brittany. He was given the monumental task of building the impregnable Western Wall of Europe.

Von Rundstedt did not believe it was possible to build an impenetrable wall of that magnitude where the enemy could be destroyed on the beaches, and so disagreed with Hitler and Rommel. He held to the dictum of Frederick the Great that "to defend everything is to defend nothing." He wanted *Panzer* divisions and infantry just far enough back from the beach to be out of range of the naval bombardment, but mobile enough to crush the enemy troops coming off the beaches before they had the benefit of their tanks and heavy mobile artillery. Most war historians agree that Von Rundstedt and Frederick the Great were right.

Hitler's position, of course, prevailed. Since Rommel agreed with Hitler, he threw himself into the task of making *Festung Europa* (Fortress Europe) impregnable. This was no easy task because in November of 1943, by Rommel's standards, it was woefully inadequate, except for areas around port cities such as Calais and Cherbourg. The Pas-de-Calais was the most heavily fortified, being the closest to England, only 20 miles across the Channel from Dover. Rommel pressed all available manpower, including soldiers, at the expense of training exercises, into building this enormous fortress.

There were hundreds of thousands of ingenious beach obstacles of every imaginable type, most of them festooned with mines or shells that exploded on contact, laced with intertwining barbed wire, and backed by thousands of cannon and machine gun emplacements. These were buried under 8 to 12 feet of concrete and steel housing that commanded the beach. Millions of tons of concrete were poured to protect beach artillery. In addition, 200 million land mines were sown in France, most of them along a six-mile strip adjacent to the beach at a concentration of 65,000 mines per square kilometer. Rommel commented to his aide Helmuth Lang that, "We will have only one chance to stop the enemy and that is while he is in the water. Everything we have must be on the coast. Believe me, Lang, the first 24 hours of the invasion will be decisive, for the Allies as well as for Germany; it will be the longest day." It was from this quotation that D-Day at Normandy became known as *The Longest Day,* used as the title for Cornelius Ryan's popular book.

The Western Allies, to maintain secrecy, were forced to seal off virtually the entire coast of England from the rest of the country to everyone, except those with security clearance, for approximately ten miles inland. All diplomatic channels out of England were censored as well, except for Russia and the United States. Stalin was denied his request to have a complete copy of the invasion plans including maps and dates for fear of leaks.

OPERATION FORTITUDE

Almost as important as secrecy was developing and carrying out a plan of deception that would fool the Germans into concentrating their main defensive forces at a fake invasion site, believing the real invasion was only a feint to draw them away.

To carry out this elaborate fiction, *Operation Fortitude* was established, with two main centers, one in northeastern England to include Scotland, called Fortitude North, which had Norway as its ostensible target (the site of the Nazi's U-boat bases), and Fortitude South, with the Pas-de-Calais as the presumed target. The latter was an easier ploy because Hitler, Rommel, and Von Rundstedt already believed that the Pas-de-Calais with its twenty-mile proximity to Dover was the most likely invasion site.

To lead Germany to believe that an assault at both the Norway and Pas-de-Calais locations was possible, they had to be made to believe that there were twice as many troops available in England than there really were. This ruse, *The Double Cross System,* was accomplished through fake military radio traffic within England, known to be monitored in Germany, or by German agents in Britain. The headquarters of the fake British Fourth Army was northern Scotland. The First U.S. Army Group (FUSAG) was not a fake, but had its numbers considerably inflated. It was headquartered in Dover. The real invasion headquarter was Southwick House in Portsmouth.

To give credibility to FUSAG, the Allies assigned General George Patton to head it up, and newspapers were allowed to print the news of his arrival in England. Patton was assigned to lead an Infantry division in France, but not on D-Day.

Dummy landing craft, docks, planes, tanks, artillery and army barracks were built and deployed along the coast of Northeastern England and Scotland, which gave greater credibility to the sham army. To extend the ruse even further, the Allied Air Force staged many more reconnaissance flights and bombing runs over the fake target areas than over Normandy.

The most help for *Double Cross* was provided by two or three German double agents in England. They confirmed the build-up of the huge Allied invasion force and the "authenticity" of the dummy military installations.

The success of *Operation Fortitude* was apparent in May, because by then Germany estimated that the invasion forces were eighty-nine divisions strong, when there were actually only forty-seven, and that the Allies had enough landing craft to deliver twenty-two divisions to Europe when in reality they had barely enough for six divisions. The threat to Norway and the U-boat bases seemed so real to Hitler that he stationed thirteen army divisions in Norway plus 90,000 naval and 60,000 *Luftwaffe* personnel. This greatly reduced their defensive potential on D-Day against the real invasion at Normandy. Rommel begged Hitler to release five infantry divisions for the defense of Western France, but he refused.

The British Joint Intelligence Committee, through *Ultra* intercepts of German High-Command reports, were pleased to learn that the Germans anticipated the primary invasion target to be Pas-de-Calais and secondarily Norway, with fake diversionary attacks at Normandy, the Bay of Biscay, and Southern France.

On the first of June, 1944, with all the exhausting and arduous planning completed, SHAEF issued the order to load up the ships and prepare for the main event. With the rumbling roar and tremors of thousands of troops, tanks, trucks, and artillery moving down the streets toward the docks and beaches, the local population in all the port towns knew that the fateful, long awaited D-Day was at hand. Everything was moving perfectly according to plan. Everything, that is, except the weather.

May had been a beautiful month, and it was probably too much to expect that it would last for another week. The high pressure system that had lingered over the Channel for much of May suddenly gave way to a low pressure storm system moving up from the Azores. The Allies had a much better weather forecasting system than the Germans, with ships dedicated to that function scattered around the Atlantic. The on-site SHAEF weatherman, whose duty it was to correlate all the reports and make a best judgment prediction of local Channel weather for a period of at least two days, was Captain J.M. Stagg, a 28-year-old canny Scotsman. It was his unpleasant duty to inform the Supreme Headquarters Staff that the storm, just beginning to move in, would reach almost hurricane proportion by the morning of June 5, D-Day. With the ships already underway to France, there was no alternative but to issue an immediate order for all of them to return to England.

What followed was the most agonizing period of the war for Eisenhower and his *Operation Overlord* staff. They had to decide in a very short time whether to hold the ships in readiness for one more day, hoping for a break in the weather, or delay the whole project for two weeks, which would create a great security risk. With wind and rain increasing steadily, the hope for a return to France on June 6 seemed out of the question.

It was at this low point that Stagg returned to the War Operation's Room with a flicker of a smile on his usually dour face to report that there appeared to be a temporary easing of the storm with some opening skies and lower winds for a period of 36 hours, beginning late on the night of June 5. He didn't think this clearing could last longer than 36 hours at most.

Then began one of the most fateful discussions in the history of warfare; to go or not to go. There was only about a half-hour to decide. Eisenhower allowed every member of the Supreme Command to voice an opinion, with Leigh-Mallory opposed and Montgomery in favor. After all the members had spoken, in the end, Ike was left alone with the ultimate decision. He waited silently for a few moments, lost in his own thoughts, and then announced, "I am quite positive we must give the order. I don't like it but there it is. I don't see how we could possibly do anything else."

And so the order was given and passed along the chain of command to all ships and air-force units that the "show" was on again and that June 6 was to be *the* day. One Admiral, leaving Southwick House in the driving rain was heard to mutter, "Bloody nonsense, I call it."

In retrospect, the invasion day storm was a deeply disguised but marvelous blessing for the Allies because the Germans totally discounted the possibility of an invasion during the miserable weather that lashed the French coast. Their forecast was for the storm to last at least one week and possibly two. They couldn't "see" the brief hiatus in the storm that Stagg reported. As a consequence, having been on super-alert for the whole month of May when weather conditions were perfect for an invasion, most of the officers took the night of June 5 off to visit friends or family or attend a concert or have a party. Some left for Brittany to participate in war game exercises at Rennes.

Rommel decided to take a few days' holiday early in June to visit his home in Ulm, Germany, and to celebrate his wife Lucie-Marie's birthday, on June 6. He bought her shoes in Paris as a present. It wasn't only the storm that caused him to relax his vigilance at this time, but he also didn't believe that the tide would be right early in June for an invasion. The Channel storm only reaffirmed his decision to take a break away from the front. Although he would be the last to admit it, Rommel was very tired and badly in need of a rest. He put in 18 hours of hard work every day, and seldom slept more than five hours a night. People who had known him a long time were shocked to see how much he had aged in the past year. He was only fifty-two.

The Allies' decision "to go" immediately activated the ponderous chain of command that carried the Supreme Commander's order to all ships and aircraft to prepare for the assault on June 6th, exactly 24 hours after the canceled attempt. The order was received with jubilation by all the troops and naval personnel who were sick of being cooped up on the rolling ships in such tight and crowded quarters. Psychologically, they were more than ready to attack the foe. Anything would be better than languishing here. The men who were most inconvenienced by the delay were the Midget Submarine personnel who had to stay under water just off the French coast in very cramped quarters for 48 instead of 24 hours. Their job was to surface and place marker flares along the outer extremes of the invasion beaches shortly before the landings.

The invasion plan was to have the parachute and glider troops land on either flank of the Normandy beach shortly after midnight to knock out telephone lines, bridges, and to secure roads leading off the beaches—in short, to protect the beachhead from German counterattack until they were firmly established. Through coded messages from BBC over French radio, the French Resistance Fighters were informed that the invasion was beginning now, which triggered them to begin their sabotage of all means of communication, including telephone, cable, electric lines, railroad tracks, and strategic roads.

The final coded message received by the French Underground that heralded the imminent invasion was the last line of August Verlaine's poem, *Ode to Autumn,* "Wound my heart with a dull languor." *Abwehr,* the German Intelligence Agency, through its spy system, also recognized that line as the invasion signal, and this word was passed to all German defense forces, except the German Seventh Army, which happened to be located closest to the Normandy beach. This oversight has never been explained, even by German war historians. Von Rundstedt dismissed the warning as a false alarm and retorted,

"Does anyone really think the enemy would be stupid enough to announce it over the radio?" He also had been assured by naval advisors that the Channel was much too rough for an invasion.

Operation Overlord— The Airborne Attack

When airborne troops took off from England late on the night of June 5, there were scattered clouds and a partial moon. This was the largest airborne operation in history, with 1,400 transport planes (460 British transports and 940 U.S. C-47s), 18,000 troops and 3,500 gliders. It was made up of the U.S. Army 82nd Airborne Division, under the command of General Matthew B. Ridgeway, the 101st Airborne Division under General Maxwell B. Taylor, and the British 6th Airborne Division under Major General R.N. Gale.

Although the C-47 was a rugged plane, designed for transporting troops and cargo, it was neither armed nor armored. There was no protection for its gas tanks, which were not self-sealing as were all fighter and bomber tanks. The plane was 65 feet long with a wing span of 95 feet. The armada that flew to France the night of June 5, 1944, was nine planes wide and 300 miles long!

The vanguard group, made up of specially trained paratroopers known as Pathfinders, preceded the main drops by one to two hours. It was their job to mark drop zones with automatic direction-finding radios and uniquely designed halophone lights.

The planes were to cross the Channel at a 500-foot elevation to avoid radar detection, then rise to over 1,600 feet to avoid coastal anti-aircraft batteries, and were then to descend to 600 feet and slow their speed to 90 miles per hour for the drop. That was the plan. In actuality, scattered clouds and heavier than expected anti-aircraft fire caused drops to occur far from the planned sites and under less than optimal conditions. Some planes went up over the clouds to drop their troops at 2,500 feet, much too high, resulting in landings miles away from the marked targets. Others went under the clouds, dropping their paratroop "sticks" at 300 feet or less, resulting in many chute failures, injuries and death. Some planes took evasive action from anti-aircraft fire and in panic dropped their chutists at speeds of over 150 m.p.h. which in itself caused frequent injury from the severe jerk upon chute-opening, disabling the soldier even before he hit the ground.

There were other problems as well. The recently flooded fields and marshes just west of Utah beach with depths of four to seven feet accounted for many drownings when soldiers landing here couldn't get free of their chute lines or their over-weighted equipment. Some troops were dropped too early and drowned in the Channel, just short of the French shore. One group drifted down right into the town of Sainte-Mère-Église, and many of these were shot like fish in a barrel by German soldiers and police. One parachutist, Private John Steele, dropped on the town church with his chute draped over the steeple, and hung there for over two hours. He had a bullet wound in his foot, but his main disability was deafness that lasted for weeks from the incessant clanging of the church bells. He was taken prisoner but later escaped, and was immortalized in Cornelius Ryan's book and movie, *The Longest Day*.

Part of the reason for the erratic deviation from the planned airborne assault was the lack of military experience of the transport pilots. They were not accustomed to enemy fire, and many were just plain "scared" and panicked. With the tracer shells arching all around the planes, some of the parachutists also panicked and refused to jump. These soldiers faced severe disciplinary action on their return to England.

The British Airborne troops had somewhat better success than did the American. One combined paratroops-and-glider operation, directed against the Orne River and Caen Canal Bridges and the powerful Merville Battery, was textbook perfect. Led by Major John Howard, the two vital bridges were captured intact shortly after the landings, and the Merville Battery was knocked out shortly thereafter by direct man-to-man assault.

Many gliders were wrecked when they slammed into the unexpectedly high (six-foot) French hedgerows. The Allied intelligence reports of French terrain inexplicably missed this very important impediment to landing a glider. The hedgerows took a much greater toll on Allied gliders than Rommel's spiked poles, also known as "Rommel's asparagus." Of all the gliders that participated in the D-Day attack, only 49 British and 52 American gliders landed safely and accurately to deliver their jeeps and anti-tank guns which were essential to the success of the entire operation.

With the somewhat haphazard paratroops delivery and associated 16 percent personnel casualty rate, at first it appeared that British Air Chief Marshal Leigh-Mallory was right in his opinion that the airborne assault would fail. One of Eisenhower's most difficult tasks was to go ahead with the paratroop landings in spite of his air chief's objection. Ike insisted that Leigh-Mallory say nothing that might demoralize his troops.

The ultimate success of the airborne invasion, in spite of the initial setbacks, has been attributed to the creative and courageous action of the surviving parachute and glider troops, who quickly, upon landing, organized the widely scattered troops, and under great duress, accomplished almost all of their objectives.

The success of these troops is also attributable to the delay in German awareness that the invasion had begun, and by the help of the French Underground. Further, the scattering of the Allied paratroops over such a large area confused the German defenders, causing them to think these may simply be drops to refurbish the French Underground. Moreover, many of the German commanding officers were away, greatly delaying German counterattacks. At least three divisions could not be brought into battle without Hitler's specific order, and Hitler was asleep at Berchtesgaden. Field-Marshal Kietel, who received the report, refused to awaken Hitler because he believed it was a false alarm and that the real invasion would be at Calais. Three or four hours of valuable response time was lost with this decision. For days after the Allied landings at Normandy, Hitler believed the main attack was yet to come at the Pas-de-Calais, and held his 15th Army in readiness there.

The German defenders were further confused with the Allied release of large numbers of aluminum strips called "windows," which on German radar looked like hundreds of invading aircraft and channel ships. In addition, large numbers of straw-filled dummy paratroopers were dropped near Rouen, Caen, and Avranches which kept German troops busy many miles away from the actual drops.

The confused, slow, German response time plus the rapid, innovative action of the Allied parachute and glider troops, won the day for the Allies. Together with the French Underground, they created havoc in the whole Cotentin

Peninsula and Orne river estuary by cutting communications, knocking out bridges, and destroying many gun batteries. They accomplished their original objective of providing protection to the flanks of the invading seaborne troops that were shortly to land.

OVERLORD NEPTUNE—
ASSAULT FROM THE SEA

The mighty D-Day armada of some 5,000 ships was divided into two commands, the Eastern Task Force under British Admiral Vian, responsible for Sword, Juno, and Gold beaches, and the Western Task Force, under Rear Admiral Kirk, whose command ship was the cruiser, USS *Augusta*. Omaha and Utah beaches were his target. These two main forces were further divided into five convoys, one for each of the five beaches. (MAP 3)

Two hundred fifty-five mine sweepers preceded all other ships. Destroyers, and destroyer escorts, protected the flanks from E-boat or submarine attack. By this time, mines were virtually the only effective German naval defense. E-boats could be devastating to individual ships, but were a nuisance rather than a serious threat to the whole operation—more like hornets at a picnic.

There were 137 warships deployed for preliminary bombardment. Six of these were battle ships, three British and three American, including the battleships *Texas, Nevada,* and *Arkansas.* The *Nevada* had been resurrected from its sinking at Pearl Harbor. The battleships could fire effectively from six miles off shore, the 68 destroyers from three miles, and the 23 cruisers from somewhere in between.

Most of the armada was made up of transports: LSTs (landing ship tanks), LCIs (landing craft infantry), LCMs (landing craft medium), LCTs (landing craft tanks), and other amphibious craft. LCVPs (landing craft vehicle-person-nel-Higgins boats) were carried over on LSTs. The LCTs followed immediately behind the mine-sweepers. Carrying four *S*herman swimming tanks (Ducks), weighing 32 tons each, and four jeeps plus their crews, the LCTs were slow and difficult to maneuver. They had little freeboard and no keel. The Ducks were to be launched five kilometers from the beach just before the troop assault. Their assignment was to knock out any remaining gun positions after completion of the naval bombardment.

The LSTs towed large rhino ferries (barges) constructed from multiple pontoons. They were 176 feet long and 42 feet wide and could carry 40 vehicles. After being loaded and released from their mother ship in the transport area, they were propelled by two large outboard motors for their trip into the beach. The rhinos were expendable, the LSTs were not.

Although the seemingly endless columns of Allied ships stretched all the way from the Isle of Wight off the English coast to the beaches of Normandy, the Germans were totally unaware of their presence until 0345 on June 6. This was due in part to the disabling of so many of their radar stations by earlier bombing missions, but mainly to their false assumption that an invasion would not be launched in such bad weather. All the E-boats were taken off patrol and were battened down in the safety of their respective port cities.

At 0530, the German big guns began firing at the Allied warships. They were generally ineffective at the three to six mile range, but from 400 yards off the beach, they were devastating, particularly at Omaha beach.

The Allied preliminary naval bombardment was only moderately effective on all beaches except Omaha, where it was totally ineffective. This was because the bombardment was too short in duration and from too great a distance. In addition, the German gun emplacements were so stoutly constructed that even direct hits would often not destroy them. At Omaha the German 88 caliber cannons were set back deep in the cliffs within concrete and steel casements. They were not knocked out until Allied destroyers moved up to within 1,200 yards off shore and blasted them at point-blank range.

In the two months preceding D-Day, the Allied air offensive succeeded in destroying so much of the French railroad system, roads, and bridges, that it virtually isolated the beachhead from the rest of Normandy. The Allies also bombed and strafed all military traffic during daylight hours. Their biggest accomplishment, however, was to gain almost total air supremacy by destroying most of the *Luftwaffe* and driving it out of France. The price for this air dominance was high, with the loss of 12,000 men and 2,000 planes in the short span of only two months.

On D-Day the Allies filled the air with 3,467 heavy bombers, 1,645 medium bombers, and 5,409 fighters. Nazi flak batteries shot down 113 planes, but not one was downed by the *Luftwaffe*.

For all the Allied planes launched against the German gun sites in Normandy on D-Day, only the bombing of Utah beach was successful. The other Nazi beach batteries were largely untouched, either because of poor visibility from clouds, smoke or fog, or because the Allied bombers, for fear of striking too close to advancing soldiers on the beaches, dropped their bombs too far inland.

Ground-air coordination was not well developed until December, 1944, when it was used effectively in the Battle of the Bulge. There was virtually no ground-air coordination on D-Day except for spotter planes to guide naval bombardment.

The Utah beach invasion by the American Fourth Infantry Division was a smashing success. In 15 hours more than 20,000 American troops and 17,000 vehicles were put ashore, although winds and ocean currents carried the landings 4,000 yards away from the planned target site. Casualties were light, with 12 killed and approximately 175 wounded, most of these by mines. The Fourth Division lost twenty times as many men at the Slapton Sands training exercise than they did on D-Day at Utah beach. By the morning of June 7, they were ready to move on into the Cotentin Peninsula to join up with the 101st and 82nd Airborne Divisions. The airborne divisions played an important role in the Utah landings, and made it possible for the Fourth Division to move rapidly inland by confusing the German defenders, interrupting telephone lines, and knocking out key defensive batteries.

Omaha beach was a different story. Here the combined strength of the U.S. First Infantry Division with the 116th Regiment of the Twenty-ninth Division were scheduled to put 40,000 soldiers and 3,500 motorized vehicles on the beach early on D-Day morning. This didn't happen, and no significant landings were made until after 1300.

The defensive attributes of Omaha beach made it the most formidable beach of the invasion. This overall defensive terrain included gun-infested hills, underwater obstacles, numerous land mines, and the close proximity of the German 352nd Army Division. Early on, some consideration was given by SHAEF to bypassing the four-mile stretch of Omaha beach because of its defensive strength, but this plan was ultimately discarded for fear the Germans might drive a fatal wedge between the Allied landings from this beach.

Navy destroyers finally saved the day for the *Omaha* assault when they moved in close to the shoreline and from there systematically knocked out the gun emplacements at close range.

The battle for Omaha beach raged on all morning with carnage and death the only reward for those brash enough to venture within range of the German 88 cannons or machine guns. Many Higgins boats, to avoid destruction, dropped their ramps in water too deep, and the hapless troops charged off the ramps only to drown, weighed down as they were with heavy equipment. Most of the swimming Sherman tanks (Ducks) that were launched too far from shore capsized in the rough seas before they had a chance to get on the beach.

After 1300, with destroyer attrition gradually eliminating Nazi gun nests, scattered pockets of infantry managed to dash and crawl their way up to the protecting shale wall where they huddled in increasing numbers waiting orders to charge up the mined exits to the ground above and behind the gun emplacements. The sea side of the wall became packed with an almost solid mass of bodies—living, dead, and wounded—waiting.

Slowly the deadly enemy fire let up and individual platoons in spurts of frenzied activity opened gaps in the barbed wire and cleared mines in the passes up from the beach. Some of the Sherman tank captains still at sea, seeing what was happening to tanks discharged too far away from shore, insisted on bringing their Ducks almost to the beach. These survived to be of great help to the advancing soldiers.

Finally, sensing that the battle was turning in the Allies' favor, Colonel Taylor at about 1300 shouted over his bull horn, "Two kinds of people are staying on this beach, the dead and those who are going to die. Now let's get the hell out of here!"

The battle for Omaha was won, but the beach and shallows were strewn with over 2,000 dead and dying soldiers and sailors. A less experienced infantry division might not have been capable of sustaining this magnitude of loss and still go on to win the battle.

Navy and Army medics, including some doctors, gave life-saving emergency care to the wounded on the beach under extremely adverse conditions, and prepared them for transfer back to England on LSTs. These were the wounded we received on our tank deck on D-Day and the days following. It was our responsibility to keep them alive and to relieve their pain and suffering.

Compared to the harrowing assault on Omaha, the landings on the British and Canadian beaches were almost like a routine military training exercise. The terrain was flatter and defensive positions not nearly as strong. Further, the British used a longer preliminary bombardment than the Americans against gun emplacements that were not as well protected. Once on the beach, General Hobart's flailing minesweeping tanks rapidly cleared paths for the invading soldiers. The U.S. Infantry at Omaha had refused to use this odd-looking Hobart "funny," depending on sappers (specially trained soldiers) to clear the paths, a slower and more hazardous process.

By 0900 European time, on June 7, 1944, Eisenhower announced to the world that the Normandy invasion was a success. The Second Front to conquer Germany and liberate Europe had begun.

THE MARCH EAST ACROSS FRANCE

....

WHILE THE WESTERN WORLD CHEERED AND CELEBRATED THE successful landings at Normandy, the German press and radio put a different spin on the events. German media explained that the Allies had fallen into the trap that Germany had set for them and would soon be surrounded and pushed back into the sea. Propaganda aside, had it not been for the surprise and confusion among the German defenders from Hitler on down during the early hours of D-Day, the Allies might not have been thrown back into the sea, but they would have had a much tougher time and sustained significantly greater losses. Although not all D-Day objectives had been attained by D+1, Bayeux fell to the British forces on that day, and they had advanced to within three miles of Caen before being stopped by tough counterattacking German tanks. The German *Tiger* and *Panther* tanks were better armed and armored than any of the Allied tanks, and the German defenders were more familiar with the Normandy terrain. For example, German tank officers took greater advantage of the bocage country hedgerows than the Allies.

CAEN

Capturing Caen on D-Day was one of the Allies' objectives that didn't materialize. The Canadians also failed in their D-Day goal of taking the adjacent Carpiquet Airfield. The German resistance was so fierce that it was not until July 9, after a massive Allied bombing attack, that the Allies were able to take most of Caen and the airfield. Caen was a key defensive position on the road to Paris and its fall was a severe blow to the Germans, but its loss only heightened their resolve to fight more fanatically for every yard of French soil. The stubborn resistance and fierce counterattacks of the *Panzer* divisions, though outnumbered and without air support, reflected the desperation that motivated the German defenders. Von Rundstedt and Rommel begged Hitler to allow them to fall back to a better defensive line, at least out of the range of the Allied naval bombardment, but with his usual paranoid, siege-mentality, Hitler stoutly refused. German Army Group B then proceeded to fight one of the greatest defensive battles in history in spite of the shackles imposed by *der Fuhrer*. By the middle of June the Germans had drawn an almost complete perimeter around the Allied troops, and the attrition exacted by German forces against the Allied armies posed a serious problem in the latter part of June and first three weeks of July. Battle fatigue within the Allied troops reached almost epidemic proportion, and Churchill expressed serious concern that a dangerous stalemate seemed to be developing that could bog down the Allied offensive for the entire winter. The infantrymen sustained the greatest losses. About 75 percent of British and 85 percent of American casualties were foot soldiers.

CHERBOURG FALLS

The Americans, at the western end of the beach-head, were having troubles of their own joining up with the beleaguered 82nd and 101st Airborne Divisions. Once the Germans recovered from their initial D-Day shock and confusion, they began to offer increasing resistance to Bradley's advance into the Cotentin Peninsula. Cherbourg didn't fall until June 27, 1944, after bitter fighting, and the rest of the peninsula wasn't secured until June 30. Before surrendering Cherbourg, the Germans totally destroyed the port, denying any appreciable use of its facilities for receiving military supplies until well into September. This loss was compounded by extensive damage to the two Mulberry ports by one of the most severe Channel storms ever recorded. This hurricane-like storm began on June 19, and lasted for three days. The destruction of the Mulberry port at Omaha was almost complete and the port opposite the British beach was also severely damaged. Had the Normandy invasion been postponed to June 19, as almost became necessary, it would have had to be canceled again because this storm was much more severe than that of D-Day. The disruption of supplies posed a serious threat to the Allies and forced a temporary halt to any offensive action.

The amount of supplies consumed by a fighting army is difficult to comprehend, as for example, 400,000 gallons of fuel per army per day, and 740 tons of supplies per division per day. The Allied armies were quite wasteful, using more than three times the war materiel used by the German armies. The Germans had no choice and had to make do with less because their two-front war was grinding up more military supplies and equipment than they could replace.

Soon the port facilities were repaired and with few interruptions the Allied Army's needs were met. What isn't commonly appreciated is that more men were killed or wounded every day in the fighting after D-Day than on D-Day itself. The British and Canadian armies began to run out of replacements as, of course, did the Germans. Only the Americans had sufficient reserves to not only replace losses but to add new units as well. The two most important factors responsible for the Allied victory in Europe were General George C. Marshall's Selective Service System that built the American fighting forces up to 7.2 million men by D-Day and the prodigious military production of American industry. Of course, without the British Isles from which to launch the Second Front and the British Navy and Air Force, the battle for Europe would have had a different outcome. At the very least it would have lasted much longer and would have had a much stronger Russian flavor. It would probably have ended in a brokered peace rather than an unconditional surrender.

BREAKTHROUGH

The frustrating and enervating July stalemate was suddenly broken, when on July 25, after a devastating carpet bombing by the Allied Bomber Command, the American First Army, in *Operation Cobra,* broke through the German lines and fanned out to the south and west in the fields behind them. They reached Avranches on July 31, and were here joined by General Patton's Third Army.

The entire western half of the German Army collapsed as the American troops drove through Brittany pursuing the fleeing Germans toward the port cities on the Bay of Biscay.

A blow to the German cause occurred on July 17 when Rommel was seriously injured during a strafing by Allied planes on one of his inspection trips to the front lines. The automobile in which he was riding crashed into a tree stump and Rommel was thrown out of the car, striking his head on the pavement. He sustained a severe cranio-cerebral injury and was replaced by Marshal Gunther Hans von Kluge, who was transferred from the Eastern Front.

When von Kluge apprised Hitler of the difficult problems the Seventh Army was having without air support, Hitler shocked him by ordering an immediate counterattack aimed at severing the American line through Mortain to Avranches. Responding reluctantly, Von Kluge's army developed a deep westward pocket into the Allied line but was then stopped. This left it completely surrounded except for an eastern gap between Falaise on the north, and Argentan on the south, which the Allies fought to close. Patton's troops reached Argentan by August 13, but Montgomery's troops moving down from the North didn't reach Falaise to close the trap until August 17. By the time the ring was tightly closed on August 20, more than 40,000 German troops escaped east to the Seine. By now the Normandy battle had cost the Germans 450,000 casualties, 1,500 tanks, 3,500 guns and 20,000 vehicles. Forty German divisions had been destroyed. Von Kluge was blamed by Hitler for the Mortain debacle and was ordered back to headquarters in disgrace. He knew what would be waiting for him there and chose suicide instead. The pressure put on German generals and the price of failure can be appreciated with the knowledge that over one hundred of them committed suicide during the course of WWII.

Bitter recriminations among the American and British commanders followed the tardy appearance of the British Army in Falaise. Eisenhower was hard pressed to keep peace in the family.

With the remarkable advance of the Allied armies all across France, driving a badly mauled German Army of some 300,000 men and 25,000 vehicles before them, arguments about Falaise subsided and a golden euphoria embraced the Allies. Paris would soon be won and Germany couldn't hang on much longer. Getting home by Christmas now did not seem like such an impossible dream.

CLOSE CALL FOR HITLER

As the Allies consolidated their gains in France and Russia prepared for its long-delayed drive west to Germany, a large group of dissident German military officers, realizing that the Nazi dream of conquest had become a horrible nightmare, were convinced that the only hope Germany had for a reasonable settlement with the Allied powers was to assassinate Hitler and establish a new German government.

Thirty-seven-year-old Lieutenant Klaus Von Stauffenberg, a decorated Nazi Army officer who now hated Hitler, and his accomplice in Berlin, a similarly disenchanted officer, German Home Army Deputy Commander General Friedrich Olbricht, were the "would be" assassins for this coup d'état.

On July 20, 1944, Von Stauffenberg at a meeting of the German High Command in Rastenburg, East Prussia, placed his briefcase containing a powerful time-bomb within a few feet from where Hitler sat at the huge oak conference table and then quickly left the building to return to Berlin. By a random quirk of fate, one of the attendees, to make room for his feet and totally unaware of the portent of his action, moved the briefcase to the other side of the massive table leg from Hitler. Moments later the bomb exploded and blew the room apart. Four men were killed outright and twenty more were seriously wounded. Hitler was burned, deafened, and temporarily paralyzed, but miraculously survived and was even able to receive Mussolini in consultation a short time later.

Von Stauffenberg, because he had checked out before the explosion, was immediately suspected as the bomber. Both he and Olbrich were apprehended in Berlin, interrogated, and summarily shot. Fifteen thousand other suspected traitors were rounded up and tried in a so-called "People's Court." Five thousand of them were executed, and many others committed suicide to avoid torture and painful execution. A number of condemned military officers were hung with piano wire by the neck from meat hooks. As they dangled, kicking and clawing, they slowly strangled, their faces swelling and turning purple before they died. Movies of these hangings were shown to selected groups of officers as a deterrent to anarchy.

Rommel, suspected of being one of the conspirators, was given the choice of suicide by cyanide ingestion or appearing before the People's Court for trial. Knowing the trial would be a sham and fearing retribution to his family, Rommel chose cyanide. To prevent any backlash from the German people who loved Rommel, the official explanation attributed his death to complications following a head injury he had sustained in the auto accident of a few months earlier. He was accorded a state funeral as a Nazi hero in what was truly a masterpiece of hypocrisy. Dietrich Bonhoeffer and Alfred Delp, clergymen who were outspoken critics of Hitler and the Nazis, were also executed as conspirators.

Never one to miss an opportunity for propaganda, upon learning of Hitler's miraculous escape from death, Goebbels intoned on national radio, "Never again will the Almighty reveal himself as he has just done in saving the Fuhrer. His intention was to let us know that it is for us now to work for victory. Let us go to it."

Paris Regained

Liberating Paris was a ticklish business. The German contingent within the city numbered over 5,000 men, led by General Dietrich von Choltitz. Under orders from Hitler, von Choltitz had placed demolition explosives beneath all the bridges, power plants, railway stations, and all important buildings. He was told by Hitler that "Paris must not fall to the enemy except as a field of ruins." Von Choltitz, known for his blind obedience to Hitler, became motivated by an obligation higher than even der Fuhrer: civilization itself. He permitted Swedish mediator Raoul Nordling to pass through German lines to the Allies and tell them to take the city as quickly as possible and they would meet with only token resistance. They could then defuse all the explosive devices. This dereliction of duty on the part of one of Hitler's most loyal followers, in the greater interest of all humanity, was one of the war's most unusual and outstanding events.

Eisenhower, to help calm General de Gaulle, permitted The Free French Army, led by General LeClerc, to enter the city first on August 23, and selected troops of the Allied armies to follow. On August 29, the Allies marched triumphantly down the Champs Élysées before the top army brass. This was indeed a thrilling moment in history.

By September 4, Antwerp and Brussels were liberated and the entire Western Front was moving rapidly towards the German border. Two thousand Allied tanks were chasing fewer than one hundred Nazi tanks, and Allied aircraft outnumbered German aircraft 14,000 to 570. The end of the European war seemed imminent and everyone was celebrating.

As the Allies approached the Rhine, however, German resistance stiffened considerably and Allied losses began to mount. The German supply lines shortened as the Allied lines lengthened, and additional *Panzer* divisions from within Germany were being thrown into the Western Front.

MARKET GARDEN

To expedite clearing a path across the Rhine, Montgomery conceived a vertical attack on the Rhine bridges at Arnheim in the Netherlands, called *Operation Market Garden*. This was a risky venture for Montgomery. It involved 20,000 U.S. troops from the 82nd and 101st Airborne divisions and approximately 9,000 British Airborne troops. Unfortunately, the preparation and execution of *Operation Market Garden* was seriously flawed. In addition it was infected with the deadly virus of "overconfidence." For the British paratroops the operation became a debacle. Over 6,000 troops were taken prisoner. The American troops fared better but the operation overall proved to be a disappointing failure.

Although the Allied troops continued to make modest progress, they had been slowed considerably. Moreover, the cloudy and rainy weather of late fall often made the Allied Air Force ineffectual. Metz fell to the Allies on November 19, and Strasbourg on November 23, but progress was again measured in yards rather than miles. The entire German population as well as its armed forces worked and fought with a fanatic zeal that stemmed from the knowledge they were facing unconditional surrender to an enemy they feared would reduce their country to pastureland, and force their people into slavery or worse. They particularly feared the Russians because they knew how cruel and ruthless they were on the Eastern Front. They also realized there was good reason for the Russians to hate them. German soldiers would much rather fall prisoner to the Western Allies than to Russian troops.

ARDENNES DEBACLE

Although the Allies were disappointed at their slow progress during the early days of December, there was never any doubt that they would ultimately be victorious. They just wouldn't be home for Christmas.

Suddenly, at 1730 on December 16, the freshly-arrived, untested U.S. 106th Division, stationed in the Ardennes Forest, was horribly shocked and totally surprised. German soldiers who seemed to come out of nowhere charged with violent fury upon the hapless Americans. There were only four American divisions in this sector of the Allied line. They were being attacked by twenty German divisions, seven of which were *Panzer* tank divisions. The Americans were completely unprepared for this massive assault and sustained a huge number of casualties. The Germans also captured more than 7,000 prisoners.

This defeat was the most serious loss for the Americans during the entire European operation. The shock of this totally unexpected counterattack caught all Allied forces by surprise, including Allied Intelligence. No one in their right mind would have undertaken such a hare-brained operation. No one, of course, except Hitler. Even his own generals, to a man, thought the idea was insane, but there was no deterring Der Fuhrer. When news of the German offensive reached Bradley, he shouted, "Where the hell has this sonofabitch gotten all of his strength?"

Bastogne and the Battle of the Bulge

....

AFTER TWO DAYS OF FLOUNDERING, THE AMERICAN TROOPS DUG IN. BY December 20, they had stopped the advancing Germans, but only after their advance had created a huge bulge westward just short of Dinant on the Meuse River. German troops had bypassed the vital transportation hub-city, Bastogne, which came under heavy siege from the 20th to the 26th of December by the celebrated *2nd Panzer, Panzer Lehr,* and *26th Volksgrenadier* Divisions. The city was being held only tenuously by the 101st Airborne Division, led by Brigadier-General Anthony G. McAuliffe, plus tanks of the 9th Armored Division and two battalions of engineers. With the city totally surrounded by German troops, when given the option of surrender by the German commander, McAuliffe responded with his now famous response, "Nuts!"

The fog and clouds lifted after a week of desperate fighting, and with renewed air support, the Allies' fortunes began to improve considerably. The siege was finally lifted and the Germans were forced back by units of Patton's Third Army and his Fourth Armored Division driving up from the south, plus a combined British and American force led by Montgomery attacking from the north.

More than 600,000 American troops were involved in the Battle of the Bulge. They sustained 81,000 casualties; 19,000 were killed and 15,000 captured. The British, who entered the battle late, sustained only 1,400 casualties. The Germans however, were the big losers. Over 100,000 German soldiers were killed, wounded or taken prisoner, 800 German tanks destroyed, and hundreds of German planes were shot down. These could never be replaced. Most of the Allied troops and equipment losses were replaced in a few days. The Allied leadership, though chagrined and humbled by the unexpected and damaging German onslaught, estimated that the net effect, aside from the substantial and tragic human losses, would be to delay Germany's defeat for not more than six weeks. Hitler's Ardennes folly on the other hand, guaranteed Germany's unconditional surrender. He had hoped that the Ardennes counterattack, together with winter weather, would have delayed the Allies at least long enough to set the stage for a negotiated peace. He also had great hope for his V-2 missile offensive against London.

The smoldering resentment that developed between the British and the American generals boiled over on Christmas Day when Montgomery blamed the whole debacle on Eisenhower for not permitting him to make a single thrust via the northern route into Germany. He then had the gall to tell the news media that British troops had saved the day for the Americans. When he arrived at General Hodges' headquarters, according to one staff officer, he acted like "Christ come to clean the temple." Montgomery also upbraided General Bradley for his army's defeat.

In reality, everyone knew that the Ardennes battle was an American campaign and the British role in it was minor. After all his criticism of the Americans, it was Montgomery who refused to act swiftly on the opportunity to close the base of the bulge and trap at least two German divisions. They would not have made it back to Germany to fight again. The Allies decisively won the Battle of the Bulge, but the victory could have been even greater had they followed up on their advantage more expeditiously. Montgomery deserves most of the blame for this tactical error.

During the first weeks of January, 1945, the Allied armies made gradual progress against very stubborn German resistance. Every village, road, and bridge yielded only after a tough and bloody battle. It was then that the Allies realized how costly was their failure to counterattack at least a week earlier and close the gap.

THE YALTA CONFERENCE

With the inexorable march of the Allies toward Berlin from the west and the punishing advance of the huge Soviet Army from the east, Roosevelt, Stalin, and Churchill met in the recently liberated Crimean city of Yalta, on the Black Sea, February 4, 1945, for what has been considered the most important conference of the war. Here important issues were decided upon, such as how to avoid clashes between the Russian Army driving from the east and the American and British armies advancing from the west as they would inevitably meet on enemy soil. Other issues were: 1) how to divide up post-war Germany and Berlin into four occupation zones, one each for Russia, Britain, France and the United States with Russia agreeing to an occupation zone for France only if it came out of the Anglo-American Zone; 2) ceding to Russia all of Poland east of the Curzon line; 3) obtaining Russia's commitment to enter the war against Japan after Germany's surrender; 4) guaranteeing return to Russia all lands lost to Japan in the war of 1904–05. The exchange of deserters and prisoners of war and "free" elections in previously occupied countries were among many other decisions made at this conference.

Roosevelt was frail and obviously not well during this meeting of the big three, and many historians believe that he made too many concessions to Stalin with whom he boasted he had a special "insider" relationship. They attribute the birth of the Cold War to the concessions made to Stalin at the Yalta Conference. This allegation was stoutly denied by U.S. Secretary of State, Edward Stettinius, who attended the conference, and who blamed the Cold War on Russia's failure to abide by the decisions made at Yalta. The most disillusioned country after publication of the Yalta Agreements was Poland, who not only had to concede land to Russia, but had no guarantee that their choice of post-war government, exiled in London, would be respected.

RUSSIA MOVES AGAIN

While the Allies were slowly but surely moving into Germany, the long stalled Russian offensive in Poland began to move again. Stalin waited long enough to insure the destruction of the noncommunist partisans in Warsaw. On January 13, 1945, he began his drive toward Germany. Warsaw fell on the 17th and the Russian Army advanced over 100 miles along a 400 mile front in a week. By the end of February the Russians had advanced to within 60 miles of Berlin. Here they halted to re-supply and prepare for the final drive into the heart of Germany. With the German lines becoming shorter and closer to their supply source and with their obsessive and justifiable fear of Russian revenge, they exacted a terrible price for every mile gained by the Russians. In March, Germany sent all the reinforcements they had to fight on the Eastern Front, which weakened to some extent its resistance on the Western Front.

CROSSING THE RHINE

....

ON MARCH 7, 1945, ALLIED ARMIES REACHED THE LAST NATURAL BARRIER to central Germany, the Rhine River. The U.S. First Army prepared to seize the vital railroad bridge at Remagen. By an amazing, almost miraculous stroke of good luck, a German prisoner of war informed one of his guards that at exactly 1600 on this day, in 45 minutes, the entire Remagen bridge was timed to blow up. The Commanding Officer immediately dispatched a special U.S. force to the bridge where they found and defused the main explosive charges just minutes before they would have exploded. Several smaller detonations did occur, but the bridge was saved, permitting the army to cross the swollen river in record time. Ten days later the wounded bridge collapsed, but by that time the army had established a bridgehead on the east side of the river, and pontoon bridges had been emplaced to accommodate subsequent crossings.

Hitler was so enraged that the bridge wasn't destroyed as planned that he had four officers in charge executed. Hitler also replaced Commanding Officer Field Marshal Gerd von Rundstedt with Field Marshal Albert Kesselring. None of those punished were responsible for what had happened.

From this new powerful east Rhine River position, the U.S. armies were now prepared to continue their advance into Germany. At this juncture, however, to their dismay, Eisenhower ordered them to halt their advance until Montgomery's northern armies had made it across the great river. At Montgomery's deliberate pace, this didn't occur until some three weeks later. This was another example of Eisenhower's effort to keep peace in the family.

Another reason for Eisenhower's delay was that he believed it was of greater strategic importance to surround and destroy German Army units west of Berlin than to march into the city itself. This position was also more compatible with Stalin's expectations.

On March 5, the U.S. Third Armored Division marched into Cologne and found it reduced to rubble. It wasn't until March 23 when Montgomery's massive forces crossed the Rhine at Wesenland that the ponderous move toward Berlin began again, hampered almost as much by roads choked with wrecked equipment as by enemy resistance.

DESPERATE MEASURES

....

ONE LITTLE KNOWN FACT IS THAT THE GERMANS, LIKE THE JAPANESE, in the latter weeks of the war, utilized suicide air squadrons to ram Allied bombers. In one day, 184 volunteer pilots, flying Messerschmitt 109s, destroyed 23 Flying Fortress bombers by deliberate in-flight collisions.

Fortunately for the Allies, the advanced weapons systems developed by Germany were not used until too late in the war to make any appreciable difference in its outcome. Germany's Willi Messerschmitt built the world's first jet plane late in the war. The planes could achieve speeds up to 540 m.p.h. and were capable of knocking down Allied fighter planes with ease and without getting hit. The fastest propeller plane was easy prey to the Me-262. When an ecstatic Göring reported the spectacular success of this plane to Hitler and requisitioned more of them, he was angrily rebuked. Hitler shouted that he wanted only bombers and not fighters. "Your fighters are no damned good!" he screamed. After watching a demonstration of the plane's attributes he grudgingly authorized building more Me-262 jet planes, but only on the condition they would be fighter-bombers. Converting the Me-262 to an effective bomber was impossible because it had neither the range nor the carrying capacity to fulfill this role. Again Hitler's interference with sound military judgment in an area that he had little expertise greatly hampered the German war effort.

The V-1 and V-2 rocket and missile bomb armaments were ahead of their time, but nevertheless arrived too late to help the German cause. During the first half of the war Hitler delayed development of the V-2 missile program in favor of conventional weapons, believing that these exotic bombing devices would not be necessary. In the latter part of the war, however, as the German prospects of winning faded, he pushed the production and deployment of the

V-2 missiles in a mood of revenge and also in the hope of gaining a more favorable armistice.

The main experimental rocket center was at Peenemundi on the Baltic Sea. Launching sites were scattered, with the principle sites being in Holland. Montgomery's failure to follow up his capture of Antwerp by seizing the northeastern approach to the city where the missile sites were located, permitted Germany to use these launch pads for a much longer time than would otherwise have been possible.

The V-1 rockets, small pilotless airplanes were loaded with explosives, dubbed "buzz bombs" by the English for the loud, rasping sound they made coming in. These relatively slow weapons (450 mph), with low trajectory, could quite often be destroyed by anti-aircraft fire or interceptor planes.

In 1944, 8,500 V-1 rockets were fired at Britain but only 2,420 successfully reached their target. Starting in September, 1944, approximately 1,100 of the much more destructive V-2 missiles (46 feet long, 14 tons with high explosive warheads) struck London, devastating hundreds of buildings and causing thousands of casualties. The V-1 and V-2 attacks on England created a constant, pervasive atmosphere of dread, particularly in London, but it had no influence on the war's outcome. Had the missile program been started earlier, it might well have resulted in some kind of armistice for Germany rather than unconditional surrender.

In pushing the rocket program, Hitler unwittingly did the Allies and the entire world, for that matter, a great favor, because he did it at the expense of the German nuclear research project which was under the direction of the very capable nuclear scientist, Werner Heisenberg at the Kaiser Wilhelm Institute. Hitler was caught in the dilemma of lacking the means to run parallel rocket and atomic programs.

Germany was producing heavy water (H_2O_2) necessary for developing an atomic bomb at Rjukan, Norway, but production was stalemated by Allied bombing attacks and saboteurs. Moreover, a time bomb destroyed a shipload of heavy water en route to Germany from Norway. In spite of these interruptions, the atomic program in Germany was moving along well until, at Hitler's direction, it was shut down in favor of Werner Von Braun's rockets.

Fortunately for mankind, the war in Europe ended before Germany could arm their missiles with the ultimate weapon, the atom bomb. There is little doubt that had the atomic bomb been available to Germany in time, Hitler would have used it without a qualm.

Diary: January 10, 1944 to June 24, 1944

....

JANUARY 10, 1944: *Along with 39 other young apprehensive medical officers, on this date I reported to the United States Naval Hospital in Newport, Rhode Island. This was an immaculate "spit and polish" hospital steeped in Navy regulations and burdened by excessive bureaucracy. I was assigned to the surgical service with no responsibilities except to observe and to learn Navy regulations and record-keeping. Filling out the right forms in the approved manner seemed to take precedence over patient care, and a great to-do was made of the most minor procedures. For example, a simple diagnostic spinal puncture such as we would do alone on the wards at the Boston City Hospital was done here in a special procedures room with two assistants, surgical draping, and elaborate equipment. Whereas our procedure was noted with one line in the progress sheet, here a formal operative report was required.*

The lack of any medical or surgical responsibility in this "holding pattern" resulted in frequent "get acquainted" parties which were fun and excellent therapy for the nagging apprehension we all felt, but we weren't learning anything about emergency surgery.

....

JANUARY 17, 1944: *Seven of us received orders to report to Lido Beach, Long Island, New York for training prior to duty out. That dispatch produced a maelstrom of excitement and, of course, provided a perfect excuse for another party.*

The prevailing rumor (and there were many) had it that we were to be a part of the European invasion assigned to an amphibious unit. Medical officers would be in the third wave. This news increased the level of anxiety in our entire group several notches. I would often awaken at 3:00 AM in a cold sweat with a strong sense of impending doom and a heavy feeling in my chest. All the news media were abuzz with the "where" and "when" of the Allied assault on the European Continent, and the predicted cost in men and materiel, which didn't help.

....

FEBRUARY 11, 1944: *At one of our morning training sessions, we were informed that we were definitely going to be involved in the much-heralded amphibious landing somewhere in Europe, most of us to be assigned to an LST (Landing Ship Tank). The lecturing Navy Chief Petty Officer, who had survived the invasion on the beaches of Salerno, vividly detailed how tough it was, and how much worse the invasion of Europe would be. He must have sensed our heightened level of apprehension because he took time to point out to us that the anticipation of battle was worse than the battle itself, and that "After the first shot is fired, you will feel much better." We all hoped and prayed he was right because we were all gripped by a pervasive, extremely unpleasant foreboding. One of our group went AWOL, and another was discharged from the service for "psychiatric reasons." He apparently couldn't handle the pressure. Most of us were confronting our own mortality for the first time in a very real way.*

....

FEBRUARY 18, 1944: *We were issued our gear which included both arctic and tropical clothing and .45 caliber revolvers. Based on the gear we were given, we didn't have a clue where we were going.*

....

FEBRUARY 21, 1944: *Groups 20 and 21, comprised of forty corpsmen and two medical officers, Elroy Peterson (a medical school chum) and I, mustered outside our barracks (A-1) and then marched in formation to the railroad station.*

What a sight! It was out of this world! Pete and I in our dress blues and great coats and pistols at our sides, leading forty smart-stepping blue jackets, all with carbines on their shoulders, marching down the middle of the main street.

We rode the troop train to Penn Station, New York City, and were conveyed by truck and station wagon to Pier 45, where our ship, LST-52, was docked. After touring the ship with USNR (U.S. Navy Reserve) Captain Robert Freeman and a few other line officers, a miracle happened! The horrible pervasive anxiety and fear

*that had been weighing down my spirits every day and often during the night sud-
denly disappeared and I felt "free!" I was ecstatic with my new lightness of being,
and wondered if this was an answer to prayer, or did it represent the normal psychological reaction of fear disappearing because I had become actively involved in
the perceived danger, as the Navy Chief said it would, "when the first shot is fired."*

*As we toured the ship we were regaled with stories by the ship's crew who had
sailed up to New York from Charleston, South Carolina, of how rough the trip was,
and how they thought the ship would break apart, and how terribly seasick they
all were. Even with these horror stories, the old icy fingers of fear didn't grab at my
throat and chest as they had before. Whatever the cause of this blessed relief, Divine
intervention, or a normal psychological response, I did utter a prayer of thanks for
the remarkable deliverance I had experienced from my debilitating anxiety.*

*The ship appeared to be much larger than I had expected, being well over 300
feet in length and displacing some 4,000 tons. The bottom was flat, drawing only
six feet, fore and fourteen feet, aft. The shallow draft permitted the LST to glide up
on the beach, open its bow doors, drop the ramp, and discharge its cargo from the
tank deck: trucks, tanks, troops or whatever, right onto the beach. If the beach was
"hot," as it would be on D-Day, the LST would unload its cargo onto flat, motorized
"rhino" barges several miles offshore that would transport the load to the beach.*

*Most of the army troops were taken ashore in LCVPs (Landing Craft Vehicle
Personnel), also known as "Higgins boats" (after their founder, Andrew Jackson
Higgins from New Orleans). These were made of Philippine mahogany, were 36
feet long, 10½ feet wide, and were lowered from davits on the top deck of the LST
into the sea. They could carry a platoon of 36 men or a jeep and a squad of 12 men.
The troops clambered into them from rope ladders or cargo nets hung over the
side. Upon hitting the beach, the bow doors dropped down and the troops charged
ashore. The propellers were protected, and the LCVP could back off the beach, turn
around in a hurry, and return to the LST for another load. The crewmen may not
have always liked their assignment, but they loved their Higgins boats.*

*The LSTs were in short supply and much too valuable to take the chance of
losing them on the beach during the initial invasion. After emptying, the tank deck
was used as a huge hospital ward to carry the wounded back to England. This
would be our workplace.*

*The very characteristics that permitted the LST to land on the beach made it a
poor ocean-going vessel. It was slow (5 to 7 knots) and affectionately called, "Long*

Slow Target," or "Last Slow Trip." The flat bottom and shallow draft caused it to roll violently in heavy seas, often creating the feeling that it would roll all the way over.

We were happy to learn that on our trip across the Atlantic our cargo would be a load of pontoons—the best load you could have in the event you were hit by a torpedo or struck a mine.

The vulnerability of the LST to rapid sinking upon taking a hit was related to the large tank deck, which occupied some 70% of the total below-deck volume of the ship. If a torpedo or mine explosion breached the tank deck it would immediately fill with water and the small lateral airtight compartments couldn't prevent the ship from going down fast. There were usually few survivors.

The officer's quarters were adequate with small double rooms containing two bunks and a desk, and a fairly large dining area known as the ward room. This served principally as a mess hall, but also doubled as an operating room for surgical emergencies. There were several long rectangular tables in the mess hall, bolted down to the steel deck. Around the table-top edges were sliding wood panels that could be pushed up two to three inches to be used during rough weather to prevent dishes from sliding off onto the deck. The food was generally very good.

We had one annoying problem on our ship. The boilers would "conk out" once in awhile, and until they could be fixed, which often took all day, the ship was a refrigerator. On one occasion the water froze in the pipes.

....

FEBRUARY 22, 1944: *Two tugs pulled us away from the pier and out into the Hudson River. The night was dark and misty as we slipped under the Brooklyn Bridge into the East River and then into the Sound. The fog became so heavy we almost rammed a barge, so we anchored for the night. The following day we sailed up to Providence, Rhode Island, and then on February 27th to Boston Harbor via the beautiful Cape Cod Canal. We docked at a South Boston pier.*

We were informed by Captain Best, Royal Canadian Navy, that we were to conduct a seasickness prevention study on our trip from Boston to Halifax, Nova Scotia. Dr. Denny-Brown, chief of neurology at Massachusetts General Hospital, would be the on-board principal investigator. This was to be a double-blind study with three different seasickness preventive drugs and one placebo. These capsules were in boxes marked I to IV. We were to distribute them sometime after leaving Boston Harbor, but before we hit rough seas.

We were in a convoy of 26 transport ships with three corvettes as escorts. We were the third ship in the sixth column which was a pretty good place to be. Unfortunately, our electric steering device broke down twice today so we had to drop back to take up the rear of our column to avoid a collision. This was a more precarious location. General quarters alarm drills were conducted twice daily for one hour at dawn and dusk.

....

MARCH 4, 1944: *During the night the seas became rough and stormy. The ship rolled up and down and around like a drunken sailor. Trying to dress, Pete was thrown across the cabin twice. I put on my clothes lying in the bunk. All but four of our forty corpsmen were seasick.*

Pete and I were both nauseated, but managed to get by until we had to go below decks to visit the sick and check up on the seasickness experiment. Below decks the troop compartments were a mess with broken dishes, vomitus, and prostrate men. Helmets were used for emesis basins. I became so ill with the ship's rolling and the stench, that as I made my rounds examining sick crew members and checking on the experiment, I would have to turn away every three to four minutes to vomit into a pail I had carried along. I have never been as miserable in my entire life! There seemed to be no difference in efficacy between the three anti-seasickness drugs and the placebo, because nearly everybody was sick except for a few of the "old salts." We could only conclude that in seas this rough, nothing worked. The ocean was an immense expanse of deep valleys and high mountains.

....

MARCH 5, 1944: *This was a red letter day for me because when I got out of my bunk, with the ship still rolling violently, I felt no nausea. Pete felt better too. We ate good breakfasts with legs wrapped around a table leg and cereal dish in hand. For fun, we would let go of the leg, slide across the room, hit the bulkhead, and slide back again. I couldn't believe my good fortune in making this adaptation so soon. Many of the crew were still afflicted. Dr. Denny-Brown never got seasick and left the ship for Boston after we anchored in Halifax harbor.*

MARCH 13, 1944: *The harbor is almost totally filled with ships. I learned from ship-Captain Freeman that our convoy leaves early tomorrow for England. There will be 70 ships plus escorts. We have the dubious honor of occupying what is known as "coffin corner," the last ship in the second column. This is right next to the least enviable position: last ship in the first column, called "torpedo junction."*

Captain Freeman bet me $25 that the invasion of Europe would happen before April 15th, 1944. I took the bet because I couldn't see how they could get everything together that soon, but maybe he knows something I don't know.

After tonight, "No pajamas." Captain's order: "Everyone sleeps in their clothes."

The North Atlantic has been the premier hunting ground for the Nazi Submarine "Wolf Packs." Thousand of Allied ships have been sunk by these predatory submarines. Even though the rate of loss diminished considerably after mid-1943, the danger of "U" boat attack still exists, and everyone takes the risk seriously. Travel by convoy with an escort is the only reasonably safe way to go. Transport ships traveling alone, which seldom occurred, or in convoy without escorts, were in great danger of disaster.

....

MARCH 14, 1944: *Today, our convoy slipped quietly out of the harbor at 1300 on a day that was warm, bright, and calm. We were number 50 to leave.*

Soon, however, as we proceeded further into the North Atlantic, the winds came up and the sea responded with choppy breakers and rising waves. LST-52 resumed its joyous, wanton rolling, and we had a reprise of our seasickness, though not quite as severe as the first time.

The night became rougher and more hectic, and we were thrown all over our bunks. One Higgins boat broke loose from its moorings and several men were thrown to the deck and injured. Seasickness, however, was again the scourge of the ship, and other illnesses and injuries were mild by comparison.

....

MARCH 15, 1944: *Today was more of the same; dark, windy, and rough. We could eat only crackers while lying flat on our bunks, and would vomit whenever we got up to move around.*

MARCH 16, 1944: *Today we felt better, but the morning hours dragged interminably. Gradually, both Pete and I regained our sea legs, and, thank God, were able to start eating again. The vestibular apparatus was finally making its rather retarded adaptation.*

Every day of the ten-day stretch from March 16 to 26 was almost identical-excruciatingly slow, rough and often nauseous.

....

MARCH 26, 1944: *General Quarters Alarm! A Submarine had been detected by one of the escorts and depth charges were dropped. There was lots of excitement, but no losses.*

....

MARCH 27, 1944: *We were getting close to the southern tip of Ireland and could detect the sweet odor of spring grass.*

....

MARCH 28, 1944: *We rounded northern Ireland and passed within 100 yards of a floating mine. I learned that ninety miles away, Bristol was bombed.*

The time of testing draws close. London was bombed heavily last night; Berlin, too. Anzio beach is at a stalemate.

....

MARCH 30, 1944: *Today Army troops disembarked at Milford Haven, Wales. Tomorrow we sail to Southampton. We are only 65 miles from France. Things are getting hotter.*

....

MARCH 31, 1944: *Last year at this time I wondered about the unknown of actual combat. I now have developed a strange mind-set. I cannot conjure any plan for the future because I can't see or imagine beyond the present, or at least beyond the "Big Event," the invasion of Europe. I wonder if I have very much time to live. Today is my 26th birthday.*

The day is beautiful, blue sky with billowing clouds. LST-52 is staying close to shore amongst a forest of barrage balloons. Except for them, it is hard to believe we are at war.

....

APRIL 1, 1944: *Foggy, rain, rough seas. Seasick again. Even the captain felt it. I spent most of the day in the sack.*

....

APRIL 12, 1944: *Palm Sunday: Entered Southampton Harbor today. Many amphibious units present. Captain Freeman predicts Easter Sunday will be D-Day. I doubt it.*

....

APRIL 5, 1944: *Visited Queen Victoria Hospital at Netly. Spring flowers, yellow jonquil, and narcissus grow in abundance; wonderful sights, smells, and sounds. The hospital grounds are beautiful but little to see of note inside.*

Solid earth has a strange feel when you first get off the ship. You are so accustomed to absorbing the rocking with your knees, and entire body for that matter, that when you walk on terra firma and nothing "gives," you experience an odd, almost sickish feeling for awhile. Sailors call it "land sickness." Fortunately it doesn't last.

I had fish and chips at a small restaurant, Winstons, today, where an elderly lady told me about the severe rationing in Britain: one egg per month, two ounces of cheese and one shilling's worth of meat per week, never ice cream. They live on fish, bread, porridge, and cheese.

Bombing destruction is extensive. Hardly a square block escaped serious damage. Many buildings were totally leveled. Beautiful St. Mary's Church was a shell: no roof, no windows, no interior, only pillars and walls. Churches seemed particularly hard hit.

Several of us attempted to get into Guildhall for the service-men's dance, but it was packed. We then went to Chantry Hall to dance for awhile and then accompanied two WAACS to their railroad station. After running for a mile or so to the docks we barely caught the last Higgins boat to the ship. Full moon, bright and beautiful, but are we tired!

APRIL 8, 1944: *Southampton again today. Spam and chips at Winstons. Read in "Stars and Stripes," the U.S. Armed Service Newspaper, that Russia had encircled Odessa. I predict the end of the German war by summer, 1945, or sooner. Saw the movie, "Road to Happiness," or as it is called in the U.S., "Intermezzo."*

Southampton is a veritable army camp. Everything is buzzing with excitement with more soldiers pouring into town every day and the harbor loaded with all types of amphibious craft: LCTs, LSTs, LCPs, pontoon barges, transports and floating concrete piers. The pontoons were unloaded from our tank deck. The vast number of cranes all around look like a burned-over pine forest.

....

APRIL 9, 1944: *Easter Sunday: I went to St. Michael's Church, a high Episcopalian Church of England, with all ritual and no sermon. Beautiful ceremony but not the format I would choose for my regular worship.*

....

APRIL 10, 1944: *Orders were received today to report to a base at Plymouth on April 13th for training exercises. Sister Melba's birthday today. With the pontoons gone, we played basketball on the tank deck; four officers vs. four enlisted men. Great fun!*

....

APRIL 11, 1944: *At 0400 we slipped quietly out of the harbor into the Channel, a calm, clear day. There were 16 escorts and only 5 or 6 merchant ships. We passed within 60 miles of one of the largest German U-boat and E-boat bases. Eight Mustangs zoomed over us bound for the French coast.*

There was a rumor from the Commanding Officer's ship that because Hitler would rather have the Western Allies take Berlin than have Russia do it, he would put up only token resistance to the European invasion. Although this would be wonderful, I doubt sincerely that it would happen. It's going to be a tough go, but right now I would be disappointed if for any reason I would have to miss it. This is in stark contrast to my feeling of impending doom before I boarded LST-52 in New York City only a few months ago. Strange!

We entered Plymouth Harbor about 1800. There were only a few ships in the harbor, most of them having left, apparently for training exercises.

Tonight, several of us had a long discussion with the Captain, whose conversation was peppered with colorful clichés and metaphors; "No strain no pain," "In any way, shape, or form," " You're crazier than a shit-house rat," "He sticks closer than the cover on a piss-pot."

....

APRIL 12, 1944: *This was our most unhappy day so far. We learned from orders that both Pete and I were to transfer off LST-52 for good and that, after one week of amphibious training at Fowey, we were to be split up with each of us taking twenty of the forty corpsmen.*

Both of us suddenly realized how much we had come to like and depend on each other and how much we had in common. We were very disheartened and to add to our misery, still no mail and no pay. It's been over two months without mail and one month without pay. No one knows what happened to the mail.

There was a little sunshine on this gray day—apple pie à la mode for lunch on the ship and chocolate cake à la mode in town at Naval Headquarters.

We spent an hour or two strolling the Plymouth streets and found the center of town to be a crumbling mess of ruined buildings. The destruction was more extensive than Southampton, and it hadn't been cleaned up as well. There were standing partitions, half walls, split towers, charred timbers, and piles of bricks. Little children played amidst the ruins, piling up the bricks and playing "hide and go seek" behind the walls. To brighten the somber, beaten city, there were scattered clumps of yellow daffodils, green grass, buds on the trees, and warm spring breezes.

....

APRIL 13, 1944: *At 0500 we were awakened for our early departure. After breakfast, we climbed into Lieberman's small boat and regretfully left LST-52, temperamental boiler and all, our home for almost two months.*

As usual we waited an hour for a ride to the depot and another hour for the train. The train was quaint and of the compartment type. The countryside was beautiful.

Our destination and temporary quarters was the dilapidated Greenbank Hotel at Fowey, Cornwall. Crigler, Thomas, Pete, and I are rooming together in a cold, bare room. One bright spot—there was a fireplace!

We had dinner at the base and then heard a lecture on the invasion plan by Lieutenant Faux. No details such as actual location were divulged. Faux said that our job, as planned, was tough, and after he had read about it, he hadn't slept for two nights. He assured us, though, that we will be successful; but at what cost? He didn't say.

Oddly enough, we had to turn in our guns before the battle! I guess someone else must need them more than we.

Saw the movie, "Song of Bernadette." Long, but good.

....

APRIL 14, 1944: *Rain, mud, and darkness, but the day was outstanding because we received our mail. It was wonderful to read the news from home.*

The CO here demands dress blues, so we slogged through sticky clay, splashing mud on pants and coats. We were inappropriately dressed considering the weather.

Today we learned at lecture what a tremendous task this invasion will be. I hope and pray I will be equal to my part.

....

APRIL 15, 1944: *Because the invasion had not begun by midnight, I won my bet from Captain Freeman. The problem now is to collect. Actually, that worries me little because Freeman is a straight shooter, but will we cross paths again? I hope so, and not just to collect the bet.*

Today's weather the same with drizzling rain, muck, and goo. Oh, for the life of a sailor! No muck aboard ship. There were more lectures and two training films on today's program.

....

APRIL 17, 1944: *Today was devoted to gas warfare lectures by Commander Ely. The use of gas to repel an invasion attempt was considered a very real possibility. This would really make a rough situation a lot rougher.*

....

APRIL 18, 1944: *More "gas" lectures. After hearing from the various speakers who have been through amphibious operations in Italy how tough this next one will be, we all feel we will be unusually lucky to live through it. Oddly enough, no one seems perturbed as yet, at least not externally. The men who had gone through those hot landings were more concerned about what they faced in this coming battle than we were. In this case our naiveté minimized our anxiety.*

Howard Scal, a good friend of mine from New York City, and I went for a long walk in the countryside tonight and discussed some of the thoughts we were experiencing. On the subject of what happens to you after you're dead, Scal said he did not believe in eternal life. "When I croak, I'll stay croaked," he said, "and no part of me will survive in any form." I felt chilled at these words, but he didn't seem to evince any concern or depression about this belief. Such good friends with such diverse beliefs.

....

APRIL 19, 1944: *Today Pete and I were separated, each taking with him half the corpsmen. I am to remain here another five days, and then report to LST-6, at Milford Haven on April 25. Pete is going to LST-316 at Penarth. Pete, Crigler, and Thomas leave tomorrow at 0700; Thomas to LST-307, and Crigler to LST-5. Tension is mounting. All diplomatic communications are being censored.*

....

APRIL 20, 1944: *Today was Hitler's 55th birthday. It was fascinating to hear the English and then the German commentator's birthday evaluations. The English: "Today marks the birthday of the world's worst enemy." The German: "On this day, 55 years ago was born the savior of the German people—yes, of the entire world."*

After helping to arrange train and truck schedules for the departing doctors and their crews, I moved bag and baggage from the Hotel into Fowey House. It is infinitely more enjoyable here. One of my new roommates, John Dodrill, is a beach master, and the other, Carlson, is in the supply corps.

....

APRIL 21, 1944: *We were disgusted to learn today that the London bus and street car workers went on strike, and the military had to take over their jobs to prevent a crippling work stoppage. I am sure the workers had gripes; low pay being the foremost. Still, their country was deeply involved in a war for its very survival, and their replacements, military personnel, were deprived of much-needed training on that account.*

This morning we had another session on gas warfare, then a quiz.

APRIL 22, 1944: *I was invited for tea and dinner to a Dr. and Mrs. Singer's home, two miles outside of Fowey. They lived in a huge rambling brick house surrounded by trees, lawns, and flowers that overlooked the sea. Both Doctor and Mrs. Singer were fascinating individuals and we had so much to talk about. He had been professor of the History and Science of Medicine at Oxford and was now at the University of London. He has written several books, and was currently writing a biography of Vesalius. Mrs. Singer was equally knowledgeable.*

The day was deep June. We strolled through their well groomed gardens, graced by carefully trained pear and apple trees and an abundance of flowers. Later we walked through the adjacent woods where "blue-bells" covered the ground. The dinner was very good considering the food shortage.

I stopped by the Fowey dance hall on the way home. Quiet but fun.

Two-thirds of my corpsmen have come down with a severe dysentery which began two days ago. We thought it would be over in 24 to 48 hours, but they are still sick, with severe abdominal cramping pain, watery, occasionally bloody diarrhea, headache, generalized aches and pains, and temperatures from 100 to 104 degrees Fahrenheit. There are now 600 cases in camp, and the ambulances have been busy night and day taking the sickest patients to the hospital for intravenous fluids. In addition to regular beds the hospital dispensary and wards have cots everywhere It took me 36 hours before I could locate two of my men.

....

APRIL 23, 1944: *Checked all my men again and found only nine that were well enough to leave with me for Milford Haven tomorrow morning. The rest are still sick with fever, aches, pains, and diarrhea. They will meet us later. We still have no idea what the infecting organism or the source of the infection is, but there obviously has to be some food or water contamination to have so many get sick at once.*

In the afternoon I hiked up to Menabilly, where Browning had lived and where Daphne Du Maurier now lived. I saw Daphne and her daughter strolling down a pasture path, but I didn't go over to speak to them because I felt they probably appreciated their privacy.

I have recently had the good fortune to be rooming with four men who had been through the Bizerte, Sicily, and Salerno invasions: Dr. Faux, Mr. Foches, Mr. Du Charmes, and "Tex" Carlson.

Last night we were awakened by an excited sailor shouting "Get up! Get to your stations! Air Raid Alert!"

My bed partners hardly stirred, and when the sailor returned, repeating his frantic call, one of them managed to mumble that our stations were right here. We all stayed in bed. Later, the all clear sounded. If I hadn't been so tired and the air so chilly I would have gone outside to see the show. We had no assigned stations.

....

APRIL 24, 1944: *Most of the day was spent on a train; nine men and myself, traveling first-class with plenty of room. Changed trains at Trenton, Cardiff, and finally Johnstown.*

The countryside was beautiful, all covered with a heavy, lush carpet of green. The land was neatly divided by ancient hedges into varied shaped and sized fields. Some were plowed and harrowed and a faint sheen of green could be seen. The winter wheat, or "corn" crop, as they call it in England, was making its first appearance from under the brown soil.

There were no unkempt, sooty buildings adjoining the tracks as is so commonly seen in our country. It was as well kept next to the tracks as away from them.

We passed by several large "flying fields" covered by grass in the center of the farm land that made them almost indistinguishable from the adjacent pastures. Cows and sheep grazed unconcerned as low-flying bombers made their landings.

....

APRIL 27, 1944: *Another train, another unknown destination. This time, the town of Swansea. Here we reported to the U.S. Port Office and were then transferred by Higgins boat to the LST-6, anchored in the harbor, fifteen minutes before it was set to sail. We hurried the luggage aboard as fast as we could, but with some of it still unloaded, the Higgins boat was hoisted up on the davits as the LST-6 got underway. No time wasted here! This is real navy!*

The captain of this ship, Captain Benjamin Franklin, was regular USN (U.S. Navy) as opposed to USNR (United States Naval Reserve) and prided himself in running a "tight ship." He had little respect for the 90-day wonders, the reservists, who made up the majority of naval officers, and he would never deviate from an assigned departure time no matter what. I soon learned that the Captain knew his navy regulations and ship management backwards and forwards, and he expected his officers and crew to follow protocol to the letter. Offenders would be punished. The other officers said he was a first-class sourpuss, and except for navy regulations, quite ignorant besides. He had disdain for the college graduate naval reserve, and he let this attitude be known. Although I sympathized with the officers, I was happy to know that he knew his seamanship and was super alert at all times. There was a grudging respect for Captain Franklin, and a definite feeling of confidence prevailed throughout the ship even though privately "they hated his guts." The food on this ship is better than I have had thus far in the navy, and its crew is experienced, having participated in the Sicilian occupation in July, and the Salerno landings in September, 1943.

We arrived in Portland around 2030 accompanied by approximately fifty small craft: LCIs, LCMs, LCTs and others. They looked like a swarm of water beetles. Our PC escorts made a submarine contact close by and dropped several depth charges that shook the entire ship.

....

APRIL 29, 1944: *The day was spent in Portland harbor with hundreds of other amphibious craft. Many indications of the impending invasion were evident. The operational plan for a large-scale training maneuver was delivered today and all liberty was stopped. Many large transport ships entered the harbor; I stopped counting at seven and still they came.*

This would be the dress rehearsal for the main event. We were informed that yesterday three LSTs of the 500 series were sunk just off the coast of England near Slapton Sands, Devonshire, during a training operation called Tiger. *There were over 400 casualties!*

All but one of our sick pharmacist mates returned to duty. An additional 45 new sailors, young and fresh from boot camp, were added to our roster.

The sullen atmosphere present when the Captain is around is none too pleasant. Sinking my teeth into this job is what will keep me going.

....

APRIL 30, 1944: *I went into Portland today to pick up the last of my sick pharmacist mates, but he was not well enough to come aboard.*

The harbor was even more crowded today with ten transports, several destroyers, at least 50 LSTs, PT boats, LCTs, and rocket ships. There were long lines of jeeps, trucks and "Ducks" preparing to "go to sea."

Yesterday German reconnaissance planes flew over, probably to take photographs. No bombs were dropped, but we are preparing for an air raid soon.

I taught our pharmacist mates how to do intravenous injections today. We began to load our tank deck at 0100. The main engines are roaring now for the trip into the landing beach area called the "hard." We have exactly four hours in which to load.

....

MAY 1, 1944: *When I awoke this morning, the ship was entirely loaded with vehicles and army personnel. In our tank deck were 6 cranes, 10 trucks, and several jeeps. On the main deck were 16 trucks and 8 jeeps.*

There are 18 army officers and 250 soldiers aboard. The ship is packed tighter than the proverbial "can of sardines." Men are sleeping outside on the deck, under and on top of the trucks, and on the decks below. What a mess if we took a torpedo.

These soldiers said they were much more concerned about being killed or drowned while on our ship than they will be on land facing enemy fire because there they could dig foxholes or dive into trenches. On the ship they were so exposed and they didn't like the thought of drowning.

We practiced hoisting simulated casualties on board today. Received and studied the operational plan for today's maneuvers, which will be the dress rehearsal for the main event. This is called the "Fabius Operation."

The Captain reported that the losses at the Slapton Sands training maneuvers two days ago were 1,300 instead of the 400 that were first reported!

....

MAY 2, 1944: *We left the confines of Portland Harbor and anchored outside with about 70 other ships. A heavy wind raised large waves, and today I felt depressed to the point of despondency. Everything seems so hopeless, so tragic. So much time and talent murdered. I longed for the woods and lakes of northern Minnesota—to get away from ships, guns, and men. How will I feel when the shooting actually begins? Better, I hope, because then there will be work to do. I must stay focused on the ultimate objective of this war, defeating the Nazis, restoring Europe, and then going home.*

MAY 3, 1944: *At 1300 our large ungainly task force got underway. We were about the fifth LST in a long column of these ships. Each towed two pontoon barges to be used for unloading vehicles and equipment from offshore positions. There were two French destroyers on either side of our column.*

'H' hour is tomorrow at 0730 and the army personnel will leave our ship in the Higgins boats.

We have our organization set for casualty handling. This is much less depressing than waiting around in a safe harbor. Again, action conquers mood.

....

MAY 4, 1944: *General alarm threw us out of bed at 0230. In the moonlit semi-darkness the soldiers quietly but swiftly prepared to make their departure. Most of them debarked in the Higgins boats, but a large number went into the beach with the vehicles on the barges.*

Maybe because we were so well prepared to handle the casualties there were none, either real or simulated. We could hear the support fire from the beach, but were told that it was nothing compared to what we will hear during the real thing.

We anchored close to shore tonight. Captain Franklin confined the first lieutenant to his room without head privileges (except for a bucket in the room) because one of the lines on a davit was too short. This captain is quite a lu-lu.

....

MAY 5, 1944: *The day slipped by rather pleasantly and quite uneventfully. The core of the day consisted of treating a number of minor medical problems. There was a classical case of scabies, one septic arthritis, one impetigo, one wart removal, and one insurance physical examination.*

The first lieutenant was freed from his room today.

Ben Roberts and I played catch on the now-empty, cavernous tank deck.

....

MAY 6, 1944: *Single file, like cattle filing into the barn yard at twilight, we entered Portland Harbor, one of ten LSTs.*

I rode the liberty boat into Weymouth and was amazed at what I saw. The streets and sidewalks were literally jammed with American and British soldiers and sailors, mostly American.

All public bars, dance halls and hotel bars were closed in the middle of the week because they had run out of wine and spirits. The only place open today was the American Red Cross Service Club, and to squeeze even one more person into that overly packed building was impossible. And so the streets were jam-packed with shouting, swearing, singing, laughing servicemen. Many were drunk, and others were well on the way. I don't know where they got the spirits, but it was probably the ubiquitous combination of ethyl-alcohol and canned grapefruit juice.

A colored soldier was playing a jazzed-up version of the popular song, "Stormy Weather" in the center of the street, and black and white soldiers alike, hungry for fun and excitement, jitterbugged to the hot sax.

There were a few girls on the street, all traveling in convoy with "destroyer escorts" numbering up to eight sailors for each girl.

A full moon drenched the city in a silvery blue light. My time was spent strolling through a park with deep lavender lilacs and bright yellow tulips, trying to fathom the meaning, if any, of all of this. It struck me that this would be the kind of a night that would be ideal for the invasion.

Soon these streets would be empty and the reveling men would have left for France, and then Berlin.

....

MAY 7, 1944: *Today we had a "light" breakfast of fried eggs, fried chicken, and a chocolate sundae for dessert. This was a little like the "last meal" before an execution.*

George Kopas of LST-705 and I went into Weymouth for a lunch of fish and chips, and as we were walking back on St. Thomas Street, we spied two beautiful young ladies watching us from a casement window above "Crabbe-the-Tailor" shop. We took a couple more steps and then without a word or a moment's hesitation we did an about face and knocked on their door. Their names were Ann and Vicki Shirley, and we learned over bitters at the Gloucester Hotel that they worked ten hours a day in an aircraft factory for one shilling (20 cents) an hour. We would liked to have visited longer, but we had to catch the last liberty ship leaving the pier.

....

MAY 8, 1944: *We left Portland this morning, a clear, sunny, windless day. Because the moon was full and we had but one escort, we anchored for the night in Torquay*

Harbor, instead of going on to Dartmouth, our intended destination. German E-boats and submarines were respected by all.

Six of us went into Torquay and found it to be a lovely town with beautiful homes, lawns, trees, churches, and even an occasional castle. We spent the evening at the Imperial Hotel, quite a swank spot, where there was no shortage of spirits. I danced with a beautiful girl named Pamela Eddy who lived in Paignton. Her Plymouth home had been destroyed by bombs when she was away.

The moon hung full and bright and paved a sparkling golden path on the water as we cruised back to our ship.

....

MAY 9, 1944: *The day was spent sailing from Torquay to Falmouth. We traveled with the unfortunate LST-289, which was one of the torpedoed ships at Slapton Sands. The stern almost to the deck house was completely blown off. I don't know how it managed to navigate.*

After lunch, I lectured on gas warfare defense to about 60 men. We still need more training.

....

MAY 10, 1944: *Conducted gas mask drill for the entire crew today, and then for my own men.*

Casualty-handling stations aboard ship were planned in more detail with my chief pharmacist mate. Our invasion casualty supplies and equipment came aboard this afternoon, and we were thrilled to see all the stuff: blood pressure cuffs, surgical instruments, ophthalmoscopes, and a ton of other supplies.

....

MAY 11, 1944: *Today more medical supplies were delivered, enough to fill three Higgins boats. There were 200 stretchers, eight cases of wool blankets (250 to a case), eight cases of plasma, splints, more surgical instruments, and scads of dressings, tape, and bandages. Are we being equipped with more than the usual hospital LST? I have no idea.*

Received a new sheet of confidential material on gas warfare. They really expect it to be used. My Chief Pharmacist Mate was drunk again yesterday and hungover today. Quite a drag!

MAY 12, 1944: *I lectured on respiration and digestion, and spent the entire evening on the new material on gas warfare. The future doesn't appear too bright from here.*

....

MAY 13, 1944: *Dry dock today. The entire hull was scraped and painted and a new screw (propeller) installed in only seven hours. That's fast! Now we are just waiting for the paint to dry. Tonight, Tracy, Ben, Hitchcock, and I went to a dance in the Princess Ballroom at the Falmouth Hotel. I spent most of my time with a lovely blonde girl named Barbara Richmond. She is enlisted in the Women's Land Army and makes 36 shillings ($7.70) a week.*

....

MAY 14, 1944: *We left dry dock today and anchored four miles up the Fal River along with six other LSTs. I lectured to the officers on gas warfare defense and then checked all the surgical instruments, wondering what some of them were for. With my internal medicine training, the sight of all those strange-looking utensils makes me nervous.*

....

MAY 15, 1944: *Went through the degaussing range today which should protect us from magnetic mines. Learned that at least one doctor that started with us at Lido Beach went down with the three LSTs sunk at Slapton Sands.*

....

MAY 16, 1944: *Went into Falmouth to have our surgical dressing packs autoclaved. Heard today that Germany has developed some new nerve gas that we know nothing about. How hideous this coming battle will be! Many feel that next week will hold the fateful D-Day.*

....

MAY 17, 1944: *Left Falmouth for Portland today and stopped for the night at Torquay out of respect for the E-boats.*

MAY 18, 1944: *Portland this afternoon. The harbor was loaded with LSTs. Most of our flotilla is now here. All our records were ordered ashore. A certain tension in the air foreshadows the nearing invasion. The U.S. radio predicted May 25th as D-Day. We will soon see.*

....

MAY 19, 1944: *Saw the paymaster today and got my $10,000 life insurance policy squared away. What a relief! Met Pete, Moody, Knight, and Chapman in Weymouth today. We talked and drank a few dark ales before we split up to return to our respective ships. Pete said that all mail from now on will be held in London until after the invasion.*

....

MAY 20, 1944: *Captain's inspection today lasted two and one-half hours. We received 12 bedpans, 7 urinals, heating pads, and water bottles today. Heard we are getting another MD aboard.*

....

MAY 21, 1944: *Our turn (LST-6) for target practice today. We shot at a flying sleeve. What a racket! They expect an air raid tonight. Tension mounts.*

....

MAY 22, 1944: *Air raid alert tonight. Smoke screen totally obscures the harbor.*

....

MAY 23, 1944: *Had one chocolate and one strawberry sundae today. Delicious! New MD, Dr. Dick Greenleaf, reported aboard tonight. Unfortunately, he hasn't had any surgical experience either! To insure secrecy, the Captain now keeps his cabin door locked at all times. Small boat men have painted white stripes on their helmets. Ships slated for "Diamond Beach" (wherever that is) are to have diamond-shaped logos painted on their hulls. All health records were sent ashore. We feel now that the big event will be the first week in June.*

Today the captain was angry and told me that either I cure the fungous infection on a mess-boy's hand or get one of my pharmacist's mates to take his place. Nice guy!

MAY 24, 1944: *All my patients feel better today, which makes me happy.*

We are tied to the transport, Melville, today. Socks, their ship's dog, fell between the ships into the water. He was heroically rescued by one of the Melville's sailors.

We wrapped syringes, needles, and instruments for autoclaving this morning.

I danced with Vicki again at the Officer's Club tonight, and learned from some army officers that tonight was their last liberty. Scuttlebutt has it that we will be "secured" (confined to our ship) starting tomorrow. We are painting a diamond on our bow tomorrow.

....

MAY 25, 1944: *Today, King George, Admirals Kirk and Hall, plus several British admirals inspected Portland Harbor. We were sandwiched in between the huge Melville and LST-332 and couldn't see the water, let alone the King's retinue. We were as obscure as a rat in a hole; nevertheless the Captain ordered that the entire ship's company, in their dress blues, stand at strict attention until all the big wheels departed, which was at least one-half hour.*

I took Vicki out again tonight. She is a bitterly disillusioned young lady, which makes her hard to get along with once the initial boy-meets-girl novelty wears off.

The army men ashore were called out of theaters and dance halls to be restricted to their base. D-Day approaches rapidly,

....

MAY 26, 1944: *Tonight, our anticipated army surgeon arrived on board with two technicians. He is a tall, suave Kentuckian of 35 years, Gus Eith, who has had quite a bit of surgical experience. What a relief to have him aboard!*

....

MAY 27, 1944: *Fog enveloped the entire harbor this morning causing our firing practice to be canceled. By now the fog has dispersed and we are greeted by a clear, beautiful day.*

At about 1530, a German reconnaissance plane flew over so high it couldn't be seen, and it drew only a few desultory shots from the local land artillery. His photographs must have held great interest to Der Fuhrer, with Portland-Weymouth Harbor literally packed full of ships of all shapes and sizes.

There is a conspicuous absence of American soldiers in town tonight. Saw Vicki tonight and she said that all the people in town predict the invasion will be this weekend. They should know!

....

MAY 28, 1944: *At 0100 I was awakened by the ominous general quarters alarm. I got up from my bunk, crawled into my pants rather leisurely thinking it was just another alert, when I heard two loud crashes that shook the ship. Immediately thereafter I heard an airplane's diving roar and the sharp staccato of thousands of anti-aircraft guns. Madly, I threw myself into my painfully stubborn clothing and life jacket, grabbed my medical kit and helmet, and hurried to the outside deck. Three more bombs burst close by, again shaking the ship. Tracy sauntered by. "They're coming close, Doc, old boy." I believed him, but didn't feel any better for it.*

Outside was a gorgeous display of fireworks that I would have enjoyed more if I had been seated in the grandstand at the State Fair. The sky was filled with 20-millimeter tracer shells from hundreds of guns on shore as well as from ships in the harbor. There were occasional bursts of heavy artillery fire, higher than the rest, brilliant silver flashes. Long white search light beams probed the sky in unceasing, almost frantic movement, but the raiders couldn't be seen. Overall this riotous confusion, myriad bright silent stars looked calmly and coldly down. A crescent moon hung low over the horizon, casting an all-too-bright yellow light on the water. I froze next to the deck house, my knees shaking and my stomach up in my mouth. I was glad it was dark enough so no one could see my visible fright. I managed to talk and act quite calmly, but it was a cover for seething emotions. One rational thought haunted me. Maybe this minute will be my last. The next second may bring a bomb crashing into our ship instead of landing 100 yards away. This was my first introduction to what war was really like and it wasn't at all pleasant!

Suddenly the spot lights found a plane and all converged. A large-four engine bomber was clearly seen—white against a background of midnight blue. It was higher than it appeared to us below. A frenzied burst of anti-aircraft fire filled the air, but all seemed to fall short or just plain missed, and the bomber cruised serenely on out of range of guns and searchlights. The bomber was held in the lights with intense surrounding fire for at least a minute, and how it survived the barrage was a mystery. I had hoped to see the plane burst into flames, but it departed unscathed. Some mother in Germany was probably praying for that pilot tonight. What a peculiar world! Soon the firing ceased, and after rehashing the attack, we all turned in to sleep until morning.

Morning dawned bright and beautiful. Small boats had begun their usual morning traffic when several loud explosions were heard and an LCVP, 500 yards off our bow, blew up. The harbor had been sown with mines and delayed-action bombs. The night visitor had left a few calling cards.

Small boats were restricted until the harbor was swept, but Tracy and I went into church at 0845, before the restriction order had been given. Every minute on the way in I expected an explosion to send us airborne, but we made it without event. In shore we learned that three small boats had hit mines.

Tonight we made up surgical packs. Essential surgical equipment was stashed in the ward room, our operating theater for the duration. Another reconnaissance plane flew over, so we can expect another attack tonight.

....

MAY 29, 1944: *General alarm threw me out of the sack at 0130 this morning, and after last night's experience I lost no time getting dressed. My throat and eyes burned and the room was filled with smoke. This was phosphorous smoke from hundreds of smoke pots all around the shore that covered all the ships in a huge white blanket. My chest burned with every breath and finally in desperation I donned my gas mask. There were only a few anti-aircraft bursts and no bombs were dropped. I tried to sleep with my gas mask on but couldn't.*

When I awoke again later in the morning my throat and lungs burned and I ached in all my joints. My eyes were sore and I had a headache. What misery! And this was "benign" smoke, designed not to injure. What would gas warfare be like? Human beings were never designed to suffer this kind of noxious exposure and this is only the beginning. Everyone on board felt punk today from smoke inhalation.

I felt better this evening and Gus Eith, Dick Greenleaf, and I went for a long hike into the hills surrounding Portland. The weather was hot, sultry, with no breeze. We are more worried about the smoke screen tonight than an air raid.

....

MAY 30, 1944: *Today we were sealed! This means we cannot leave the ship except on business of extreme importance and then only under guard. Captain Thompson, army engineer, is back with us to supervise loading, which takes place tomorrow. Events are moving fast!*

This morning I attended a medical meeting with 40 other doctors aboard the Ancon. *Captain Gough presented the operational plan. Our ship is to be in the initial assault wave. Gus, Dick, and I got together on our ship later to make additional provisions for the coming ordeal. We still have lots to do and hope there won't be any bombing attacks or smoke tonight.*

....

MAY 31, 1944: *Loading was postponed one day. The tempo of our preparation has increased. Emphasis is being placed on surgical nursing. I worked out a plan of duty.*

Tracy showed me a detailed map of the beach our assault force will attack. It lies between _____ and _____. To be supplied later. There are four main types of underwater obstacles in addition to mines and barbed wire. The odds now of the Germans using gas are one in four.

....

JUNE 1, 1944: *"For what is so rare as a day in June." There were no delays today. We are loaded to the gills with trucks, ambulances, cranes, jeeps, and "Ducks." There are now five of us sleeping in my small single cabin. The same army personnel is aboard now as were with us on the* Fabius Operation. *We are jammed in so tight you couldn't get out in a hurry unless you tore through a bulkhead.*

An army captain showed me his invasion map and told me about their operation. Involved are parachute troops, assault troops, and thousands of planes. The attack on Europe will occur from Western France, Southern France, Norway, and later, Yugoslavia.

We had our last medical meeting today with all the medical officers of our flotilla in attendance.

Twelve quarts of blood and three million units of penicillin were received aboard today. These are "just before the battle" items: not much, but our quota.

There was much wagering concerning the time and date of D-Day. Consensus has it that it must be either Sunday, Monday, or Tuesday of next week. The moon would then be full and the tide right. I expect an air raid tonight. The night is clear, cool, and the moon is half full.

....

JUNE 2, 1944: *The expected air raid never materialized. This prolonged quiet is foreboding. This is a sunny, cool day with a light breeze from across the Channel.*

Just before sunset I stood on the bridge and watched the huge red sun sink beyond the English coast. It reminded me of so many sunsets that I had watched over the water at Lake Minnewashta. Aside from the familiar flaming gold path on the water, however, all other surroundings were foreign.

All craft in the harbor were fully loaded. Outside the harbor, slick cruisers and destroyers lay quietly at anchor. Blinker signal messages flashed between ship and shore as silent but important information filled a super-charged atmosphere. The invader is poised to strike and he hopes to keep it a secret from his enemy.

Our ship is in the first assault wave. We will arrive in the transport area ten miles off the French coast before H-hour and should leave it about H+3 or H+4 hours.

Time drags interminably as we impatiently await D-Day. The officer quarters are crowded and we eat in two shifts. The army officers read pocket books, play cards, and none of them seem at all perturbed. There are no weighty or important utterances made at this dramatic hour in history. Everyone seems so normal and usual.

....

JUNE 3, 1944: *At 1200 we left Portland Harbor to anchor just outside the break-waters. The other LSTs in our flotilla (about ten) joined us. As I watched them slip through the harbor gate in single file they again reminded me of solemn, plodding cattle leaving their corral to go to pasture.*

We are surrounded by fifteen to twenty destroyers, four to five cruisers, one old French battle ship, innumerable tugs, and smaller craft. There is one old, black, heavy French cruiser that is loaded with concrete to serve as a buttress for the pier in the new port the Allies plan to build on the French shore.

The day began with sunshine and a warm, pleasant breeze. This morning the corpsmen went through a dress rehearsal casualty drill. All day was spent getting last minute details straightened out. We sterilized vaseline gauze, checked all first aid boxes, built dressing trays, rigged up an oxygen tank, and checked on bed pans.

After dinner I met with all the pharmacist mates, briefly reviewed first aid equipment, then handed out Red Cross arm bands. It was like the last minute rush that precedes putting on a play. The players have rehearsed long weeks, have waited and waited, and now "opening night" was at hand. Did they know their parts? This show had to be a success!

Toward evening a stiff breeze blew up off shore and the sky became overcast. It's quite chilly.

I learned just now from Conyers that D-Day is Monday, June 5, and H-hour 0700. We leave here tonight to rendezvous some place in the Channel with other convoys. Twenty-four hours from now I probably won't be turning in.

The hour is almost at hand that all the world has waited for these past two years. It is a fateful, portentous hour; millions hang breathlessly on its arrival and its outcome. I can't grasp the significance so close, but I know it must be successful! So far, I'm glad that I'm here.

....

JUNE 4, 1944, SUNDAY: *D-Day has been postponed for 24 hours! What a letdown! How we all wish it would start so we could get it over with!*

The weather turned bad forcing the delay. We had started on our way at 0200 this morning, but were ordered to return to Portland when SHAEF headquarters realized that the weather would be too bad Monday morning to hit the beaches.

And so, anticlimactically, after breakfast, we grudgingly limped back to Portland Bay to wait some more. The wind had increased filling the bay with whitecaps. Toward evening the sky became cloudy and dark and a heavy rain began pelting our ship with the wind increasing. I stood on the bridge, watched the unheeding weather as it altered man's best plans, and shivered as I looked down at the cold, green, angry sea.

The day passed rather quietly. I read my "Manual of Therapy" and also an article in the JAMA, "Opportunities for Doctors Following the War." I played bridge in the afternoon with Andresen (support boat officer and scout), Gus Eith, and Dick Greenleaf. After dinner I gave a short first aid lecture to the engine-room crew.

The best part of the day was receiving mail from home. Sailors from the Portland Base braved the rain and the high seas to bring all the ships outside the harbor their mail. These letters couldn't have come at a more opportune time, and they made me feel infinitely better. Holding the mail in London was a false rumor.

Before bed, an army chaplain from Oklahoma conducted a short worship service in the officer's ward room.

D-Day is now definitely set for Tuesday morning, June 6, barring worse weather. The experts apparently feel that the weather will be adequate because we are to get underway at 0300 this morning.

MONDAY, JUNE 5, 1944: *No turning back today. At first our convoy headed southwest, somewhat along the coast of England, then at about 1800 we changed course to southeast, straight toward the coast of France.*

Our convoy consists of LSTs 314, 357, 6, 316, 310, 315 and 317, in that order. Each LST tows a rhino barge. Far off, barely visible on the horizon, can be seen the comforting silhouettes of many destroyers and cruisers. Trailing behind are a host of LCTs. Overhead, P-38s on patrol duty can be seen every ten to fifteen minutes. There are ships in every direction as far as the eye can see. All the planes have three white stripes on the fuselage and the wings.

The day is cold and windy with an overcast sky. The Channel is rough, and we are rolling madly from side to side. The small LCCs are tossed about like chips. They dive into a valley and it looks as though they have gone down for good, but then they shoot up again high on a crest. I admire and sympathize with these men and the men on the rhino barges. It's cold, wet, and miserable where they are, and they still have a long way to go.

I have slept on and off all day. The rocking has made me somewhat seasick again.

It is about 0230 and we are about ten miles from our transport area, which will be somewhere between ten and two miles from the beach. From the bridge, anti-aircraft fire, flares, and rockets can be seen in the direction of the French coast. As yet we have not been attacked nor has general quarters been sounded.

The quiet is ominous. Our engines continue their steady churning as we draw closer to our destination and destiny. The quiet must soon be broken.

At 1400, two divisions of American paratroopers landed on the Cotentin Peninsula, somewhere behind (east of) the port city of Cherbourg.

H-hour is 0630. We heard the wonderful news by radio that Rome has been taken by the Allies.

....

D-DAY, TUESDAY, JUNE 6, 1944: *Night crept along—still no attack—nothing but flares and ack-ack with an occasional red or green rocket over the distant beaches could be seen.*

The night was still cloudy; only rarely did the moon peep through. The wind slowed briefly, but then started afresh in almost gale-like severity.

We arrived in the transport area and still no attack. It seemed too good to be true!

The small boats (LCVPs) with Tracy and Carbonaro, 25 coxswains and the rocket boats, with Andresen, Halupka, and Lajko, were lowered into the tumultu-

ous sea where they rallied briefly before going into the beach. The choppy sea made it almost impossible to marry the rhino and the "6." For a time we feared having to delay this joining process all day or until the wind stopped. Fortunately, after two hours, we were able to fasten the rhino to the ramp and drive the first truck on. By 0800 the barge was loaded, and together with the soldiers started into the beach.

At 0550 the Navy heavy cruisers, including the Augusta, opened fire on the fortifications in the hills above the beach. They blasted away for more than an hour without interruption.

The skies cleared but the wind blew heavy and the sea was high. We lay at anchor with transports and other LSTs and never an attack of any sort. We could hardly believe it!

During mid-afternoon we learned that all was not as peaceful on the beach as we had thought. An LCT, quite badly damaged by gunfire, moored alongside. Her officers and crew were visibly shaken. They shouted up, "We have two bodies aboard. You must take them because it is impossible to get a living human being on the beach, much less a dead one."

They told us of the horrible situation on Omaha Beach. The preliminary bombardment and naval fire failed to destroy a large number of well entrenched enemy guns that still commanded the beach. Demolition crews, who were supposed to have cleared out the underwater obstructions—the hedgehogs, railway spikes, and mines—had been killed or wounded, and now small craft were trapped, exposed to withering fire, and unable to go forward or retreat. The beaches were strewn with the dead, and bodies were seen floating everywhere in the water off the beach. No sizable forces nor equipment had been landed by noon, when these men left the area, and H-hour was at 0630. They were pessimistic and felt that "Omaha Beach" would be lost.

Andresen came back, pale, drawn, and wide-eyed. He too was badly shaken. "She's tougher than hell in there, Doc," he shouted.

It wasn't until 1600 that troops managed to land in any significant numbers, but were still only about 300 yards up from the water's edge. Andresen said that he thought the beachhead would be taken through sheer force of power, but that the price in lives would be very high.

Tracy and Carbonaro came back about suppertime. Carbonaro had lost his boat. Was I glad to see them!

They told the same story. They were lucky to be alive! They had been through Africa, Sicily, and Salerno, but this was by far the worst.

They said that all the small boats milled around an area just beyond the range of the 88 guns, which was about 400 yards out from the water's edge. Any that advanced closer were blasted out of the water. The squadron leader implored them to go in, but none responded. Finally, he prevailed upon all of them to charge ashore at one time, behind two boats with a chain lashed between them, clearing the obstacles and diffusing the targets. Although this attack wasn't mounted until 1230, six hours late, it proved successful and a small contingent of soldiers made it up the beach. The cost was high.

After dinner an LCI brought us 18 wounded. It was a tough job transferring them in the rough sea, but we did it without incident. These wounded, together with those we had received earlier, totaled 27.

What tragic sights they were! They were all so young and so bewildered. One had his lower jaw shot away, another had lost both eyes to shrapnel. A third had been shot through the anus and lower rectum, a fourth through the chest, and a fifth had a gunshot wound in his head. There was one "shell shocked" lad, with no visible injury, who was dazed and totally disoriented. The terrible thing about these injuries was their total randomness with no regard for any part of the human body; not at all like the neat bullet wound to the chest seen in a Hollywood war movie. These were so gross and so indiscriminate.

We lowered them by elevator to the tank deck and began to treat them. Their bloody clothing was removed and they were wrapped in dry blankets. Plasma was started on most of them and morphine was given as needed. The chest injury had sealed itself and didn't require specific treatment other than an occlusive dressing. Wounds were washed and dressed, and after a short time, most of the wounded were able to eat and they all felt so much better with rising spirits.

One soldier had an abdominal shrapnel wound penetrating his left loin that we felt certain must have perforated his sigmoid colon. We took him up to our makeshift ward room operating theater. Placing him on one of the mess tables, we opened him up. Gus Eith was the surgeon, I, the assistant, and Dick Greenleaf, the anesthetist. Aside from the instruments being thrown to the deck a few times from the rolling of the ship and poor catgut that broke too easily, the operation progressed smoothly and was completed at 0300, 55 minutes from start time. Fortunately, the shrapnel had followed the planes of the flat abdominal muscles and had not penetrated the abdominal cavity, so there was no colon injury. At 0330 we trudged off to bed.

Our ship left the transport area for England at about 2100. Looking back an hour later we saw terrific anti-aircraft fire from the ships remaining and we knew we had just missed an air raid. All the way back we passed through convoys headed for France.

....

JUNE 7, 1944: *Got up for breakfast and was thrilled to see Portland Harbor. I never knew I would be so happy to see the shores of England.*

We discharged our dead and wounded to the army in the afternoon. We were told that we had taken back the most casualties so far and had done an exceptionally fine job, which was nice to hear.

The "6" was immediately loaded and we withdrew again into the harbor to wait. At 0100 we leave again for the coast of France. They aren't wasting any time! Will our beach be secured?

....

JUNE 8, 1944: *When I arose this morning, we were again nearing the beaches of Normandy. There were six LSTs and one destroyer escort in our convoy. The Channel was choppy, but not as rough as it was on D-Day. Wherever you looked you could see convoys coming from every direction, all headed for the same strip of beach. Innumerable Allied planes, in various-sized squadrons, passed overhead.*

When we came within sight of the French coast, an unforgettable sight met our eyes. There were Allied ships as far as you could see in every direction. There were literally thousands of ships of all types in this area.

We anchored about one mile off the beach to wait until 0200 when we are to beach the ship and unload.

There were a few air raids on our ships around 0100. Two German planes were hit and I watched one of them explode and crash in flames into the sea.

One of the beach battalion soldiers who had been injured in the air raid was hoisted aboard with a nasty shrapnel wound involving his left lower leg. He told us that their outfit had suffered 60 percent casualties. The American forces were only six miles inland at this point and the fighting was heavy. The infantry needed tanks and heavy artillery soon. The British had penetrated twenty miles in one place because they took no prisoners. Taking prisoners is time-consuming. "We have over 600 prisoners on our beach alone," the injured soldier reported. "Many were only fourteen or fifteen years old. All seemed arrogant and cocky. They said they knew four days before the landings occurred exactly where they would be and were ready. They were surprised that the beach was taken. There were several Japanese prisoners wearing German uniforms."

The Nazi beach fortifications were fantastic. There were steel Quonset huts buried eight feet underground which held guns and gunners.

German 88 cannons were housed in heavy concrete bunkers and concealed deep in the hills overlooking the beach. By now they had been silenced, but the beach was strewn with the dead and wounded, awaiting evacuation, victims of the hillside guns.

At 0300 we headed into the beach but ignominiously foundered on a sandbar 200 yards off shore. We are stuck, and all efforts to break loose have been to no avail. Lovely place to spend an evening.

....

JUNE 9, 1944: *This morning found us high and dry on "Fox Green" beach. There were wrecked, overturned, and riddled landing craft up and down the beach. We were alongside LCI-497 which had hit two mines. There were still three dead sailors aboard. Some of our crew scavenged clothing, knives, and other items from this ship.*

The engineers had already constructed some good roads leading inland from the beach. The assault engineers had suffered an 80 percent casualty loss.

We took on twenty-one wounded. One marine's left arm had been almost shot off. His company had advanced eleven miles inland when they were trapped by German 88 guns and dive bombers. All but three or four of 180 men were wiped out. He said that they were forced to kill their eighty prisoners, which they did by shooting them through the head. He ran around with his arm dangling trying to find someone to stop the bleeding. Finally a medic reached him and stopped the bleeding with a tent-rope tourniquet.

There was no way to salvage the injured soldier's left arm, so we completed the amputation already begun by the gunshot wound. We couldn't, however, amputate his horrifying memories.

We managed to get off the beach at high tide. We learned the sobering, tragic news that two of the ships in our immediate group, the LSTs 314 and 376 were sunk last night by E-boats. There were two doctors on each ship that I had known from our original group who were killed.

Tonight as we sail through the darkness back to Portland we are all very tense and expectant. One of our LSTs fired at a friendly motor launch, mistaking it for an E-boat. Fortunately they missed. We have put a special E-boat watch on duty starting tonight.

···

JUNE 10, 1944: *Arrived safely in Portland this morning. There were only a few others that had made two trips.*

Malcolm Pitt, support boat officer, who had been with us for awhile, was wounded the day following D-Day. He was standing on the top deck of LST-52, my first ship, when an 88-mm shell exploded near by, driving a piece of shrapnel into his liver. He was operated on aboard his ship and the laceration in his liver sutured. I don't think they could remove the piece of shrapnel. I visited him today and he looked pretty good, but was in a lot of pain. This may be a blessing in disguise for him because he may be sent back to the States.

Greenleaf, Gus, and I went into Weymouth tonight. I'll always love the sensation of getting my feet on solid ground after being at sea.

Ann Shirley joined us and we went to the Officer's Club. The town was crowded with servicemen again, on their way to France. There were numerous riots and street fights all through town. The English servicemen and the American Blacks were fighting the American White servicemen. How crazy can things get?

Long lines of ambulances were loading wounded servicemen at the Weymouth docks. One LST brought in 415 and another 131.

These are only the wounded. The dead are now being buried in France. France is becoming one of America's largest cemeteries.

···

JUNE 11, 1944: *Tracy, Gus, and I went into Weymouth tonight. That town is woefully short on entertainment spots, which may be responsible for some of the rioting. We went to the Officer's Club later, where I saw Vicki again. I was genuinely happy to see her.*

There were long lines of trucks, tanks, and big guns passing through Weymouth's main street all day long.

We moved into the harbor tonight, and expect to load soon. This did not seem like Sunday.

JUNE 12, 1944: *Tracy, Carbonaro, and I went to the USS* Melville *for ice cream today where we talked to the captain and the executive officer of the ill-fated LST-314. They lost 60 percent of their personnel including four officers, two of whom were their medical officers, Landell and Hare. I knew both of them very well. I also learned that two more LSTs were sunk by E-boats, the 374 and 499. In one month I know of these LSTs having been sunk: 507, 532, 314, 376, 374, and 499. LST-289 was damaged but not sunk. The E-boats have become a grave menace. I hope we travel by day.*

Went into Weymouth again, this time to the Regent Dance Hall. The hilarity was not fitting for the times, and I left.

I learned that LST-6 was loading up at the hard in Portland. I missed our small boat but caught one from the LST-375 and reached our ship at 0130. We have a load of trucks and anti-aircraft guns aboard this time, together with 32 army officers and 600 enlisted men. Our room is crowded again.

....

JUNE 13, 1944: *We left Portland at 0500 and arrived at "Utah Beach," Normandy, at 2100. The Channel was rough with a high wind, fog, and cold. I spent the entire day in the sack.*

Arriving in French waters we saw the hulks of three large ships, apparently victims of an air raid. These Germans don't always miss.

Our current contingent of army personnel are casualty replacements. They have been in England only a few weeks and are green. They are full of confidence and hope.

....

JUNE 14, 1944: *The jerries staged a small air raid last night, which wasn't worth getting out of the sack to watch.*

We landed on "Utah Beach" at 0500 and unloaded the vehicles. One hundred and eighty casualties were brought aboard, filling our entire tank deck.

There were wounds of all types: burns, amputated legs, shot-out eyes, fractures, blast injuries, grenade wounds, shrapnel, machine gun and rifle wounds, and shell-shock.

One lad was distraught and trembling because he had bayoneted a fifteen-year-old German soldier. "I can see the little kid now," he sobbed. "He cried out to me,

'Nein! Nein!' but I ran him through anyway. God, I can't stand it! Why did I kill him?"

I tried to reassure him that had he not killed him someone else would have, or the German lad would have killed him. He seemed to calm down somewhat after that.

There were eighteen German soldiers, one Pole, one Russian, and three French civilians among the wounded on our tank deck. Most of the German wounded were friendly, but a few were quite arrogant. One wanted beer with his supper. I managed to communicate quite well with them with my halting German.

We had several paratroopers with us who complained that they had been dropped in the wrong place, and all were spread too far apart.

Caring for these wounded was a huge job because there were too many to spend much time on any one of them. We changed dressings, gave penicillin, sulfadiazine, morphine, and sodium amytal where indicated. Some of the soldiers were stuck to their stretchers with dried blood and urine, and cleaning them up was a big job in itself. Feeding this mob and providing bed pans and urinals kept all the corpsmen busy with no time to rest.

We had to post a guard on the German wounded because some of the U.S. soldiers wanted to kill them. They were really angry.

Fortunately we are going to anchor here for the night, just off "Omaha Beach," and return to England in the morning. The E-boats are becoming too effective.

There is an air raid in progress right now and four bombs have dropped close enough to jar our ship considerably. They are still coming down. Artillery shelling this afternoon came too close for comfort.

....

JUNE 15, 1944: *General alarm sounded at 0400. I rushed down to the tank deck to avert any panic, but found most of the wounded sleeping. They were too tired or sick to notice. The Jerries were dive-bombing the beach and a few offshore ships, but did not come close to us.*

All day long we worked with the wounded and used up all the penicillin and sulfa drugs quite quickly. We changed dressings innumerable times. A few of the wounded looked like they wouldn't make it.

One of the Germans said that they were sure to lose the war. He felt we would win it within six months. A Lieutenant Colonel Tincher, from Owatonna,

Minnesota, one of the wounded, said that over 15 doctors were killed when the glider planes crashed into the sharpened posts erected in every possible landing field. One whole glider unit was destroyed. These sharp posts were called "Rommel's asparagus."

We traveled back to England in a large convoy. The sea is rough but fortunately we are heading into the waves so we don't experience the rolling.

....

JUNE 16, 1944: *We arrived in Portland this morning where we unloaded the wounded. It was such a relief to get them off and into a better situation. The tank deck was so cold and dark.*

After unloading the wounded, we filled the tank deck again with army vehicles and personnel.

Tonight we are again bound for France. There are about ten LSTs, two MTBs (Motor Torpedo Boats) and one corvette in our convoy. Again we are in the "coffin corner." The night is dark and cloudy with a cool breeze and a choppy green sea. Everyone is tense. The crew all want to sleep topside so they can jump off the ship in a hurry if we take a hit. I'm sleeping with all my clothes on tonight. The E-boats have cast their spell.

....

JUNE 17, 1944: *The night was quiet and the day beautiful. This is the first really pleasant weather we have had since the invasion began.*

About 500 yards off our port side, two mine-sweepers detonated three mines simultaneously. The explosion almost capsized one of the ships, throwing several of the crew into the water. No one was killed. We waited just off the beach for a falling tide before we went on in. On the beach could be seen an occasional enemy artillery burst. At 2100 we beached right next to the LST-504.

It is 2400 (midnight) now and the long twilight has just slipped into blackness. I can hear a few bombs exploding near by, but as yet no general quarters alarm has sounded. I hope to get some sleep before it does, because I expect a big casualty list this trip.

JUNE 18, 1944: *This morning I learned there had been a few air raids during the night, but I slept through them all.*

After unloading the tank deck we received 230 survivors from a British transport that had struck a mine. We backed off the beach at noon and at 1800 were on our way back to Portland. Why they insist we travel at night is beyond me.

....

JUNE 19, 1944: *Portland again and the same routine—unload the wounded, load up at the hard, and then anchor outside the harbor to await a night's journey.*

While loading in Portland today, we saw about 500 German prisoners in a temporary prison camp. The camp is merely a heavy barbed wire enclosure with canvas rain shelters, latrines, and a food table inside. On each corner is a raised platform on which stands a guard with a machine gun. They were searching the prisoners when we walked by. As we looked at them through the fence it reminded me of a day at the zoo. But these were human beings.

I saw Pete today and he says he has become quite jumpy and irritable. I learned that LST-133 hit a mine which blew a hole clear through her center, killing many. One by one they are getting knocked off.

We are underway again for France. There is a heavy wind dashing waves against, and up over the bow. This will be a rough night.

I learned that the Cherbourg peninsula has been cut by the Americans, and advanced units are only eight miles from the port city of Cherbourg.

....

JUNE 20, 1944: *I was almost thrown out of my sack this morning by the rolling and tossing of the ship. This is a severe Channel storm, and the roughest weather so far. Just as we approached the French coast we were given orders to immediately return to England. In the distance a cargo ship could be seen burning. Why we were ordered to return when we were so close to our destination remains a mystery. The explanation given was that the bad weather had spread the mines all around the beach area, preventing the mine-sweepers from keeping a clear channel. Tracy thought there might be a pack of U-boats detected on the way into the area.*

We anchored in the harbor between Portsmouth and Southampton. There were hundreds of ships here, including battle ships, cruisers, destroyers, corvettes, and transports.

June 21, 1944: *The wind continued unabated today causing us to remain at anchor. I was initiated into the game of poker today and won $20.00. Not bad for a beginner. Read* Night Flight *and parts of a German storybook. Advanced Allied patrols are 3½ miles from Cherbourg.*

....

June 22, 1944: *The wind finally tired, and today begins as a clear brisk day with only a slight breeze. We started across the Channel at 0900, leading the group, when suddenly all of the rest of our convoy turned around and headed back. We crossed the Channel alone without an escort. Why we didn't return with the other ships was never explained to us by our captain or anyone else.*

When we came in sight of "Utah Beach" we learned why we had been ordered back to England a few days ago. There were three LSTs that had been sunk within 500 yards of each other: LST-499, LST-523, and one identifiable only by the mast protruding from the water. There was a liberty ship down by the stern and several other unrecognizable hulks looming up from the depths. The beach was cluttered with large and small craft that had been blown up by the severe winds.

In getting to the beach, we traversed a stretch of channel ahead of the minesweepers. We all expected to find a mine for them at any moment.

The news is that the Allies are now closing a ring around Cherbourg. Poker is a two-edged sword. I have now felt both edges. Today I lost $24 in two hours.

....

June 23, 1944: *When I awoke this morning we were high and dry on "Utah Beach." Gus and I went for a long walk down the beach. A land mine exploded about 500 yards away, which gave us a scare.*

The high winds of two days ago had washed 230 ships up on the beach, many of them being large cargo ships. It had almost destroyed the American Mulberry temporary concrete port as well. The men who were here during the storm said it was a terrible two days.

High tide welled up on the beach and we backed off at 1100. At 1600 we became part of a large convoy and headed back to England, this time to Southampton. There were no wounded to take back this trip because most casualties were now either being treated in advanced army emergency centers, or were flown back to England.

The Channel is perfectly calm tonight without a breeze. I have never seen it this quiet. There is a new moon and we are gliding along like a dream boat.

The Nazis still hold Cherbourg and are fighting to the last man. If they keep that up this war will last longer than six months. We'll do well to finish them in a year.

....

JUNE 24, 1944: *This was our first real summer day. The sun was bright and the breezes warm. We lazied out in the harbor until 1600 and then went into the hard to load.*

Detachment orders came for Gus, and I won a pound-sterling from him, he betting that they hadn't arrived. Tracy and I went for a long walk and when we returned, Gus came rushing up to me shouting, "Doc, I'll bet you a pound you're detached!"

"I'll take that bet," I answered, knowing that detachment would be highly unlikely. We stormed into the Captain's office, and sure enough, there were my orders, detaching me and my corpsmen from LST-6! I was dumbfounded! We had an hour and a half to pack.

All was turmoil as I threw my clothes into sea bags and a suit case. I passed around all the excess pint bottles of medicinal brandy to the officers, said goodbye to all the wonderful friends and walked off the ship a very happy and relieved man.

I could hardly believe that I had lived through the Normandy Invasion. When I first received my orders into the Amphibious Navy six months ago, I thought for sure I was doomed.

Photographs

....

ALL OF THE FOLLOWING PHOTOGRAPHS, EXCEPT THE FIRST TWO,
WERE TAKEN BY ME AS THE SHIP'S PHOTOGRAPHER ON THE LST-6
AND THE AKA-103 IN THE ATLANTIC AND PACIFIC BATTLE AREAS.
I SELECTED THESE IMAGES FROM APPROXIMATELY 150 PHOTOS
THAT I TOOK, DEVELOPED, AND PRINTED ABOARD SHIP.

My father, Private Henry P. Linner, Spanish American War

Floyd Peterson, a student at Gustavus Adolphus College and
close friend of mine, received this sweatshirt from one of his
German pen-pals in 1938

Top: Rhino barge approaching LST-6 to load for trip into Omaha Beach

Bottom: Rhino barge to Omaha beach—D-Day

Top: An LST unloading on Omaha
Beach, June 9, 1944

Bottom: LST-6 with vehicles to be
transferred to rhino barge for Omaha
Beach on D-Day

TOP: Emptying tank
deck preparing to
receive casualties,
June 9, 1944

BOTTOM: Bringing
in wounded to LST-
6, June 9, 1944

TOP: Transferring
wounded from
jeep to LST-6

BOTTOM:
Transferring
wounded soldier
from LCVP to
LST-6

Top: The USS *Rankin*   Bottom: USS *Rankin* crew at attention during commissioning ceremony, February 24, 1945, Charleston, South Carolina

TOP: (*from left to right*) USS *Rankin* Department Heads: Gunnery, Damico; Medical, Linner; Navigator, Brent; First Lt., White; Supply Officer, Chamberlain; Chief Engineer, Modell

LEFT: USS *Rankin* Skipper, Lt. Cmdr. T.D. Price and Exec. Officer R. Tepper

BOTTOM: USS *Rankin* Medical Department

TOP: USS *Rankin (right)*
meets tanker *(center)* in
Panama Canal

CENTER: Temporary
bridge over Pasig River,
Manila, September, 1945

BOTTOM: Sunken ship,
Manila Harbor

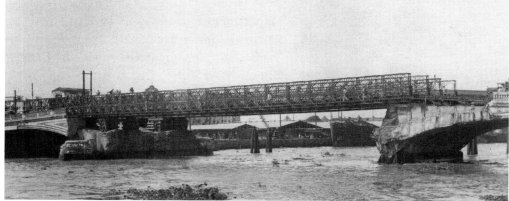

TOP AND CENTER: Manila destruction, bombed by both Japan and United States

BOTTOM LEFT AND RIGHT: Bombed-out cathedral, still functioning

TOP: Nothing escaped destruction
in downtown Manila

BOTTOM: Group of young ladies with
a chaperone, Manila

FAR LEFT: Mother and child, Manila

LEFT: Perfect balance

BELOW: Future Filipino leaders at school

BOTTOM: New Manila shop (one of hundreds) and Supply Officer Chamberlain

TOP AND BOTTOM: Unloading ammunition from USS *Rankin*,
Okinawa Harbor, June 11–27, 1945

TOP: Wakayama, Japan; quick adjustment to new reality

CENTER: United States occupation troop, Wakayama, Japan

BOTTOM: Taxi, anyone? Wakayama, Japan

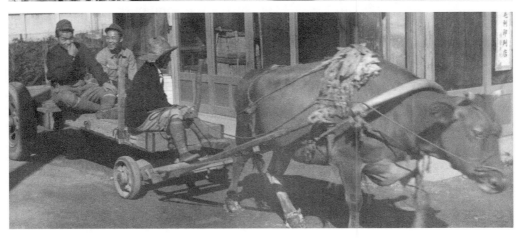

TOP LEFT: Downtown, Wakanura, Japan

TOP RIGHT: Japanese children in Wakanura

CENTER: Shore leave, Wakanura

BOTTOM LEFT: Our backstreet guide to Wakanura, Japan

BOTTOM RIGHT: He survived the bombings

TOP: *Geisha* compound converted to the Officers' Club, Wakanura, Japan

BOTTOM: *Geisha* staff, the Officers' Club

TOP AND BOTTOM: Nagoya, Japan; some areas escaped destruction

PART TWO

....

WAR IN THE PACIFIC

Background

....

JAPAN'S ATTACK ON PEARL HARBOR ON DECEMBER 7, 1941, CAME AS A surprise and shock to most Americans. To the Japanese it was an essential stratagem in a war they had undertaken years before to control all of the Pacific Ocean west of Midway Island. They euphemistically called this area the "Greater East Asia Co-Prosperity Sphere."

Japan was engaged in a high-stakes game against China and the Allied Powers, principally the United States and England, on an immense chess board that included more than half the Pacific Ocean, with its islands, and its Pacific Rim countries.

The conflict began by Japan defeating the Russian fleet at Port Arthur on the China coast in 1904, gaining the southern half of Russia's Sakhalin Island and all of Korea. Similar to the Pearl Harbor attack, there was no declaration of war nor any warning given prior to the Port Arthur attack. They next invaded Manchuria in 1931 on trumped up charges, without declaring war, and set up a new puppet state, Manchuoko, in 1932. From these opening moves, which met no effective opposition from targeted countries, nor any sanctions from the League of Nations, Japan continued to acquire most of the eastern third of China, including Shanghai, Nanking, and Peiping. In Nanking they slaughtered over 250,000 civilians. In 1939, an appeasement policy by Britain, similar to that granted Germany, permitted Japan to cross Thailand, enter Burma, and close the Burma Road, China's only effective supply route for war materiel from India and Burma. Britain was criticized by China for doing this, but with the German threat in Europe looming large, Britain didn't dare confront Japan at this time. Instead Britain chose appeasement. After Germany defeated France in 1940, Japan moved into French Indo-China (Vietnam, Cambodia, and Laos) with the tacit approval of Vichy France. Together they served as the new colonial landholders. At first they were hailed as deliverers by the local population, but soon, when their true intent became known, they were viewed with fear and disenchantment.

Japan felt totally justified in her imperial ambitions, citing the absence of raw material in her own country, as well as the example set by other great powers that had extended their colonial holdings for economic advantage. In fact, most of the islands and countries Japan planned to invade had previously been acquired and to varying degrees exploited by others. A further stimulus to Japan's expansionism was the fantastic success of Germany's military exploits in Europe in 1939 and 1940, which Japan tried to emulate. Japan quickly signed a tripartite pact with Germany and Italy, even though none of the signers trusted one another. Japan admired Hitler's triumphs but was offended by Germany's "pure Aryan race" dogma.

After Germany's surprise attack on Russia, Hitler urged Japan to attack Russia from the east. Japan considered this option for a time, but decided its interests would be better served by exploiting the riches of the Pacific, as it had been doing. A non-aggression pact was then signed with Russia, and Japan reveled in the fact that all the major powers who could interfere with her imperial designs were too involved with the war in Europe to interfere. China had been effectively neutralized as a threat to Japan's ambitions from the west, and Britain was fighting for her very existence in Europe, so could be discounted as a serious adversary in the Pacific.

Only one country could possibly spoil the dream of empire for Japan, and that was the United States. The United States would have to be neutralized in the Pacific by destroying her fleet and then conquering all of her Pacific holdings west of Midway Island, especially the Philippines.

The militarists in Japan, rising to power in their own country by intimidation and assassination, were emboldened by their success both at home and abroad, and did not shrink at the audacity of attacking a power so much greater than themselves. Hideki Tojo engineered his own move upward from Minister of War to Prime Minister, and Emperor Hirohito, a good man but primarily a figurehead, was cast in the role of a great military leader. There were moderate voices in the government who abhorred and feared the idea of war with the United States, but they were shouted down and shunted aside by the rising power of the military.

The chess-master who planned the Pearl Harbor move designed to checkmate the United States was the brilliant, American-educated, Admiral Isokura Yamamoto. He was not only a master tactician, but was reputed to be an inveterate gambler as well. It was perhaps a combination of these two characteristics that fuelled his determination to strike Pearl Harbor. He believed that a surprise, knockout blow to Pearl Harbor, the principal anchorage of the U.S. Pacific Fleet, would cripple any immediate offensive action by America. By the time it could rebuild its Pacific naval forces and launch any effective counterattack, Japan would be so solidly entrenched, the United States would have to accept the new extended Japanese Empire.

Japan's intelligence information confirmed Yamomoto's belief that the American people would not permit a long costly war in the far reaches of the Pacific to reclaim islands they had never heard of. In Yamamoto's opinion, the Pearl Harbor strike would be tantamount to checkmate. His one significant caveat was that Japan would have to complete the destruction of the U.S. Fleet and seize its Pacific military bases in one year or less because he knew it could not win a protracted war against the industrial might of the United States. The fact that the blow against Pearl Harbor was a sneak attack with no warning did not pose an ethical or moral dilemma to Japan. It was simply considered a necessary military strategy for its success. Japan was dependent on the U.S. accepting a negotiated peace on Japanese terms. It would then have achieved its objective of controlling the Greater East Asia Co-Prosperity Sphere and all of its riches.

During the pre-WWII period of Japanese aggression in China, not only did the United States offer no resistance to Japan, but also it continued to sell scrap iron, steel, and oil to Japan right up until their move into French Indo-China in 1940. Shortly thereafter the United States declared an embargo on all military supplies to Japan, and froze all their U.S. assets. They also condemned Japan's war against China and included China in the Lend-Lease program initiated for Britain and later extended to Russia. Britain was encouraged to reopen the 700-mile Burma Road that extended from Lasio, Burma, to Chunking, China, and had been closed for three months. Later Japan closed the road again by force of arms.

Most Americans were unaware of the magnitude of the Sino-Japanese war in this pre-Pearl Harbor era, during which time Japan had conquered all Chinese port cities and had disrupted all overland and air-access routes to China as well. China was spared total defeat only by virtue of its huge land mass, mountainous terrain, the steadfast refusal of the Chinese armies to surrender, and the stout support of the Allied forces in the India-Burma theater.

One of the factors of vital importance during 1943 and 1944 to China's survival was the establishment of an air-supply route from India to China over the

Himalaya mountains (the hump) by Claire L. Chennault and his intrepid Flying Tigers. Japanese jungle armies had effectively closed the supply route over the Burma and Ledo roads. Only after sufficient armed strength was provided by forces under British Major General Orde Wingate and American Brigadier General Frank D. Merrill were the Japanese gradually forced out of Burma and the supply roads opened. Wingate's troops were called Chindits, and Merrill's termed Marauders. With help from two Chinese divisions, the Twenty-second and the Thirty-ninth, plus Burmese natives, the jungle-wise Japanese were fought in their adopted habitat using Japanese methods of infiltration and sneak attack. Airborne Allied troops were dropped behind Japanese lines and were supplied totally by air. This was unbelievably hazardous duty, but the Allies refused to give up despite heavy losses.

The China-Burma-India phase of the Pacific war was extremely complex and difficult not only from the point of view of the terrain and the well entrenched enemy, but for political reasons as well. Churchill felt strongly that the Allies should not be involved at all in this jungle morass. He agreed with United States Admirals King and Nimitz that at this stage the war against Japan should be waged only from the sea, island by island. Roosevelt, on the other hand, backed Generalissimo Chiang Kai-shek's demand that the Japanese be defeated in Burma and then in China. The Generalissimo's most important agenda was to defeat the Chinese Communists while the Allied armies fought the Japanese on the ground. Churchill had little regard for Chiang or the Chinese Army, but grudgingly agreed at the Casablanca Conference in early 1943 to back the Burmese operation. Churchill appointed Lord Louis Mountbatten to head up the India-Burma operation.

General Joseph "Vinegar Joe" Stilwell was assigned as Chief of Staff to General Chiang Kai-shek, but he had no respect for Chiang or his armies. In addition, he totally disagreed with Chennault's bombing operations. Stilwell was courageous and tough, but became so irascible he was relieved of his command. He was succeeded by Major General Albert C. Wedemeyer.

By the time Japan surrendered to the Allies in September, 1945, Japan had 1.3 million troops in China. The commitment of this large an army to the China campaign, plus the effectiveness of the Allied forces in Burma, was largely responsible for Japan's decision not to invade India or Australia. This had been one of its goals early in the war.

During the Sino-Japanese war the Chinese Army sustained over three million casualties and the civilian population lost six million. China suffered greatly from Japan's depredations, but Japan ultimately had little to show for its costly invasion of China.

Japan's defeat, however, did not end the travail for China because now the Chinese civil war between Chairman Mao Zedong's Communists and Generalissimo Chiang Kai-shek's Nationalists began in earnest. Despite support from the United States, the Nationalists, assailed by squabbles between the warlords and rampant corruption at all levels, were defeated on the mainland by the single-minded, determined Communists. By 1949 the Nationalists were forced to retreat to the adjacent island of Formosa (Taiwan).

With this brief background, the course of the war in the Pacific Theater from the Pearl Harbor attack on December 7, 1941, to Japan's formal surrender in Tokyo Harbor on September 12, 1945, can perhaps be better understood.

PEARL HARBOR

....

THE PEARL HARBOR ATTACK CAME AS A COMPLETE SURPRISE TO THE average American, but was no surprise to President Roosevelt and the U.S. Joint Chiefs of Staff. They didn't know the exact place or time of the attack, but they knew the United States was on a collision course with Japan and that neither side would yield on the principal sticking points that confounded a diplomatic resolution: Japan's continuing presence in China and its move into Indo-China. The United States' embargo on oil and other military supplies, plus the freezing of Japan's assets in the United States, virtually guaranteed war because Japan's only other available source of oil was the Netherlands East Indies, and that was off-limits as far as the U.S. was concerned.

Although the United States' Congress had approved the Lend-Lease program to send military equipment to Britain in March of 1941, the overwhelming sentiment in the country was still one of isolationism. For this reason, and because the President during his 1940 election campaign had promised to keep "our boys" out of the war in Europe and the Far East, it was strict U. S. policy to not fire the first shot. If there was to be a war in the Pacific, the United States authorities wanted Japan to open hostilities and bear the blame. They expected the opening salvos to be against a British or Dutch colony or possibly one of the more distant United States bases such as Wake, Guam, or the Philippines. They didn't dream that the opening blow would be a devastating strike on home soil.

As horrifying as the death and destruction at Pearl Harbor was to the United States' leadership, this dark cloud did have a silver lining. It eliminated American isolationism overnight and united the entire population in dedication to the total defeat and unconditional surrender of Japan. With Germany and Italy's declaration of war on the United States shortly thereafter, all the Axis Powers were included in America's resolve to fight and win the war as quickly and decisively as possible. Even though Churchill decried the destruction at Pearl Harbor, he was delighted that the United States would now become a full partner in the war against "the powers of evil." What had been largely a European Theater conflict suddenly became a world-wide conflagration. World War II was now truly global!

After the initial shock and horror of Pearl Harbor had somewhat abated, there was the general feeling that we would whip this impertinent little country, Japan, in a hurry. A cartoon in the *Minneapolis Star* newspaper, shortly after Pearl Harbor, depicted Japan as a tiger leaping from a tree to its obvious sudden death onto the upraised bayonets of a platoon of American soldiers. Only gradually did the extent of the damage to our fleet and planes and the surprising strength of Japan's military forces dawn on most Americans. We slowly and painfully began to realize that our involvement in this global war would be for a long time and at tremendous cost. It soon became apparent that the attack on Pearl Harbor was only one facet of a giant multi-pronged Japanese offensive erupting all across the vast reaches of the Pacific.

There were several reasons why the attack on Pearl Harbor, rather than on some more distant base, came as such a surprise to the United States military, especially to the command at Pearl Harbor. First, even though the Japanese diplomatic code (termed *Magic*) had been broken, the amount of material to decode was so large during the period prior to Pearl Harbor that it was difficult for cryptographers to evaluate the significant portions. Further, the Japanese fleet had gathered at their launch site in the far northwestern corner of the Pacific, just north of the Japanese main islands, under strict radio silence. United States intelligence was tracking a large Japanese fleet moving across the South Pacific toward the Dutch East Indies where the first blow was expected to be struck. In addition, the command at Pearl Harbor, Admiral Husband E. Kimmel and Lieutenant General Walter C. Short, did not have direct access to *Magic* so had to depend upon the Joint Chiefs for their information. They were told that war could break out at any time and to prepare accordingly. Because no one believed that the opening target would be the Hawaiian Islands, General Short took the warning to mean "take measures against sabotage." He accordingly had all the planes cobbled close together so they could be more easily watched and all ammunition put under lock and key.

Adding to the surprise were the earnest negotiations in Washington between Secretary of State Cordell Hull and two Japanese representatives, Ambassador Nomura and Special Envoy Kurusu, who were themselves totally ignorant of the impending attack.

The final factors that insured complete surprise were the timing of the strike for early Sunday morning after most military personnel had been out the night before, including Kimmel and Short, with the whole base in a state of Sunday relaxation. Added to that was the extremely unfortunate misinterpretation by the early warning radar operators that the large squadron of planes visualized on their screen was American and not Japanese.

Some historians have speculated that had Roosevelt not moved the Pacific Fleet from its San Diego anchorage to Pearl Harbor in May of 1941 (over the objections of the Commanding Officer who was fired and replaced by Kimmel), the attack would never have happened, at least not at Pearl Harbor, and very unlikely at San Diego. We will never know. Roosevelt's rationale for stationing the Pacific Fleet at Pearl Harbor was to locate it closer to the threatening hostilities in the Pacific and also as a deterrent.

One strange occurrence that has never been explained satisfactorily is that in January of 1941, Ambassador Joseph Grew, stationed in Tokyo, reported that Japan "may attempt a surprise attack on Pearl Harbor using all their military facilities." C. L. Sulzberger, in his fascinating book, *American Heritage History of World War II,* offered this explanation. "Analysis in Washington was unimaginative; intelligence was faulty and communications were slack and mixed up." He also attributed the United States' lack of preparation to an unrealistic underestimation of the "myopic," bespectacled Japanese.

In his book, *Day of Deceit,* author Robert Stinnett presents evidence about who knew what prior to Japan's attack on Pearl Harbor, especially the role of President Roosevelt. His evidence is based on a comprehensive study of previously withheld documents released following the Freedom of Information Act (FOIA) of 1987, plus interviews of many key people involved with these issues during 1940–1941. This extremely well documented and annotated book, in my view, presents strong evidence, contrary to most WWII historical accounts, that the Japanese code had been broken over a year before Pearl Harbor. Further, the Japanese attacking fleet did not observe radio silence prior to the attack. According to Stinnett, U.S. Intelligence knew a week or more before the Pearl Harbor attack where the fleet was located, that it was heading for Pearl Harbor, and that the date scheduled for the attack was on or close to December 7, 1941. This information was routed through channels to the Commander in Chief, President Roosevelt, but was never forwarded to Admiral Husband E. Kimmel or Lieutenant General Walter Short, commanders of the Navy and Army forces at Pearl Harbor. According to Stinnett, this oversight was by design and not by accident.

An opposite view, based on evaluation of the same coded material, has been advanced by Stephen Budiansky, correspondent for the *Atlantic Monthly*, and author of the book, *Battle of Wits*. He claims Stinnett is obsessed with a conspiracy theory against Roosevelt and that his interpretation of the recently released code documents is erroneous. Where the truth lies is unclear.

Stinnett, however, is not alone in concluding, based on good evidence, that the Pearl Harbor debacle was part of a broad plan by Roosevelt and a few of his advisors to get the United States involved in the European war through a provoked attack against the United States by Japan that would reverse the hardened position of the isolationists in America. Others argue that the steps taken by the United States against Japanese interests in the Pacific prior to Pearl Harbor virtually guaranteed that Japan would launch a military strike against the U.S. somewhere in the Pacific that would provide the excuse to declare war on Japan. Because of the tripartite pact Japan had with Germany and Italy, declaration of war against Japan would obligate the Axis powers to declare war on us, guaranteeing our involvement in the war in Europe, which was the main objective of the Pearl Harbor tactic. This indeed proved to be the case. Roosevelt's earlier decision to move the Pacific Fleet from San Diego to Hawaii was considered unwise by top Navy brass because of inadequate facilities in Oahu, and also unnecessary exposure to attack. Roosevelt overrode all objections, insisting that the Pacific fleet remain in Hawaii.

In spite of these well documented allegations against President Roosevelt, Stinnett considered him to be a great president during the course of the war who, in his zeal to enter the global conflict against the Axis powers before the fall of Britain, employed a method that exceeded in destructive force his strategic intention. He truly believed that all of Western Civilization as we knew it would be destroyed if the Axis powers were triumphant in Europe.

All the evidence prior to FOIA was buried in classified files or shredded until the recent release of much, but not all of it. Kimmel and Short were found guilty of dereliction of duty, charged with having committed "errors of judgment." A later attempt (1995) to clear their names posthumously by their families was unsuccessful. Stinnett maintains that important evidence absolving them was withheld or unavailable at the time of the trial. He estimates that there are at least 143,000 Japanese naval intercepts, together with their supporting communication data, that remain sealed in the U.S. Navy or National Security Agency files. He continues to fight for their release to this day.

Stinnett writes: "Over that time, most of the U.S. military leaders, cryptographers, and intercept operators who were either participants to events leading to Pearl Harbor have died or their memories have faded with age. Because they were never called to testify for their country, we have been denied a full account of what happened from their perspectives. To those heretofore silent survivors who are represented in this book we owe an immeasurable debt. Nevertheless the major secrets of Peal Harbor are at last out in the open. After years of denial, the truth is clear: we knew."

The heartrending dilemma of Pearl Harbor will always be with us. Did the ends justify the means? As Stinnett opines, "The wisdom and moral justification that ultimately took millions of lives will be argued over for many years by people of good faith and from all political persuasions."

The details of the Pearl Harbor attack have been recounted in story and film innumerable times and will not be repeated here except in barest outline. The attacking armada was huge, consisting of six aircraft carriers, two battleships, two cruisers, nine destroyers, nine submarines (with five of the mini-submarines carried piggyback on five standard submarines), four hundred airplanes, and a number of support ships, including oilers for refueling during the 3,500-mile trip across the North Pacific to Pearl Harbor. This huge fleet began its journey on November 26, 1941, at a speed of 13 knots, expecting to arrive at its "strike site," 250 miles northwest of Hawaii very early on December 7, 1941.

The commander of this strike force, assigned by Yamamoto, was Vice-Admiral Chuichi Nagumo, First Air Fleet Commander, a man with an excellent military record. Unfortunately, he didn't agree with Yamamoto's strategy of striking Pearl Harbor first and then destroying the balance of the U.S. Pacific Fleet as quickly as possible thereafter. He had no choice in the matter, however, and was obliged to follow orders. His negative attitude made a difference, though. After the second and last bombing run, instead of making a third strike and taking out all the oil storage tanks in the area, Nagumo ordered a withdrawal and return to Japan. His air force had damaged or sunk most of the ships in the harbor as well as a large portion of the aircraft on the ground, and Nagumo felt that was quite enough in what he considered to be a flawed battle plan.

Fortunately for the United States, all three Pacific aircraft carriers, the *Lexington, Enterprise,* and *Saratoga,* were away from Pearl Harbor that Sunday morning and were spared. Nagumo was faulted by Yamamoto for not persisting until he had destroyed the oil supplies and the aircraft carriers, wherever they were. This time it was Yamamoto's obligation to accept Nagumo's decision because the commander in the field has the final authority in Japan's navy, once the battle is underway.

The damage inflicted on Pearl Harbor, though not fatal, was gut-wrenchingly horrible: a full scale disaster. There were 2,433 killed, with almost half that number below decks on the sunken battleship *Arizona,* where they reside to this day. There were 1,178 wounded. The U.S. lost 18 surface warships, badly damaged or sunk, 188 planes destroyed, and 155 damaged. Three of the five damaged battleships (the *California, Nevada,* and *West Virginia*) were eventually rehabilitated. Japan sustained minimal losses: 55 aircraft pilots, nine mini-submarine crewmen, and 65 sailors on one submarine. None of the Japanese surface ships were damaged and although they anticipated losing at least 30 percent of their aircraft, they lost only 7 percent (29 planes).

This was one of the most one-sided battles in history. Though it was a terribly painful experience for the United States, it proved to be a fatal error for the Japanese. For the embattled Russians and the British, it was like manna from heaven.

In the panic that accompanied Pearl Harbor, the U.S. government committed an egregious offense against 120,000 Japanese who happened to live on the west coast of the United States. At the urging of California's Attorney General Earl Warren, and against the advice of FBI Director J. Edgar Hoover, President Roosevelt issued an edict, without due process of law, to uproot this entire population of Japanese-American citizens and confine them to a guarded prison camp in the Arizona desert. This breach of civil rights was perpetrated solely because these people were of Japanese ancestry. In panic and fear, their democratic rights were abrogated. Although this was a crime against humanity, it doesn't compare to the much more horrible crimes committed by the Nazis or the Russians.

Over the years since the war, some restitution has been made to these Japanese families, and a memorial park is currently being developed in Washington D.C. in remembrance of these 120,000 interned Japanese-Americans. Ironically, the liberal, Earl Warren, insisted on internment without due process, and the conservative, J. Edgar Hoover, was against it.

GUAM, WAKE, AND THE PHILIPPINES

···

S HORTLY AFTER THE TERRIBLE SHOCK OF THE PEARL HARBOR DISASTER had been comprehended, if not completely digested, it became apparent that the blow to Pearl Harbor was only one part of a huge multi-focal Japanese offensive. During the ensuing weeks Japan made strikes against the United States bases at Guam, Wake Island, and the Philippines. They also mounted devastating attacks against Hong Kong, Malaya, Singapore, Burma, Thailand, the Dutch East Indies, New Guinea, and Guadalcanal. They bombed Darwin, Australia, and Ceylon (now Sri Lanka), and there was great trepidation they would soon invade Australia and probably India as well.

Guam fell in half a day, Wake in twelve days, and the Philippines in approximately five months. The Japanese attack on the Philippines occurred ten hours after Pearl Harbor, but the Philippine Command, even though aware of the strike at Pearl Harbor, did nothing by way of preparation for the blow they knew must be imminent. General Douglas MacArthur, who was in the process of developing and training the U.S. and Philippine armed forces, was aware of the Pearl Harbor debacle shortly after it happened, but remained incommunicado in his Manila penthouse apartment headquarters and did not warn his staff or even accept callers during this crucial period. It was as though he had been hypnotized or was in some kind of trance.

To this day there has been no valid explanation for this strange behavior. Some have speculated that he was afflicted by the same paralysis that seized Stalin immediately after the German assault on Russia, a kind of denial state that frustrated positive action. Others have opined that he believed, or at least speculated, that if he made no provocative moves, Japan may not strike the Philippines, at least not until later, when the partially trained Philippine armed forces were better prepared and supplied. He was also awaiting delivery of more aircraft.

During this state of suspended animation, the inevitable happened. Two hundred Japanese aircraft bombed and strafed all the parked U.S. planes on both Clark and Iba airfields adjacent to Manila. They also destroyed the Cavite Naval Base. A Japanese pilot, interrogated after the war, said, in effect, that the air raid on the planes at Clark and Iba fields was like shooting at sitting ducks. They couldn't believe the absence of any opposing planes in the air or anti-aircraft fire and how easy it was to completely annihilate so many aircraft in so short a time. There were only 80 Allied personnel killed during the Philippine attack, but the loss of aircraft, especially B-17 bombers, was devastating. Eighteen of 35 bombers, 56 of 72 P-40 fighter planes, and 25 other planes were destroyed.

For two weeks after the initial Japanese air strikes, an eerie calm settled over the Philippines. On December 22, 1941, a Japanese invading army of 40,000 soldiers under the command of General Homma landed on the beaches of Lingayen Gulf, unopposed, and began their inexorable march toward Manila. MacArthur and Philippine President Manuel Quezon declared Manila an "open city," and MacArthur with his wife, Jean Faircloth MacArthur, and three-year-old son, Arthur, moved expeditiously to the island fortress of Corregidor, at the entrance to Manila Harbor, where MacArthur set up his new headquarters. As for considering Manila an open city, Japan viewed it more as a "target" city and bombed it mercilessly.

Promises of more troops and planes for the Philippines came from both President Roosevelt and General Marshal, but because Japan had bombed Australia and threatened invasion of that country, American troops and planes were diverted to Australia at Churchill's request. Churchill's main concern was that Australia, for its own defense, would withdraw its troops from North Africa, where they were sorely needed in the desperate battle against Rommel's Afrika Korps. To prevent this from happening, Churchill and Roosevelt prom-ised more American military aid to Australia, and the appointment of General MacArthur as Supreme Military Commander of the entire South Pacific.

By this time the U.S. high command (Roosevelt and Stimson) had concluded that the Philippines could not be held for more than six months at the very most, so had in effect written it off. MacArthur, trying to make the best of a bad situation, moved his troops from Luzon to the Bataan Peninsula in what has been touted a brilliant military maneuver, credited with delaying Japan's victory in the Philippines by several months. This strategem would have been more successful if the designated troops and supplies had not been diverted.

Just as MacArthur was contemplating the miserable options his end game with Japan presented (including suicide rather than being captured), out of the blue came the startling news from Roosevelt that he had been appointed Supreme Commander of the entire South Pacific Theater to assume command of all American troops, followed by the order that he was to leave his post in the Philippines for Australia within a few days.

On March 11, 1942, General MacArthur, together with his family, their Chinese nurse, and a few of his staff officers, left Corregidor in four old PT boats to travel for 35 hours, almost 600 miles, to Mindanao. Here they were picked up by a B-17 bomber and flown to Australia. MacArthur knew his leaving Corregidor in the middle of this losing battle with Japan would be unpopular with his soldiers, and he was right. Following his departure he was referred to by his men as "Dug-out Doug," an appellation that clung to him throughout most of the war. He had, however, no choice.

BATAAN

THE ARMY MACARTHUR LEFT BEHIND ON BATAAN, TOUTED AS 200,000 strong, in actuality was made up of only 60,000 Filipino and 15,000 American soldiers, all partially trained and poorly equipped. These troops and the 26,000 civilians on Bataan had less than one month's ration of food and very little medicine. Disease and hunger were rampant. With no relief and no rein-forcements in sight, disillusionment, bordering on despair, gripped many of the men. The following ditty became popular.

> "We're the battling bastards of Bataan,
> No mama, no papa, no Uncle Sam.
> No aunts, no uncles, no cousins, no nieces,
> No rifles, no planes, or artillery pieces,
> And nobody gives a damn."

In spite of their plight, the sick and half-starved American soldiers held their ground until April 3, 1942, when 50,000 fresh and well-equipped Japanese troops forced the weakened Americans to surrender. When the Japanese dis-covered there were 75,000 troops instead of the expected 25,000, they realized they would need a much larger prison camp than the one assigned. They pro-ceeded to resolve this problem in a most inhumane way. The prisoners, in spite of their weakened condition, were forced to march 65 miles, under a blistering sun, over a period of three to five days to Camp O'Donnel, a much larger but very poorly equipped and run-down prison camp. Prisoners were beaten and whipped as they marched. If they lagged or tried to get a drink of water from a roadside spring, they were smashed with rifle butts or shot. At least 15,000 of them never made it. This sad episode in military history was well named the *Bataan Death March*. Phil Brain, a friend of mine and fellow Rotarian, was one of the soldiers on the death march who lived to write a fascinating book, *Soldier of Bataan,* about his experience as an American prisoner of war held by Japan.

After MacArthur's departure from the Philippines, General Jonathan Wainwright was appointed his successor. It was his unhappy duty, after struggling hopelessly against overwhelming odds, to surrender Corregidor and shortly thereafter, on May 6, 1942, all of the Philippines to Japan. (MAP 7)

Hong Kong and Singapore

O F ALL THE EARLY TARGETS OF JAPANESE AGGRESSION, THE MOST VITAL to Britain and Australia were Singapore, Hong Kong, and New Guinea. Singapore was particularly important as a naval base, on which the entire far eastern British naval power was dependent. Hong Kong and Singapore together were essential for the very existence of Britain's Eastern Empire. New Guinea, and especially Port Moresby on the south coast of Papua, were of paramount importance for the defense of Australia. Churchill placed top priority on holding Singapore, reflected in his order to General Arthur Percival, Commanding Officer: "Singapore must be defended to the death. No surrender can be contemplated." To back up these stern words, Churchill sent a flotilla of seven ships, sorely needed in the European war, to Singapore, including the new 35,000-ton battleship *Prince of Wales,* the battle-cruiser *Repulse,* and the aircraft carrier *Indomitable,* under the command of Admiral Sir Thomas Phillips. Unfortunately, the *Indomitable* went aground off Jamaica, and Commander Phillips, not appreciating at this time the essential role the *Indomitable* would have played in his fleet's defense, proceeded on without her.

On December 10, 1941, Sir Thomas Phillips sailed his little fleet north out of Singapore harbor, without air cover, to engage the enemy. He was attacked by 80 Japanese torpedo and dive bombers. The vaunted firepower of the two battle ships on which the Admiral had depended was ineffectual against multiple bombers attacking from all directions. The entire fleet was sunk in a few hours. There were 840 lives lost, including that of Admiral Phillips. On the bright side, two thousand sailors were rescued. Churchill recounted later that this was one of the worst blows he had received during all the years of the war. The vital lesson learned from this fiasco was that you don't engage the enemy anywhere at sea without an aircraft carrier or proximity to land-based aircraft. After this episode and after the battle of Coral Sea, it became obvious that the battleship was doomed to obsolescence. The aircraft carrier was now the principal surface weapon of the navy.

The same antiquated thinking that destroyed the *Prince of Wales* also afflicted the "impregnable" fortress, Singapore. Accused later of "blimpism," the military establishment rested secure in the dictum that Singapore could never be taken because it had the impenetrable jungle, swamps, and mountains to the north and a huge battery of 15-inch cannons facing south (out to sea). The British Military believed that this was the only direction from which the Japanese forces could strike. Even after Pearl Harbor, civilians and military alike felt quite secure from Japanese assault. Life went on as usual with cricket matches, polo, pink gin, and plenty of servants to relieve the hardships of daily living. The military boasted 85,000 troops, and Singapore was a stronghold that was expected to survive any attack.

Unfortunately for Singapore, the Japanese military didn't agree that the Malay Peninsula north of Singapore was impenetrable. General Tomoyuki Yamashita moved 200,000 specially trained Japanese soldiers from Indo-China across Thailand to the upper Malay Peninsula. From here his soldiers, clad in tennis shoes, with many on bicycles, slithered and slid down the forbidding "impossible" terrain of Malaya from north to south in just over two months. They were sporadically engaged by ineffectual troops made up of Chinese, Indian, and British soldiers who were too few and too poorly trained to slow the advancing Japanese, even temporarily.

Finally, the Strait of Jahore immediately north of Singapore was reached, which was expected to halt the advance, at least for awhile. The connecting causeway bridge had been dynamited by the British to prevent the passage of tanks, but the resourceful Japanese, anticipating that possibility, had put together a fleet of collapsible plywood landing craft which carried 30,000 troops and sufficient firepower to secure a beach-head on Singapore. They then repaired the bridge for a tank assault, which was accomplished quite readily because their airforce dominated the skies. Though outnumbered by at least two to one, on February 15, 1942, the determined Japanese forced British General Arthur Percival, now almost out of ammunition and water, to surrender.

It was later reported that at the time the island had been half conquered, British officers were seen sipping drinks at the Raffles, and civilians were standing in line to see Katharine Hepburn in *Philadelphia Story*. Though Yamashita promised humane treatment to the some 80,000 prisoners, as was so often the situation with Japanese conquerors, humaneness evaporated in favor of brutality. In addition to the usual looting and rape, over 5,000 Chinese soldiers were summarily executed. (MAP 10)

DUTCH EAST INDIES AND JAVA

In need of a secure oil supply, Japan invaded the oil-producing region of Borneo in the Dutch East Indies (Indonesia) at about the same time it was attacking Singapore. This was shortly followed by a large-scale invasion of Java. An attempt to halt this aggression was undertaken by a relatively small Allied fleet made up of American, Australian, and Dutch ships on February 27, 1942. After three days of intense naval warfare, in what has been called the *Battle of Java Sea*, the Allied fleet was totally destroyed. The United States lost a cruiser and two destroyers in this action. By March 9, 1942, the entire archipelago fell to the Japanese, ending four centuries of Dutch colonial rule. One hundred thousand prisoners were taken in another devastating Japanese victory. For the Allies in these early months, all the war news from the Pacific was bad. The Japanese were winning everywhere.

TOKYO BOMBED

Needing some kind of psychological boost for the beleaguered Allies, Roosevelt charged the Navy to find some way to bomb Japan. A submarine staff officer, Captain Francis S. Low, came up with the brilliant idea of launching long-range bombers from an aircraft carrier positioned within striking distance of Tokyo.

There was only one hitch in the plan: once launched, there was no way the planes could land on the carrier, even if they could make it back. After the bombing, they would have to fly into China and hope to land in an unoccupied area. To lead this audacious one way trip, an ex-stunt pilot, Lieutenant Colonel Jimmy Doolittle, 37 years old, was recruited. He assembled a group of eighty well-trained volunteer pilots and crew to carry out this risky mission. Sixteen long-range Army Air Force B-25 Mitchell bombers were modified to take off from the relatively short runway of an aircraft carrier. On April 18, 1942, approximately 700 miles from Japan, all 16 planes, each carrying one ton of bombs and a crew of five, successfully took off from the deck of the newly commissioned carrier *Hornet*. They dropped their bombs first on Tokyo, over a period of about six minutes, and then on five other Japanese cities. Japan was caught completely by surprise. Citizens were shocked that United States' bombers were able to breach their defenses and bomb their capital city. And from where?

Even though the damage was relatively slight, the propaganda value was immense in two ways. It boosted morale in Allied countries, especially in the United States, and it undermined the confidence of the Japanese military. None of the planes were shot down during the raid, but several had to crash-land in unfamiliar areas. Eight of the flyers were captured by the Japanese and three of these were tortured to reveal their launch site. Two were executed as a reprisal for the bombings and over 200,000 Chinese, suspected of aiding the downed flyers, were executed. One of the planes landed in Vladivostok and its crew was held until the end of the war. Seventy-one of the eighty flyers eventually made it home. When asked how the United States Navy managed to bomb Japan, Roosevelt responded that they had taken off from Shangri-La, the mystical domain in James Hilton's book, *Lost Horizon*.

THE BATTLE OF
CORAL SEA

....

I T WASN'T UNTIL LATE SPRING AND EARLY SUMMER OF 1942 THAT THE TIDE
began to turn against Japan. The United States Navy began to effectively use
the knowledge it had gained from cracking the Japanese code, *Magic,* which
Japan believed was impossible. They never suspected, for even a moment, that
some of their most vital battle plans were becoming an open book to the United
States. Breaking the code was the work of a brilliant cryptographer, Lieutenant
Commander Joseph Rochefort, and his specialty team stationed in Pearl Harbor.
This was the single most significant event, early in the war, responsible for stopping the Japanese juggernaut and starting the United States on its long, grueling
journey to Tokyo.

In early May, based on cryptographic reports, Pacific Fleet Commander
Chester Nimitz learned that Japan planned to invade Port Moresby, at the southeastern end of Papua, New Guinea, a necessary preliminary to their planned
invasion of Australia. Nimitz, to prevent the loss of this absolutely vital Allied
military base, gathered together all the ships he could muster to intercept the
Japanese fleet as it entered the Coral Sea, just southeast of New Guinea. Under
the command of Rear Admiral Frank Fletcher, a fleet of U.S. and Australian
ships, headed by two of the top United States' aircraft carriers, the *Lexington*
and the *Hornet,* engaged the enemy fleet from approximately 200 miles away.
The surface ships were never within range or even in sight of one another for
the entire two days of fighting. Only planes from the carriers were able to attack
enemy ships and their planes in this long-distance battle. This was the first time
in history that a naval battle was fought by proxy, the ships never close enough
to fire a shot except at enemy aircraft. (MAP 8)

The Battle of Coral Sea established, without question, the superiority of the aircraft carrier over all other surface ships, including the largest battleships. The battle lasted two days, May 7 and 8, 1942, and the losses between the two fleets were fairly even. In addition to a destroyer, a tanker, and 66 aircraft, the United States suffered the painful loss of the great aircraft carrier *Lexington*. The ship seemed to have miraculously survived several direct hits by bombs and torpedoes, but after all the fighting was over, mysterious explosions deep within its hull, from stored munitions, gasoline fumes, or delayed action bombs, gutted the ship and forced its abandonment. After all the survivors had been picked up, the *Lexington* was mercifully sunk by a U.S. destroyer. Japan lost a tanker, a destroyer, 77 aircraft, and the light carrier *Shoho*. Both sides claimed victory, but the United States fleet came out the real winner because it forced Japan to divert its transports away from Port Moresby and give up its plan to invade Australia.

One of the survivors who escaped the *Lexington* as it was sinking was Robert Sellstrom, a friend and classmate of mine from Gustavus Adolphus College. He was a fighter pilot on the *Lexington* when it was the only carrier in a U.S. task force in February, 1942 that penetrated deep into Japanese territory, 200 miles from Rabaul, a principal Japanese base in the South Pacific. During an air battle near Bougainville and later at Coral Sea, Bob shot down five enemy planes, for which he received the Navy Cross.

After the *Lexington* was sunk, he was assigned duty on the carrier *Saratoga*. Ironically, as a passenger on a routine training flight, with no enemy in sight, the plane crashed into the sea. Although Bob was rescued, he died shortly thereafter from the injuries he sustained. On May 18, 1943, in Houston, Texas, a new destroyer escort was named the USS *Sellstrom* in his honor.

Another friend of mine on the *Lexington,* Norman Sterrie, also won the Navy Cross for his intrepid flying in the air battles at Lae and Salamaua, New Guinea. Norm survived the war and became a very successful pediatrician in St. Louis Park, Minnesota.

BATTLE OF MIDWAY ISLANDS

....

SHORTLY AFTER THE BATTLE OF CORAL SEA, CRYPTOGRAPHERS REPORTED A Japanese battle plan of immense scale that involved invading Midway Islands, 1,100 miles northwest of Hawaii, the last United States Pacific Base west of Hawaii. This was to be coupled with an earlier diversionary invasion of the Aleutian Islands, designed to decoy the U.S. fleet away from the attack on Midway. Yamamoto, the architect of the Pearl Harbor strike, was now putting into action the second phase of his plan to defeat the United States by drawing out the last vestiges of its Navy as it responded to the attack on the Aleutians. Then, with the important element of surprise, he would destroy it with his vastly superior fleet. This time, however, the surprise would be on Yamamoto because most aspects of his ambitious plan, including the Aleutian ploy, were known to the U.S. Navy.

Even with this tremendous advantage, however, the outcome was still gravely in doubt because the Japanese fleet was so much larger and more powerful than that of the United States. It consisted of 190 ships, including the large carriers, *Akagi, Kaga, Soryu*, and *Hiryu,* several smaller carriers, 11 battleships, 23 cruisers, 65 destroyers, and 200 aircraft. Against this armada the United States could scrape together only 76 ships: three carriers (including the *Enterprise* and the *Yorktown,* which had undergone rehabilitation after damages it sustained in the Coral Sea), no battleships, and an assortment of destroyers, cruisers, tankers, and escorts.

For this epic battle, Yamamoto took personal command. He established his headquarters on the world's largest battleship, the 64,000-ton *Yamato,* boasting 18.1-inch guns having a range of 25 miles. His carrier chief was a veteran naval officer, Vice Admiral Chuichi Nagumo, the Pearl Harbor commander, who also had bombed British bases at Columbo, Ceylon, and Darwin, Australia, and had badly mauled the British navy in the Indian Ocean. This was definitely Japan's first team and their goal was nothing less than the destruction of the U.S. Pacific fleet, followed by the invasion of Midway, Hawaii, and probably even the west coast of California. Japan could then negotiate a very favorable peace.

Yamamoto split his fleet into five parts, sending Nagumo ahead with four carriers and accompanying vessels, but withholding most of his ships to pounce on the U.S. fleet when it showed up to attack Nagumo. Early on the morning of June 4, 1942, Nagumo struck a massive blow at the Midway military base with all 108 planes from his four carriers, not realizing that the U.S. 16th and 17th Task Forces, under the commands of Rear Admirals Raymond Spruance and Frank Fletcher, lay waiting 200 miles to the northeast. Exhibiting extreme daring, raw courage, and fortuitous intuition, Spruance dispatched all his planes—twenty-nine Devastator torpedo bombers, sixty-seven Dauntless dive bombers, and twenty Wildcat fighters against the attacking fleet.

By a stroke of sheer luck, Spruance's planes reached Nagumo's fleet just after most of their planes had landed and were being refueled for a second attack. Pandemonium seized the Japanese aircraft carriers as they tried to respond to this unforeseen emergency. Zero fighter planes still in the air, faster and more maneuverable than any of the U.S. planes, together with Japanese anti-aircraft fire, shot down all but one of the torpedo bombers as they flew in for their low-level torpedo runs.

Just as it appeared that total disaster had struck Spruance's offensive and Nagumo was about to score another spectacular victory, from 15,000 feet, the dive bombers, unseen by the low flying Zeros, hurtled down upon the unwitting Japanese carriers at top speed, releasing their bombs at 1,800 feet as they swooped up and away. Within ten minutes, three of Nagumo's carriers were mortally wounded, converted into burning, sinking hulks, including Nagumo's flag ship, the *Akaga*. Nagumo ignominiously had to abandon ship, to be picked up by one of his cruisers. During the four-day melee that followed, Japanese planes managed to sink the *Yorktown* and U.S. planes destroyed the remaining Japanese carrier, the *Hiryu*.

With the loss of his last carrier, Nagumo, horrified, withdrew his tattered fleet. Upon receiving Nagumo's report, Yamamoto, in a state of shock, fired him on the spot, then spent the rest of his day trying to compose a favorable message to send to Imperial Headquarters. Yamamoto finally came up with the following: "The enemy fleet, which has practically been destroyed, is retiring to the east. Immediately contact and destroy the enemy." Imperial headquarters in Japan then announced that a great triumph had been achieved, bringing "supreme power to the Pacific." The reality was, of course, quite the opposite.

Though the U.S. fleet didn't appreciate it at the time, they had scored a great victory that suddenly put Japan on the defensive. About this victory and that of the Coral Sea, Churchill wrote, "At one stroke, the dominant position of Japan in the Pacific was reversed. The annals of war at sea present no more intense, heart-shaking shock than these two battles, in which the qualities of the United States' Navy and Air Force and the American race shone forth in splendor." Yamamoto's dream of destroying the United States Pacific fleet ended at Midway.

THE ALEUTIAN ISLANDS

The Japanese occupation of Attu and Kiska in the Aleutians, designed as a feint to divert the U.S. Navy away from Midway and divide its fleet, was unopposed. Thanks to *Magic,* the deception didn't work, but the presence of Japanese soldiers on U.S. territory was anathema to the American public and the Joint Chiefs of Staff. Consequently, rather than simply bypassing these Japanese-held bases, as done at Rabaul and elsewhere, and which would have been the shrewdest military tactic, on May 11, 1943, only one year after its occupation, the U.S. Army's 7th Division, bypassing Kiska, invaded Attu. After two weeks of bitter fighting, all 2,500 Japanese defenders were killed and the island won, but at the cost of over one thousand American lives.

On August 15, 1943, Kiska was assaulted by 34,000 American and Canadian troops. To their surprise and great relief, there wasn't a single remaining Japanese soldier on the island. Protected by heavy fog, a Japanese task force had slipped through the U.S. Navy blockade on August 28 and had taken off all the 5,000 plus men on Kiska in less than 55 minutes. This was considered to be one of the most brilliant evacuations of the war. Kiska and Attu were then used as American air bases.

New Guinea

....

DENIED PORT MORESBY AT THE BATTLE OF CORAL SEA, JAPAN'S alternate strategy was to establish a base at Buna on the northeast coast of New Guinea and then drive south over the "impenetrable" Owen Stanley mountains to take Port Moresby by land. Japan knew how vital Australia was as the supply source of men and materiel for the entire Allied operation in the southwest Pacific. They needed to take New Guinea and hold their bases in the Dutch East Indies and the Solomon Islands to successfully invade Australia. At the very least, they needed Port Moresby to interdict all Allied shipping through the narrow seas between Australia and New Guinea, and the seas around and between New Guinea and the Solomon Islands. The Allied strategy was clearly the reverse: to hold Port Moresby at any cost, drive the Japanese out of New Guinea, and then begin to dislodge Japan from its bases in the Solomons to secure the Australian sea lanes. (MAP 8)

On July 21, 1942, Japan landed troops on the north coast of New Guinea at Buna and Gona and began the 120-mile march south over the Owen Stanley Mountains to Port Moresby. In about two months they had reached to within thirty miles of this coastal city. This time however, different from the battle for Singapore, they were met by a large contingent of fresh Australian troops and U.S. planes that counterattacked, stopped the advance, and then began to drive the Japanese troops back. Ten months of tough fighting was required to force the Japanese Army back across the mountain and recapture Buna. Both sides were exhausted and riddled with wounds and exotic jungle afflictions by the time Buna was won. With fresh reinforcements sent up from Australia by MacArthur, the Allied army then swung west to clear the entire north coast of Japanese troops.

When Japan attempted to reinforce its garrisons at Lae and Salamaua from the major base at Rabaul on New Britain Island, Japanese forces were met in the Bismark Sea by a host of planes: B-17s and B-25s, from the Fifth Air Force stationed on Papua and led by Major General George C. Kenney. By the time the three-day battle of the Bismark Sea was over, the Allied planes had severely damaged or sunk all ten of the Japanese warships and twelve transports, and had shot down over 102 aircraft. All but a few of the Japanese reinforcements were drowned. Shortly thereafter, New Guinea was secured for the Allies.

GUADALCANAL

....

WHILE THE BATTLE FOR NEW GUINEA WAS RAGING, ANOTHER
important front had ignited: Guadalcanal, at the southeastern end of the
Solomon Islands. Here Japan was building a new airfield to provide a base from
which to attack Allied shipping to and from Australia. To eliminate this grave
threat to its supply lines, the United States launched its first ground attack of
the war against Japan. On August 7, 1942, approximately 10,000 troops from the
First Marines, under the command of Major General Alexander A. Vandergrift,
following a three-hour heavy bombardment, successfully landed on the north
shore of Guadalcanal near the unfinished airstrip. They met surprisingly weak
resistance at first, and soon secured the field. They named it Henderson Field
in honor of Major Lofton R. Henderson, who had been killed in the battle of
Midway. (MAP 9)

The initial success was deceiving, however, because soon the Japanese
brought in large numbers of additional troops, and the fighting became vicious
and harrowing. Not only did the Japanese soldiers fight in an almost suicidal
fashion, but the jungle itself, with its swamps, poisonous snakes, scorpions, rats,
oppressive heat, and malarial mosquitoes, was a daunting adversary. The U.S.
Marines, young and with no tropical jungle experience, were fighting veteran
soldiers trained in this type of warfare and imbued with a wild fanaticism that
surprised and shocked the Marines.

The battle for Guadalcanal lasted for almost seven months. It was marked
not only by hard fought, bloody land battles, but also by the effort to stem
the flow of Japanese troops by sea. The campaign also witnessed six major
naval battles, during one of which the carrier *Hornet* was sunk. The last major
Japanese attempt to land reinforcements was during the middle of November,
1942, and resulted in the largest and most violent of all these naval battles,
the Naval Battle of Guadalcanal. For three days American ships pounded the
Japanese fleet, assisted now by U.S. Air Force planes taking off from Henderson

NORMANDY TO OKINAWA

Field. By the morning of November 15, the Japanese fleet, virtually destroyed, had been prevented from landing a single soldier.

The jungle fighting went on until February 9, 1943, when under cover of darkness, Japanese destroyers evacuated their 12,000 remaining troops from Cape Esperance on the northwestern tip of Guadalcanal. At the end of the fighting, the Americans counted 1,752 dead, and the Japanese, 24,000. The number of wounded and the sick from tropical diseases was much greater.

The United States had learned hard lessons in jungle warfare and gained valuable insights into its unorthodox enemy. Best of all, it had won its first land war in the Pacific. The battle for Guadalcanal taught the American military that though the Japanese were terribly tough, they were not invincible.

Another fortuitous break in the Japanese code revealed that on April 18, 1943, Admiral Isokura Yamamoto, Chief of Japanese Naval Operations, would fly from Rabaul to Bougainville. With that precise information, the U.S. Navy set up an ambush and shot down his plane.

Yamamoto, the gambler, had cashed in his chips.

SOLOMON ISLANDS

From Guadacanal, Admiral Ghormley's South Pacific Forces moved westward up the Solomon chain to Bougainville, the largest of the islands. It was taken only after bitter fighting and heavy losses. At the same time, MacArthur's Southwest Pacific forces were clearing out all Japanese troops from New Guinea and adjacent islands in preparation for their return to the Philippines. In this westward movement many Japanese strongholds, including Rabaul, the largest, were bombed heavily but not invaded. The supply routes to these islands were cut off and they were simply bypassed. Over 135,000 Japanese troops on major bases such as Rabaul and Truk were left to die on the vine, with no hope of rescue or resupply. This effective technique, used frequently during the Allied drive to Japan and euphemistically called "island hopping," was code named *Operation Cartwheel*. Although MacArthur claimed credit for this strategy, Nimitz definitely was its author and director.

GILBERT ISLANDS—TARAWA

After the battles of the Solomons and New Guinea, in November of 1943, Spruance's Central Pacific Forces began attacks on the Gilbert Islands, Tarawa and Makin. Tarawa had been honeycombed with interconnecting steel-reinforced concrete-coral bunkers by the Japanese and was declared impregnable. This assessment proved to be almost correct. In spite of intense preliminary bombing, the Marine landing was just barely successful, and the battle to win this island was one of the bloodiest of the war. Each buried bunker had to be individually assailed with flame-throwers and grenades. By the time all had been destroyed, the Second Marine regiment had sustained heavy losses, including over 2,000 wounded and 1,300 dead. All 4,500 Japanese defenders were killed before the island was secured. Although the American public was shocked at the high cost in lives of securing Tarawa, its defeat was essential for the westward advance of the Central Pacific Force.

MARSHALL, CAROLINE, AND PALAU ISLANDS

The Marshall Islands came next on Spruance's drive west, the two major islands to be conquered in this chain being Kwajalein and Eniwetok. Kwajalein, 66 miles long and 18 miles wide, is the largest atoll in the world. In the preliminary bombardment of Kwajalein, over 15,000 tons of bombs were dropped on the island, reducing it almost to rubble before any landings were made. In spite of this heavy bombardment, however, Japanese soldiers seemed to rise up out of the ashes and foxholes. The fight to conquer this island was much the same as all the others: destroy one bunker at a time in a scorching, bloody battle.

Finally, all the Marshall Islands were won, and the Central Forces moved westward to the Carolines, the Marianas, and the Palau Islands. Truk, in the Carolines, was bombed but bypassed, and Ulithi was taken without a shot fired.

Ulithi provided Allied forces with one of the best natural harbors in the entire Pacific for their burgeoning fleets. It could accommodate hundreds of ships at one time. Its location was ideal, being only 900 miles from Iwo Jima, 1,200 miles from Okinawa, and 1,500 miles from Japan. Nimitz called Ulithi the Navy's secret weapon. (MAPS 7 & 9)

Although there was heated argument as to whether to attack Formosa (Taiwan) first, as strongly urged by Admirals Nimitz and King because of its closer proximity to Japan, or the Philippines, as fervently championed by General MacArthur, the matter was settled by Roosevelt and Churchill in favor of the Philippines. With Roosevelt's fourth-term election looming, given MacArthur's immense popularity in the United States, this decision was probably based more on political than on military considerations. Nimitz strongly recommended bypassing the Philippines, Iwo Jima, and Okinawa to invade Formosa, then the mainland of China, and then Japan. The battle for Japan would be joined by Chiang's Nationalist Army. It was his contention that thousands fewer lives would be lost using this approach. An additional advantage of this technique might have been the prevention of the Communist takeover of China. The latter is, of course, speculation.

MacArthur was instructed to bypass Mindanao, strike Leyte first, then Luzon (location of Manila and Corregidor), and to move the invasion timetable up from December to October, 1944. To accomplish this objective, the Allies would have to destroy Japanese strongholds in the Mariana and the Palau Islands and airfields within striking distance of the Philippines and Japan.

SAIPAN

During the months of June, July, and August, 1944, Nimitz's Central Pacific forces, under Spruance, struck Saipan with an armada of 525 ships carrying 127,000 men, 80,000 of whom were Marines. Saipan was defended by approximately 32,000 well dug-in Japanese. Four days after the American invasion, a huge Japanese carrier force struck the U.S. fleet in one of the largest carrier battles of the war. Because 500 Japanese planes were shot down during this engagement, it was dubbed The Great Marianas Turkey Shoot. The U.S. lost 130 planes. In an attempt to save some of their ships, the Japanese armada broke off the fighting and retreated west toward their Philippine base, but not until three more aircraft carriers, now without air protection, were sunk.

The land battle for Saipan was rugged, characterized by fanatic *banzai* attacks. Within three weeks the island was won, but at the cost of 16,000 American casualties, including 3,426 deaths. The Japanese lost 23,811 soldiers and an untold number of civilians who jumped off the high cliffs of northern Saipan rather than be captured. The commanding officer, Lieutenant General Yamashita Saito, and most of his staff committed suicide the honorable way, by *hari-kari*. Admiral Nagumo, of Pearl Harbor fame, now demoted to the command of a small-craft fleet at Saipan, employed a less respectable but easier way out. He shot himself. (MAP 7)

TINIAN, GUAM, AND PELELIEU

Tinian and Guam fell after fierce, bloody fighting, punctuated by suicidal *banzai* attacks that inflicted some damage to the U.S. forces, but which decimated the Japanese. On Tinian, for example, 195 U.S. Marines were killed compared to approximately 5,000 Japanese. Many of the enemy were never found because they were buried in their caves by giant U.S. bulldozers during the course of the fighting.

When Agana, the capital of Guam, fell, the victors received an unexpected reward. The total Pacific supply of liquor for the Japanese forces was stored there. This included not only *sake* but good quality Scotch, bourbon, rum, beer, and wine. How it was distributed, I was unable to learn, but I don't think it went to waste.

The last stepping stone to the invasion of the Philippines was Pelelieu Island in the Palaus, which finally fell after a month of ferocious fighting. An elongated, heavily defended hill down the center of Pelelieu Island was the last to yield to the Marines. With ample reason, the Marines called it Bloody Nose Ridge. Of the 45,000 Marines and soldiers that struck Pelelieu Island, 1,800 were killed and 8,000 wounded. Eleven thousand Japanese soldiers were killed.

Though a terribly costly acquisition, Pelelieu not only provided the United States with a base close to the Philippines, but it eliminated a Japanese stronghold from which they could have bombed the newly acquired Allied anchorage at Ulithi and harried B-29 bomber flights to Japan from Saipan. The stage was now set for the invasion of the Philippines.

The Allied advance westward, island by island, met with increasing resistance and higher costs in men and materiel. The prospect of huge additional losses before the Philippines, Iwo Jima, and Okinawa could be won also loomed darkly over the Allies. Beyond that loomed the greatest blood bath of all, the invasion of Japan. (MAP 7)

Return to the Philippines

....

ALTHOUGH JAPANESE MILITARY LEADERS KNEW THE PHILIPPINES WERE targeted next for invasion, they didn't know exactly where. They suspected that it would be Leyte, but Soemu Toyoda, the new Commander in Chief of Naval Operations, being a conservative tactician and now directing a greatly reduced navy, did not want to commit any of his forces until he was sure exactly where the landing would be. To create as much confusion as possible, elements of Admiral Halsey's Third Fleet attacked air bases on Formosa from October 11–14, 1944. During the air battles these forces shot down 500 Japanese planes and lost 100 Allied planes. The Formosa attack accomplished its primary objective, and for at least a few days Toyoda was fooled into believing that Formosa was the target. When it became apparent that the invasion would be against Leyte instead, Toyoda mobilized all the naval power he could muster, now absent a large number of carrier planes. This fleet consisted of approximately 70 Japanese warships and 716 planes split into three separate commands that opposed an American force of 166 warships and 1,280 planes.

The American Sixth Army, under the immediate command of Lt. General Walter Krueger, numbering some 200,000 troops, carried by 400 transports, began their landings on October 20, 1944, on the east side of Leyte along a ten-mile stretch of beach in an operation similar to but smaller than that at Normandy. The preliminary bombardment of beach defenses was carried out by Rear-Admiral Jesse Oldendorf, under the overall command of Seventh Fleet Commander Vice-Admiral Thomas Kincaid. The Seventh Fleet was responsible for transporting all troops and supplies and providing protection for the actual landings. Halsey's Third Fleet operated at some distance from the invasion beach to interdict any assaults by Japanese war ships. (MAP 7)

Upon realizing that east Leyte was the invasion site, Toyoda divided his forces into three basic units. The smallest unit comprised four aircraft carriers (with a total of 108 planes), two carrier battleships, and a few escorts. Vice-Admiral Jisaburo Ozawa, the commander, was to lure Halsey's Third Fleet northward as far away from the invasion beach as possible. The larger remaining Japanese fleet, made up of four carriers, seven battleships, two battleship carriers, and twenty cruisers, was divided into two attack units under the commands of Admirals Takeo Kurita and Shogi Nishimura respectively. Kurita would attack Leyte beach from the north through San Bernadino Strait. Nishimura would attack from the south through Surigao Strait.

Kurita's fleet was spotted by a U.S. submarine who radioed its course and sank two heavy cruisers, damaging a third. One of the cruisers sunk was Kurita's flagship, from which he was picked up by the battleship *Yamoto*. Before reaching San Bernadino Strait, Kurito was forced to turn back by the heavy attack from planes of Marc Mitscher's Task Force 38, a part of Halsey's Third Fleet. At this point Halsey's task force fell for Ozawa's decoy maneuver and began the chase north away from Leyte, as hoped by Toyoda, and contrary to the U.S. battle plan. Halsey's unplanned diversion left San Bernadino Strait unguarded, dangerously exposing the U.S. landing forces from the north.

With relief from the heavy air attacks occasioned by Halsey's departure, Kurita returned to San Bemadino Strait toward Leyte Gulf expecting to trap the U.S. invasion force in the pincers between his and Nishimura's fleet coming up from the south. Unfortunately for Kurita, Nishimura never made the rendezvous. His fleet was detected by Admiral Kinkaid, who ordered Oldendorf to block the exit from Suragao Strait with all his ships: six old battle ships and an assortment of cruisers, destroyers, escorts, and PT boats. When Nishimura discovered the blocked exit and tried to turn around, his fleet was totally destroyed by withering broadsides. Nishimura was killed and almost all his fleet was sunk or severely damaged.

In the meantime, oblivious to the battles occurring around Leyte Gulf, on October 24, Halsey caught up with Ozawa's decoying fleet and managed to sink two of his aircraft carriers and severely damage two others. He would have continued the battle with Ozawa, but was ordered back to Leyte Gulf and sternly rebuked by Admiral Nimitz through Admiral Kincaid for having departed from the prescribed plan. His impromptu chase left the defense of the vulnerable beach landings at Leyte Gulf entirely up to Kinkaid's relatively small fleet.

With Halsey's fleet on the high seas, Kurita, coming up the San Bernadino Strait on October 25, was opposed by Admiral Thomas Sprague's small contingent of six lightly armored escort carriers and six destroyers, now the only defense available to protect the U.S. invasion forces. Facing a much larger fleet and expecting no immediate reinforcement, with great daring and courage and a superb battle instinct, Sprague went on the offensive and attacked Kurita with every ship and plane he could muster. The frenzied two-hour battle that followed, together with no communication from Ozawa, convinced Kurita that he was facing a much larger contingent. After several hours of seeing his cruisers either sunk or damaged, he broke from the melee and retreated back through San Bernadino Strait.

During this battle, the first coordinated *kamikaze* attack which translates as *divine wind* and is named for a hurricane that destroyed Kublai Khan's invading Mongol fleet in 1279 occurred, sinking the escort carrier *St. Lo* and damaging two others. As Kurita sped west, Halsey's fleet returned to the chase, but Kurita escaped with no further damage. The battle of Leyte Gulf, October 23–26, 1944, one of the greatest naval battles in history, had ended, and the land battles for the Philippines had begun. In this and the preliminary Formosa bombardment, over 1,000 Japanese planes, three battleships, and four carriers were destroyed. Serious damage was inflicted on numerous others. The threat of any significant Japanese naval opposition to America's drive to Japan had been virtually eliminated. Now Japan's hope was dependent upon its army and marine land forces and its newfound secret weapon, the *kamikaze*.

The beach landing on Leyte, with General Douglas MacArthur's triumphal "I shall return," was a success. Yet the subsequent fighting was drawn out, difficult, and bloody. Through an inexplicable U. S. intelligence failure, land designated for air strips, essential for the invasion of Luzon, proved too boggy. The only one available for use was a narrow strip at Tacloban, the capitol of Leyte. The fighting on Leyte, reminiscent of trench warfare in WW I, dragged on through November and December and into January of 1945, much longer than expected. U.S. casualties were over 15,000, and 50,000 Japanese were killed. To build more air strips for the invasion of Luzon, the island of Mindoro, closer to Luzon, was acquired in December. A typhoon on December 18, 1944, complicated that operation, but didn't derail it for long.

The invasion of Luzon, beginning on January 8, 1945, involving again about one-quarter of a million troops of Krueger's Sixth Army, was a three-pronged attack from the southern end of Lingayen Gulf, the northern end of Bataan, and the beach southwest of Manila. Naval sea and air support was again provided by the Third and Seventh Fleets. The Fifth U.S. Army Air Force, under the command of General Whitehead, provided air support. The U.S. forces were opposed by Yamashita's 280,000 well dug-in troops, who were indoctrinated to never surrender, but to fight to the death. They were supported by very limited air and naval power and by the feared and reviled *kamikaze.*

In one week of hard fighting Clark Field was retaken, providing excellent paved runways for air support for the invading army. On February 3, the outskirts of Manila were reached, but here the advance was stopped. Conquering the city was a lot more difficult than getting there. Twenty thousand Japanese troops were holed up in most of the houses. They had to be rooted out house-by-house and block-by-block in bloody battles that lasted over a month. When it was finally over, 12,000 American and 16,000 Japanese soldiers, had been killed. Manila was almost totally destroyed. During the battle for Manila, Japanese soldiers in a massacre similar to the rape of Nanking, wantonly raped and butchered over 100,000 Filippinos.

Corregidor was bombed heavily for weeks. On February 16, it was invaded by U.S. paratroopers and seaborne troops. The American troops were outnumbered, but they dug in and survived several suicidal *banzai* attacks.

On February 21 and 22, tremendous underground explosions occurred, caused by accidental gunpowder detonation or by suicidal intent, killing over 2,000 Japanese defenders. By March 1, 1945, Corregidor was won. After three years of Japanese occupation, the American flag was raised over this embattled island fortress. Fighting continued on Luzon until August when Yamashita, with only 50,000 soldiers remaining of his huge army, surrendered all of Luzon.

Iwo Jima

....

WITH THE PHILIPPINE VICTORY SECURED, THE NEXT OBJECTIVES ON THE inexorable U.S. march to Japan were Iwo Jima (Sulfur Island) in the Bonins, and Okinawa, one of the Ryukus, 350 miles from Kyushu, southernmost island of Japan.

The acquisition of Iwo Jima was essential to the U.S. plan to eliminate a Japanese fighter base that posed a threat to U.S. bomber runs from Saipan. Iwo Jima would also provide landing fields for B-29s, and for fighter escort planes.

The first B-29 raid from the Marianas (Saipan, Tinian, and Guam) occurred on November 24, 1944. These planes had a range of 1,500 miles. With their pressurized cabins, they could fly at altitudes of over 30,000 feet, well out of the range of anti-aircraft fire and most enemy fighter planes. Although these were important characteristics, as a practical matter, bombing from that height, given the prevailing winds and clouds, offered poor accuracy. Damage to Japanese military targets (ammunition and aircraft factories) was minimal.

Iwo Jima, pork-chop shaped, and only 2½ by 5 miles in size, with one high elevation, Mount Suribachi, was heavily defended by the Japanese and treated with great respect by the U.S. Marines charged with its capture. Following several weeks of heavy bombing from the air and three days of naval bombardment, three Marine divisions (the Third, Fourth, and Fifth), under the command of General Holland Smith, assaulted the volcanic island in force on February 19. They managed to land on the beaches against heavy fire. They found forward progress greatly impeded not only by the well-armed, cave-embedded enemy, but also by the deep drifts of volcanic ash, not apparent prior to the landings. The small size of the island precluded U.S. support fire from either the air or the sea for fear of striking our own troops. As a consequence, the advance up the slope of Mount Suribachi was gained literally inch by inch in bloody hand-to-hand fighting by the usual technique of flushing the enemy out of its caves and foxholes with flame-throwers and hand grenades. The top was not won until February 24, 1945, whereupon several Marines planted the American flag. This act was memorialized by Associated Press photographer Joe Rosenthal in a photograph printed in newspapers and magazines around the world. (MAP 7)

Winning Mount Suribachi by no means ended the fighting on Iwo Jima. The entire remainder of the island had to be methodically cleared of Japanese defenders by grenade, flame-thrower, and bayonet. Finally, on March 14, after a month of fierce fighting, Iwo Jima was won. Losses on both sides were heavy. Of 20,000 Japanese defenders, all but 200 were killed, including Commanding Officer General Kuribachi. The U.S. Marine toll was also heavy, with 6,000 killed and 25,000 wounded.

As soon as the island was secure, existing landing strips were repaired and lengthened by the Sea Bees (Construction Battalions). Iwo Jima became an important air base that could accommodate B-29 traffic.

As an interesting aside, just prior to the Iwo Jima invasion, the Joint Chiefs of Staff seriously considered using poison gas instead of a conventional attack to conquer the island. They argued there were no civilians there and the cost of invasion in American lives lost would be extremely high. Roosevelt denied this option, and rightly so, in my opinion, declaring that gas should only be used in retaliation for its first use by the enemy. I'm equally sure that most families who had lost loved ones at Iwo Jima wish that gas had been used and maybe their loved ones would have been spared. War so often presents extremely difficult choices.

TOKYO BOMBED AGAIN

Disappointed in the effectiveness of high-altitude daytime bombing of Japan, in the latter half of 1944, General Harold "Hap" Arnold, head of the U. S. Army Air Force, replaced General Haywood S. Hansell, chief of the Twenty-First Bomber Command, with General Curtis LeMay, at that time the chief of the Twentieth Bomber Command in China. LeMay had also had extensive bombing experience in Europe. With the change in command came a marked change in bombing strategy. Instead of high-altitude daytime bombing raids directed at military targets, now low-level nighttime incendiary (jellied gasoline and TNT) bombing raids were aimed at neighborhoods adjacent to military factories. Bombers were stripped of their armor to permit heavier bomb loads.

On the night of March 10, 1945, three hundred thirty-four B-29s, flying at low altitude over Tokyo, dropped fire bombs for three hours on a 16-square-mile area of homes and factories. The resulting inferno, driven by the wind, destroyed everything in its path. Somewhere between 80,000 to 100,000 people, mostly civilians, were killed in this raid. A similar raid was launched against Nagoya, Japan, with equally devastating results.

The bombing tactics in Europe primarily involved attacks on pinpoint military targets. The change to bombing broad population areas in Japan resulted from a change in mindset among the U.S. bombing command that stemmed from the wanton cruelty and disregard for human life of the Japanese Army. Adding to the disgust and hatred for Japanese military tactics was their increasing use of *kamikaze* attacks. A "show them no mercy" attitude began to prevail within the U.S. command.

OKINAWA

....

THE UNITED STATES' DUAL DRIVE ACROSS THE CENTRAL AND SOUTH
Pacific had now converged on the last essential objective prior to the attack
on Japan itself, the invasion of Okinawa. The U.S. military knew it would be
the costliest and most difficult achievement of the Pacific War, which it proved
to be. The only assault predicted to be worse was the invasion of Japan, which
some had estimated would cost one million Allied soldiers' lives. Because of its
location, its excellent airfields, and its large deep harbor, Okinawa was a vital
strategic step in the battle for Japan. (MAP 12)

Okinawa was defended by the Japanese Thirty-Second Army of over
100,000 men, under the command of Ushijima Mitsuru. The defense of the
island depended to a large extent upon a complicated system of caves, some
natural and some man-made, located in the mountains of southern Okinawa.

Just prior to the Okinawa invasion, the adjacent Japanese island of Kyushu
was bombed, and a small island next to Okinawa, Kerama Retto, was seized by
U.S. forces to provide a base for the repair of damaged ships and from which
Okinawa could be bombarded. Fortuitously, on Kerama Retto 300 suicide boats
designed for use against the Okinawa invasion were discovered and destroyed.

The invasion of Okinawa, code-named *Iceberg,* began on April 1, 1945.
It involved a fleet of over 1,000 ships. It was to be carried out by the newly
formed U.S. Tenth Army, under the command of Lieutenant-General Simon
B. Buckner Jr.

The initial force was made up of 150,000 troops divided into a marine division, assigned to the northern half of the island, and an army division for the
southern half. The largest contingent of Japanese soldiers was hunkered down
in the southern mountain caves where they were expected to make their stron-
gest stand. The northern half of the island offered relatively little resistance and
was secured by the U.S. Marines by April 13.

After three weeks of desperate fighting, the first Japanese defensive line, *Machinate,* was breached, and the second more heavily fortified *Shuri* Line, was attacked. The *Shuri* Line extended across mountain ridges from the city of Naha on the west coast. It was buttressed in its center by the old fortifications of *Shuri.* Here a counterattack by Lieutenant-General Mitsuru Ushijima's army was beaten back with heavy Japanese casualties. Fortuitously, many previously hidden artillery positions were revealed, making them more vulnerable to U.S. attack.

The final grueling drive to conquer the southern half of Okinawa involved the usual cave-by-cave process of burning, blasting, and hand-to-hand combat. Ushijima was forced to retreat to the southernmost tip of the island, where, after four more weeks of bitter fighting, the Japanese Thirty-Second Army was destroyed.

By June 21, the battle for Okinawa was over. Ushijima committed suicide and almost every one of his 100,000 soldiers were killed. Thousands of Okinawa civilians were also killed. U.S. casualties exceeded 75,000. Sadly, just before war's end, Lieutenant-General Simon Buckner was killed in a freakish accident. A Japanese bullet hit a rock next to where Buckner was standing. A rock fragment chipped off by the bullet's impact struck him in the forehead and killed him.

Adding to Okinawa's tragedies, Ernie Pyle, the celebrated and much beloved Pulitzer Prize-winning war correspondent, was killed April 18, 1945, during the invasion of Okinawa on Ie Shima, a small adjacent island.

As the U.S. Tenth Army fought against the Japanese soldiers on land, the U.S. Navy, with its thousands of supply and support ships, was attacked by conventional Japanese air-raids and *kamikaze* attacks on the seas around the island. There were approximately 2,000 *kamikaze* attacks on U.S. ships during the Okinawa campaign, most of them over Naha harbor where the concentration of ships was the highest.

The battle for Okinawa exacted the greatest loss of naval personnel of any battle in WWII. There were 33 ships sunk and 368 ships damaged. Four thousand nine hundred U.S. sailors were killed and 4,820 wounded at Okinawa, accounting for 20 percent of all navy dead in WWII. On our ship, the USS *Rankin,* loaded as it was with ammunition, we lived in constant fear of being struck by a *kamikaze* plane. We attributed our good fortune to the dense smoke cover utilized during an attack and to pure chance.

Other lesser known Japanese suicide devices were the *kaiten* and the *okha*. The *kaiten* was a modified long-lance torpedo which provided a longitudinal, but very cramped space, for a pilot. With a small window in the front of the torpedo and a miniaturized steering device, he could guide it to its target. As many as six of these torpedoes could be carried by a submarine to the target area.

The *okha* was a mini-rocket plane that housed one pilot and a bomb load. It was carried by a twin-engine bomber to be released near the target. Because of its rocket speed it was almost impossible to hit by anti-aircraft fire or fighter plane. However, it proved to be vulnerable because the mother plane was so slow it would frequently get shot down before it could release its manned missile.

With the battle for Okinawa successfully concluded, the attention of the Allies was now directed to the daunting final phase of the Pacific war, the invasion of the Japanese home islands.

Japan

THE ATTACK ON JAPAN WAS DIVIDED INTO TWO PHASES. THE FIRST, CODE-named *Olympic,* would be launched against the southernmost island, Kyushu. The second, *Coronet,* would assault the main island, Honshu. It was hoped that Russia would attack the Japanese army in Manchuria to prevent it from participating in the main island defense. Russia was more than happy to accommodate the Allies in this regard. (MAP 13)

U.S. intelligence estimated that the Japanese, for their defense, had approximately 10,000 planes, half of which were *kamikaze,* and two million soldiers. In addition to the soldiers, millions of civilians, too young or too old for military service, were conscripted to act as suicide barriers to the invasion. They were instructed to kill at least one invader before they were killed. The U.S. Joint Chiefs of Staff were aware of the terrible cost in American lives the Japanese invasion would bring, estimated by some to be a million or more. However, there being no clearly discernible alternative, they were prepared to pay the price. The Joint Chiefs believed that Japanese government leaders would never accept the Allied position of unconditional surrender without a fight to the death.

Even as the U.S. military was formulating its prodigious battle plans and marshalling its forces, the possibility of another course of action was unfolding. On the desert, near Alamogordo Air Base, at a test site named Trinity, in New Mexico, on July 16, 1945, at 0830 the first atomic (plutonium) bomb was exploded from the top of a 100-foot steel tower. The awesome power released from this explosion approximated 15,000 to 20,000 tons of TNT, with a core heat four times that of the sun! It literally vaporized the steel tower upon which it was fixed, and tremors from the explosion were felt hundreds of miles away.

Dr. Robert J. Oppenheimer, theoretical physicist from the University of California and scientific director of the Manhattan Project, was awed. He quoted Hindu scripture, *I am become death, the destroyer of worlds.* This event, world-shaking in its significance, would expedite the conclusion of WWII and forever control the balance of power in the world.

Atomic Bomb Project

....

R OOSEVELT NEVER DISCUSSED THE STATUS OF THE ATOMIC BOMB PROJECT with his Vice President, Harry S. Truman. After Roosevelt's death on April 12, 1945, Secretary of State James Byrnes and Secretary of War Henry Stimson apprised the new president of the status and potential of the bomb project. It became Truman's awesome responsibility to decide whether to use the atomic bomb against Japan. A summary of some of the events leading up to the successful detonation of the atomic bomb that were covered in President Truman's briefing are of great interest.

This fascinating story begins with Albert Einstein. A refugee from Germany in 1933 (the same year that both Roosevelt and Hitler came into power), Einstein was concerned over the possible development of an atomic bomb in Germany. He wrote a letter in 1939 to Roosevelt informing him that according to his theoretical calculations, the atom could be split, resulting in an immense release of energy that could possibly be developed into a bomb. Roosevelt acted on Einstein's suggestion, and, in May, 1941, established the Office of Scientific Research, under the direction of Dr. Vannevar Bush, President of the Carnegie Institute in Washington. Bush was charged with developing a method of releasing energy from the atom with the principal objective of building an atomic bomb. To provide enough space to conduct this research and test its progress, vast lands were acquired at Oak Ridge, Tennessee, Los Alamos, New Mexico, and Hanford, Washington. Soon, huge plants were built in Oak Ridge and Hanford to separate a uranium derivative, U-235, and to make plutonium.

The overall military aspects of the project were given to the U.S. Army, under the direction of the feisty and controversial General Leslie R. Groves. The project was called the Manhattan Project, so named for the city in New York where its first meeting was held. A large laboratory was established in Los

Alamos, to be directed by Dr. Oppenheimer, for the development of a warhead to deliver the bomb. Enrico Fermi achieved a chain reaction on December 2, 1942, in an atomic pile in Chicago. It was jubilantly predicted at that time that the first bomb could be completed by late 1944 with enough fissionable material available by the summer of 1945 for at least two bombs.

The Potsdam Declaration

....

By the time of the Potsdam Conference, held just outside war-torn Berlin, during the last half of July, 1945, Roosevelt, Hitler, and Mussolini were dead, and Churchill had been replaced in office by Clement Attlee. Churchill was in attendance along with Truman and Stalin. The most significant event of this somewhat rancorous conference was Truman's announcement that the U.S. had successfully detonated an atom bomb the day before the conference began and had the capability to use the bomb against Japan. Both Churchill and Stalin urged Truman to use it, and Stalin agreed to attack Japan in Manchuria. Truman, in his memoirs, stated, "Let there be no mistake about it, I regarded the bomb as a military weapon and never had any doubt that it should be used."

Accordingly, on July 26, 1945, the Potsdam Declaration was issued with an ultimatum that demanded Japan's unconditional surrender, or face the alternative, total destruction. After two days of deliberation, Premier Suzuki responded that Japan would ignore the ultimatum. This rejection initiated the already-planned U.S. response, which had been set up under the command of Lieutenant General Spatz, now Commanding General of the U.S. Army Strategic Air Force in the Pacific.

HIROSHIMA AND NAGASAKI

....

THE PLAN UNFOLDED AS FOLLOWS: TWO BOMBS, ONE OF URANIUM, called *Little Boy,* and one of plutonium, *Fat Man,* were dismantled, then sent to Tinian in the Marianas. They were reassembled there for the strikes against Japan.

A tragic event occurred shortly after delivery of *Fat Man* and *Little Boy* to Tinian. Travelling unescorted to Leyte, on the night of July 29, the heavy cruiser USS *Indianapolis* was sunk by a Japanese submarine. Electrical failure precluded sending an SOS, and none of the surviving sailors were found for over 82 hours. From a crew of 1,119, 888 succumbed. Many died of injuries and exposure, and some had been torn apart by sharks. Much worse, however, would have been a torpedo strike against a ship carrying *Fat Man* and *Little Boy.* The skipper, Captain Charles McVay III, was indicted for failure to follow navy regulations. He did not order a zigzag course in these waters and was subsequently court-martialed.

Two of four selected cities—Hiroshima, Kokura, Nagasaki, and Niigota—were to be the targets. Bombing dates would be determined by weather conditions as soon after August 3 as possible. Colonel Paul W. Tibbetts Jr., with a specially trained crew in a modified B-29, named *Enola Gay* after his mother, Enola Gay Tibbetts, was selected to drop the first bomb, *Little Boy,* on Hiroshima on August 6, 1945. The second bomb, *Fat Man,* was to be dropped by Major Charles Sweeny from a B-29 called *The Bock's Car,* on August 9, if Japan hadn't surrendered after the first bomb.

Tibbett's mission to Hiroshima on August 6 was completed without a hitch. The 12-foot-long, 9,000-pound *Little Boy,* carrying the equivalent of 20,000 tons of TNT, exploded 2,000 feet over the center of Hiroshima, totally demolishing four square miles of the city and blowing away all lightly built houses three miles beyond that. About 80 percent of all buildings were destroyed and the rest badly damaged. Approximately 80,000 people were killed and at least that many injured. Immediately after the blast, the *Enola Gay* was catapulted upward in a severe jolt. Tibbett reported that after the mushroom cloud had dispersed, the city below looked like a sea of boiling black tar.

Sweeny, on the other hand, ran into trouble from the start. His first target, Kokura, was so cloud-covered he had to change his target city to Nagasaki. Several passes were required here because of swirling smoke from a previous bombing. Finally, by 1100, two large Mitsubishi plants became visible and *Fat Man* was released over this industrial and residential center.

Although *Fat Man* was larger than *Little Boy* and more powerful, the damage to Nagasaki was actually less because of surrounding hills and water. All buildings in the valley were destroyed, but the death toll was less than Hiroshima: 40,000 to 50,000 overall. After Nagasaki, Sweeny didn't have enough fuel left to make it back to Tinian and had to make an emergency landing on Okinawa. Here, only by reversing his propellers, did he avoid smashing into a row of parked B-24s. When his plane finally came to a stop, there wasn't enough fuel left to taxi off the runway. Sweeny was a lucky man!

With Premier Suzuki's rejection of the Potsdam Declaration, on August 8, 1945, Russia declared war on Japan. The next day, a huge Russian army, encountering little resistance, rumbled across the border, decimating Japan's Kwantung Army. Within a few days it had penetrated deep into Manchuria. By the time of the Japanese formal surrender to the Soviets on August 22, the Russian Army had killed 80,000 Japanese soldiers and captured 594,000. (MAP 13)

JAPAN SURRENDERS

Even after the destructive power of the atomic bombings became apparent to the Japanese government, the Council was split, three to three, on whether to accept the surrender terms. By the night of August 14 Emperor Hirohito resolved the stalemate by insisting that Japan surrender. For the first time ever, on August 15, he recorded a message broadcast by radio throughout the country that Japan was surrendering to the Allies. Hard-line military officers attempted to seize the recording and effect a coup, but they failed.

Tokyo accepted the terms of the Potsdam Declaration, but asked that Japan be allowed to retain its Emperor. This was agreed to by President Truman, with the stipulation that the Emperor's authority would be "subject to the Supreme Commander of the Allied Powers." He also promised that the people of Japan could establish their own form of government. Other terms of the Potsdam Declaration included the surrender of all Japanese troops in China, Hong-Kong, Singapore, Formosa, Korea, and all other Japanese bases across the Pacific. At the time of the formal surrender, August 14, 1945, there were 5.4 million soldiers and 1.8 million sailors in the Japanese military.

With few exceptions, the Allied military forces were ecstatic that Japan surrendered without having to be invaded. Allied prisoners of war were the happiest, because prior to Japan's surrender they learned that at the time of the Allied invasion, whenever that was, all prisoners of war were to be slaughtered. There was no ambivalence in their minds as to whether or not the atom bomb should have been used to end the war. The luxury of those deliberations was left to the armchair philosophers and Monday morning quarterbacks.

There was considerable turmoil in the upper echelons of the Japanese government during the period just before and after the decision to surrender. On August 15, Japanese Premier Suzuki resigned and was succeeded by Prince Higashikuni, the Emperor's uncle.

SURRENDER CEREMONY

The formal surrender ceremony was staged on the battleship, *USS Missouri*, flagship of the U.S. Pacific Fleet, on September 2, 1945. For protocol reasons, Premier Higashikuni was represented at the surrender ceremony by the one-legged Foreign Minister, Mamoru Shigemitsu, who dressed formally with a top hat and striped pants. Representatives from Allied countries wore their fancy dress uniforms, except for the U.S. representatives, who dressed in their plain informal tans.

MacArthur read a magnanimous statement, after which two decorated war heroes were introduced, General Jonathan M. Wainwright, prisoner of war following Corregidor's fall, and Lieutenant General Sir Arthur Percival, prisoner of war after the fall of Singapore.

Shigemitsu signed two copies of the document, then MacArthur, Nimitz, and the Allied delegates signed too. MacArthur concluded his statement with the following: "It is my earnest hope that from this solemn occasion a better world shall emerge, a world dedicated to the dignity of man. Let us pray that peace may now be restored to the world and that God will preserve it always. These proceedings are closed."

In the days and weeks following the surrender ceremony, the peaceful occupation of Japan by American soldiers and sailors began. The U.S.S.R. requested but was denied the opportunity to participate in the occupation. The vast majority of Japanese military personnel, seven million of them, returned to Japan to participate in its rebuilding.

The Cost of War

....

With the formal surrender of Japan on September 2, 1945, after four and one-half years of bitter fighting, WWII ended and the world returned to peace. The losses, in terms of numbers of human beings killed and cities destroyed, were staggering. The U.S.S.R. sustained the greatest loss of life, with 25 million deaths, two-thirds of which were civilian. China was second, with 15 million deaths. Poland lost 6 million; Germany, 4 million (not counting the victims of the Holocaust), Japan, 2 million, Yugoslavia, 2 million, the United Kingdom and the United States, 400,000 each. The total global mortality has been estimated at 60 million, a figure beyond comprehension. It was exceeded only by the horrific mortality of the influenza pandemic of 1918: 50–100 million!

Although 400,000 U.S. military deaths is a huge figure, it is much less than the mortality of the American Civil War. In fact, Civil War mortality (673,000) was greater than that of all twentieth-century U.S. wars combined. In the Korean war there was a total of 118,515 United Nations military personnel killed, 33,729 of which were American. In the Vietnam war over 58,000 American soldiers, sailors, and marines lost their lives. United States WWII civilian deaths were minimal compared to the gargantuan losses of the war-torn countries. In these areas, in addition to the dead and wounded, over ten million people were dislocated, having been permanently expelled from their homes, or finding no homes remaining after their repatriation. This was the single largest human migration, during a short period of time, in history.

One of the greatest war costs in terms of human suffering and death occurred in what has become known as the Holocaust, termed the "Final Solution"(*Endlosung*) by the Nazis. The "Final Solution" was based on the Nazi edict that "Citizenship was to be determined by race; no Jew to be a German." Eleven million Jews had been targeted for extermination in Nazi death camps, and the Nazis had achieved more than half that goal by war's end in 1945. According to John Loftus and Mark Aarons, in their book, *The Secret War*

Against the Jews, recent evidence has revealed that over six million Jews were exterminated in death camps, and the mass killings were not limited to Jews. Between 500,000 and probably closer to one million Gypsies and approximately ten million other nationalities were eliminated in concentration compounds and death camps.

Hitler would have been willing to allow emigration of the Jewish population to any other country including Palestine, but no other country offered asylum. Jews with adequate means were allowed to leave the country, but usually at a high price, such as confiscation of their home, art works, and bank accounts. When British, French, and U.S. intelligence reported the grisly business of mass extermination of human beings in death camps, the information was kept secret and withheld from the general public.

At the Bermuda Conference held in 1943 to discuss this matter, the joint decision was made that nothing could be done about the problem anyway, so whatever was going on in German-held territory would have to run its course. They sensed that Hitler would be willing to send the Jews to any country that would have them, but there were no volunteers.

According to Loftus and Aarons, Allied planes could easily have bombed the death camps. "Bombing the gas chambers at just three death camps: Solubar, Treblinka and Auschwitz, might have shut down the killing system for months, sparing hundreds of thousands of lives." U.S. Assistant Secretary of War John McCloy determined that bombing the death camps was not cost-effective and shouldn't be done, even though military and industrial targets were being bombed all over Europe, often not far from the camps.

The Holocaust, as applied to the Jews, was genocide for no other reason than to eliminate a particular race of people. Genocide has occurred at other times and other places but usually for some political, territorial, or religious reason.

Strictly speaking, the Holocaust was not a consequence of the war but was rather a manifestation of the depravity and sickness of Hitler's mind and that of the entire Nazi party. The war provided the Nazis with the cover they needed to carry out this ghastly crime.

Stalin was also guilty of mass murder from the Ukraine to Siberia, but he managed to cover up his genocide by touting German atrocities. Sometime after the war in Poland it was discovered that mass murder had occurred in the Katyn Forest in eastern Poland. Hundreds of Polish military officers were found buried in the forest after having been shot through the head at close range. Stalin, when confronted with this hideous atrocity, blamed it on the Nazis. Later studies, however, revealed that it was the Soviet Army that had committed this heinous crime and probably at the direction of Stalin.

In another example of Stalin's vindictive nature, angry at reported defections of Chechen soldiers from the Red Army earlier in the war, he ordered ethnic cleansing for the entire country of Chechnya and its Ingush neighbor. Through the Soviet secret police (NKVD) boss, Lavrentii Beria, 478,479 Chechans and 91,250 Ingushens were evicted from their homes on February 23 and 24, 1944, and loaded into 180 special trains, 159 of which were sent to the winter wasteland of central Asia and Siberia. There the occupants were unceremoniously dumped to fend for themselves. At least one-quarter died on the trains of exposure, starvation, or typhus, and an untold number perished in the bitter cold after leaving the trains.

Journalist Thomas Goltz, in his book, *Chechnya Diary*, said that, "If the Chechens had been lacking the concept of nation before the traumatic events of 1944, they no longer had any doubts about who they were now: a self-conscious community set apart from all the other nationalities that made up the USSR. They had been branded as traitors and thieves and outcasts, but knew themselves to be survivors."

The memory of the horror of the genocide of 1944 has been kept alive and burning in all modern-day Chechens and they are dedicated to never yielding their homeland to Russia even though their capital city, Grozny, has been bombed to rubble. They are the terrorists, the fifth column in Russia today, and they have vowed to fight to the last man.

Whereas all Japanese soldiers and prisoners of war were returned to Japan, the U.S.S.R. held most of their war prisoners for many years after the war, using them as forced labor in the rebuilding of their shattered infrastructure.

The United States reduced its armed forces in Europe from 3,500,000 to 400,000 men in the short span of ten months, but the Soviet Union retained troops there for a much longer time. Soviet soldiers were permitted to wreak vengeance on the defeated Germans, which they did with rampant looting, rape, and slaughter. Other Allied powers, for the most part, did not indulge in this vindictive behavior.

All Allied countries appropriated various items of strategic military importance. The Soviet Union, having sustained such immense human and property losses, betrayed by Germany, felt completely justified in exacting maximum reparations and demonstrating unbridled revenge. The Soviets were not checked or inhibited by the United States or Britain because neither country wanted to give Russia an excuse to grab more territory than approved at Yalta. Churchill particularly did not want to risk a war with Russia at this time.

The economies of all participating nations, especially the losers, suffered immensely. Only the United States came out of the war stronger than when it entered.

The initial reaction within the U.S. leadership after the war was to crush Germany forever. Secretary of the Treasury Henry Morgenthau recommended that the Allies reduce Germany to pastureland. Even Roosevelt, on one occasion, stated that as far as he was concerned, "The Germans could live happily on soup from soup kitchens."

Truman dismissed Morgenthau and fortunately adopted a much more humane and rational approach to the management of post-war Germany and of Europe. This was exemplified by the Marshall Plan to rebuild Europe's economy, the Truman Doctrine to protect Turkey and Greece, and the formation of the North Atlantic Treaty Organization (NATO) to protect its members and preserve the peace.

The U.S.S.R., on the other hand, in addition to the impossible reparations mentioned earlier, was stoutly dedicated to regaining all eastern territories held by the Czars, including eastern Poland, the Baltic States, and East Prussia. It also wanted to insure the friendship of eastern European countries by installing within these countries sympathetic Communist regimes, then binding this ideological empire into an economic and military bloc.

War Crimes Trials

....

ON NOVEMBER 20, 1945, IN NUREMBERG, GERMANY, A TEN-MONTH TRIAL of German "war criminals" began. Held in a gray, nondescript building, one of the few still standing, a four-power court was set up to deal with an *ex post facto* body of law regarding aggressive warfare and crimes against humanity. Indictments were brought against 21 Nazis, who were given one month to prepare their defense. The prosecution presented lurid details of the gory history of Nazi extremism, including witnesses, photographs, documents, and motion pictures. That this was no "kangaroo" court was apparent with the acquittal of several high-ranking Nazi officials, including editor and propagandist Hans Fritsche, former Chancellor Franz Von-Papen, and diplomat and financial genius Hjalmar Horace Greely Schacht.

The worst offenders were found guilty and sentenced to death by hanging. These included Alfred Rosenberg, Frank Streicher, Wilhelm Frick, Fritz Saukel, Arthur Seyss-Inquart, Joachim Von Ribbentrop, Ernst Kaltenbrunner, Wilhelm Keitel, and Alfred Joseph Jodl. The S.A. *Sturm Abteilung* (Storm Troopers) boss, Martin Borman, who escaped Hitler's bunker, was at large at the time of the trial, his remains (a skull) were reportedly found in 1973. His family refused to accept his remains for burial. Herman Göring committed suicide during the trial by taking a cyanide capsule hidden in the heel of his boot. Hitler, Goebbels, and Heinrich Himmler also robbed the gallows by committing suicide.

Hitler married his mistress, Eva Braun, in the Reich-Fuhrer's Berlin bunker below the Chancellery Garden shortly before they both committed suicide on April 30, 1945. Eva swallowed poison, and Hitler shot himself through the brain with the barrel of his pistol in his mouth.

Following Hitler's specific orders, two *Schutzstaffel* (Defense Unit) men carried Hitler's body up the stairs and out into the Chancellery Garden, where he and Eva were doused thoroughly with gasoline and set on fire. No recognizable portions of their bodies were ever found. In his last message to his armed forces he accepted none of the responsibility for the defeat of the Third Reich. Instead he put all the blame on his Army General Staff. He had always detested weaklings who committed suicide, so he wanted his suicide to be kept a secret. The official story was to be that he died fighting at the head of his soldiers. Propaganda minister, Joseph Paul Goebbels, resolved his end-game dilemma by poisoning his children, then shooting his wife and himself.

Loftus and Aarons claimed that hundreds of Nazi war criminals who should have been brought to trial and punished were released from prison over a period of several years without penalty. Many were financiers and bankers. They took up residence in different countries all over the world, including the United States. A large number of them emigrated to Argentina, a country with Fascist sympathies. According to Loftus and Aarons, the greatest atrocities of WWII were the result of bigotry, greed, and stupidity.

Dr. Cabot Wohlrabe, an Army medical officer during WWII and a good friend of mine, was assigned to the Nuremberg trials. He witnessed the entire spectacle. He said that Göring was a very personable man. If you weren't familiar with his wicked past, you would think he was a good guy.

One of the reasons the Nuremberg trials were held under the auspices of the Allies was that after WW I, the Germans were allowed to conduct their own trials, which in retrospect, as noted earlier, were a farce.

War crime trials were also conducted in Japan following WWII. Seven high-ranking officials were found guilty and hanged. Two avoided the gallows by committing suicide: General Shigero Honjo and former Premier Prince Fumimaro Konoe. Tojo was found guilty, attempted suicide, but was unsuccessful. Before his hanging he wrote this poem: *It is goodbye. Over the mountains I go today, to the bosom of Buddha. So happy am I.*

Emperor Hirohito was stripped of all but his symbolic status. He issued an Imperial Rescript to his people stating that his position as Emperor, "was predicated on the false assumption that the Emperor is divine, and further, that the Japanese people are not superior to all other races, nor destined to rule the world."

According to author Herbert P. Bix, professor of history at Harvard University, Hirohito was not a totally passive, symbolic figurehead as MacArthur and his General Headquarters staff described him and as presented by the press and subsequent history books. Instead, Hirohito was very much involved as head of state. He not only approved the militarists' plan to extend the Japanese Empire, but also he provided leadership in the war against China, the attack on Pearl Harbor, and the conduct of the war throughout the South Pacific. He condoned the use of chemical and biological weapons against China, but forbade their use against the United States for fear of retaliation in kind. Tojo, who served as minister of war and later as prime minister, received most of the condemnation for Japan's aggression and inhumanities. Tojo, together with many of his cabinet and armed services chiefs, were tried as war criminals and executed.

MacArthur insisted on exempting Hirohito from the war crimes trials to retain him as a stripped-down emperor who would serve as symbolic head of state without power, secular or divine. MacArthur's strong feelings on this point can be appreciated in his telegram to Truman, the concluding paragraph of which is quoted by Bix as follows: "His indictment will unquestionably cause a tremendous convulsion among the Japanese people, the repercussions of which cannot be overestimated. He is a symbol which unites all Japanese. Destroy him and the nation will disintegrate. It is quite possible that a million troops would be required which would have to be maintained for an indefinite number of years."

With the backing of Truman and the State Department, all efforts to force Hirohito to abdicate and face trial were squelched. Even Tojo was careful during his trial to not implicate Hirohito in any of Japan's depredations, nor was Japan formally condemned for the use of chemical weapons. Russia considered Hirohito to be a war criminal and strongly urged that he come to trial.

Article 9 of Japan's new post-war constitution forbade Japan to sustain any armed forces nor resort to war for any reason. The constitution also modified the role of the emperor: "The emperor would be the symbol of the state and of the unity of the nation, deriving his position from the will of the nation with whom resides sovereign power."

Because of this failure to expose the whole truth to the Japanese people and to hold Hirohito responsible for his central role in Japan's aggressions, Japan has never really recognized or apologized for the war or for its inhumane behavior. Current Japanese school textbooks say virtually nothing about WWII and cast Japan as a victim of the war, citing Hiroshima and Nagasaki as examples. Not too subtle pressure is being applied by the current Japanese prime minister, Junichiro Koizumi, to scrap the 1946 constitution and replace it with one that eliminates Article 9. He would also restore a more active role for the emperor as head of state with divine lineage (*genshu*) instead of his current status as symbol only (*shocho*).

One year after Hirohito's death in 1989, his son, Akihito, was enthroned as emperor, cast in the *shocho* tradition. With the current political ferment in Japan, it may not be too long before pre-war *genshu* returns.

When reflecting on the high cost of the war to the United States, the alternative to remaining aloof from it, thereby guaranteeing an Axis victory, is too horrible to imagine. All of Europe would have been under control of the evil and immoral Nazi regime, and Japan would rule the Pacific. Being the only bastion of freedom in the world, the United States would, sooner or later, have to face the combined strength of all the Axis powers, including Japan. The cost of that war is incalculable, even if we were fortunate enough to win it. That is why most WWII historians have counted it a blessing that Japan did us the unwitting favor of attacking Pearl Harbor. No one will ever know how long it would have taken for the U.S. to get into the war if that event had not occurred.

Pat Buchanan, potential Reform Party presidential candidate during the 2000 election, in his book, *A Republic, Not an Empire*, expressed an entirely different view. He believes that because of the military weakness of both England and France in 1939, they should not have declared war on Germany following its attack on Poland. Instead they should have waited until Germany carried out its master plan of first attacking Russia. Then the two evil empires would fight it out to the death or debilitation of both countries. During this time the Allied countries could build up their military strength, and when the German-Russian war ended, they would not only be invulnerable to attack, but would be in a very strong position to determine the framework of a new Europe. In that scenario, the United States would have strengthened its military, but would not have needed to enter the European war. Hundreds of thousands of American lives would have been spared.

The problem with this thesis, in my opinion, is that Germany, given its vastly superior military strength early in the war, would most likely have defeated Russia. Further, with only one front to support, the Germans would undoubtedly have started earlier in the spring instead of late June, because they would not have to contend with battles in Greece and Yugoslavia, which delayed their planned invasion of Russia in 1941. At that time, even though they were fighting on two fronts and contending with severe winter weather, they almost defeated Russia. A victorious Germany in the east that could apply its full strength to the new Western Front would be extremely difficult, if not impossible, to defeat given the lack of preparedness of the Allied countries at that time. This, too, is speculative.

The twentieth century has been the bloodiest in history. There is no doubt that the WWII generation made a huge contribution to saving our country and the world. This fact is underscored in Tom Brokaw's excellent book, *Reflections on the Greatest Generation*. I am equally certain that given the same set of circumstances, today's generation would commit itself just as honorably and effectively as did ours. None of the wars and military actions since WWII, especially Vietnam, have had the clear rationale for patriotic duty and sacrifice as was present in WWII with Japan's attack on Pearl Harbor and Germany's threat to the entire free world.

Diary: June 25, 1944 to December 19, 1945

···

JUNE 25, 1944: *The day was warm and sunny—such a rare treat in England. After a short walk around Southampton, we boarded the 1236 train for Plymouth. Flowers in the parks were in full bloom—the roses particularly beautiful.*

The truck ride from the American Red Cross to the station was among my most harrowing experiences. Though we were 30 minutes early, the truck driver must have thought we were late because he drove like a madman through the narrow congested streets. I asked if he was a taxi driver from New York City. He said "No, a truck driver from Boston." This was adequate explanation.

We were crowded on the train, but the six hours went by quickly with the various "docs" relating their experiences. When we arrived at Plymouth it was pouring rain. This was more like it! Now England was her old self again.

Trucks carried us to Vicarage Barracks, which we learned is primarily a survivor's camp, where we unloaded. There were many of the Lido Beach gang already here: Woody, Eckstam, Panter, Czerny, La Royan, Boylston, Thomas, and about twenty others.

The scuttlebutt is that we are going to be sent back to the States—but no one really knows. I will believe it only when we are underway.

To celebrate this great occasion, Yorkoff brought along a half gallon of 95 percent ethyl alcohol which he mixed with grapefruit juice. It tasted so good and seemed so innocuous, I had no idea that it packed such a wallop. In a short time, the whole room was spinning and I barely managed to climb into my upper bunk.

JUNE 27, 1944: *Morning, and how my head pounds! I don't dare turn it for fear it will fall off. How miserable I feel! All the men are groaning and cursing the night before. "Never again!" is the cry. I managed on unsteady legs to drag myself to lunch and even eat a little. This afternoon I felt much better and after dinner felt good enough to go to an officer's dance at the Continental Hotel.*

....

JUNE 28, 1944: *Early this morning, Dick Greenleaf, Hilary Holmes, and I went shopping. We first picked up 60 clothing points. There was very little to buy in the stores. I settled for a head scarf for Mother, a loud necktie for Dad, and a few souvenirs.*

It was announced this morning that Cherbourg had been captured by American troops.

I spent the afternoon painting my sea chest and repacking my clothes.

There are about six doctor survivors here from our group who were either on mined or torpedoed ships. The LSTs sunk that I am definitely sure about, having either seen the sunken ships myself or talked to survivors, are: the 507, the 531, and the 289 (Fabius operation—sunk by E-boats). Panter and Eckstam were on the 507. They were picked up after three hours in the icy channel water (46 degrees F). They were unconscious when rescued and only survived because they had tied themselves to the life raft. Dr. Manning and probably his partner (though I don't know for sure) went down with the 532. Then there are these: LST-499 (struck a mine—Boylston and partner—injured but survived), LST-496 (Dr. Henderson killed), LST-133 (struck a mine, one or two doctors killed), LST-523 (mine, one or two doctors killed), LST-376 (E-boats, Gerber survived), LST-314 (E-boats, Drs. Landahl and Hare killed).

There are rumors of others sunk but these cannot be trusted until you have a firsthand source. Because these sinkings are kept secret, there are undoubtedly others unknown to me.

Jim Thomas' ship was shelled on D+8 on the British beach. Five 88 mm shells hit their LST, causing 19 casualties, including ten deaths. I guess I have been plenty lucky.

JUNE 29, 1944: *This was another of England's typical days: fog, rain, and cold. The food here is lousy, our Quonset hut is cold, and we are out of toilet paper. What a joint! We complain all day long, of course, but to no avail.*

My men were ordered back to the States today, as well as Pete and his men. As yet there have been no orders for me. There are about twenty of us docs left behind and scuttlebutt has it that we are going to form a new beach battalion. I don't believe it!

Learned at noon today that the LST-282 was sunk. Every day we hear of new sinkings.

Walked through the rain tonight to a local pub for a few beers. The place was typical, with dart games, dark beer and local gossip.

Again I go to bed wondering what will be my fate. Such prolonged suspense doesn't agree with me.

....

JUNE 30, 1944: *Rain, fog, cold; another depressing day. Food was worse than ever: stale bacon, crummy French toast, soggy breakfast food. Lunch and supper were no better. Even the cake served for dessert was burned. Though all of us here are so lucky, we still could find something to complain about.*

Crigler and I went to the Guildhall Officer's dance. All around the buildings were smashed. Fortunately, the dance floor was intact and there were a few nice gals present. I'm getting quite smooth with the British dance, the "Polyglide."

No news of our fate yet, but Dr. Lane says, "Anything might happen to you boys."

A Liberty ship survivor came in tonight and reported that three Liberty ships were sunk in mid-afternoon in the Channel.

....

JULY 1, 1944: *Still raining. Received two boxes of candy in the mail from Mother today. Excellent! Went to the Guildhall dance again tonight and danced all evening with a very small but very cute girl, Phyllis Williams. She had recently had her heart broken by an American soldier. He was engaged to her, then she discovered he was married. She seemed to be recovering quite rapidly. Walked her home in the deep wet fog. I felt like a character out of Sherlock Holmes as I walked through the fog-bound streets of Plymouth.*

JULY 2, 1944: *Pouring rain again today. Will this never cease? Crigler and I picked up the mail. Another box of candy from Mother. Went to the local cinema,* Son of the Navy, *starring Jimmy Dunn. After the movie, Al Moody, Mark Anutz, and I walked to Tomarton, a small town about three miles away. The countryside was so lush and beautiful. No lack of moisture here.*

....

JULY 3, 1944: *Morning and evening were clear, but of course it rained all afternoon.*

Lew Harmon and I went to the dentist at Manadon Field, then saw the movie, Rosie the Riveter. *Howard Scal came along with us to the dance at the Continental. He says he's becoming very schizoid and I'm not surprised. He has the right type of personality, being very introverted and extremely sensitive. He is no way psychotic.*

The moon is bright and beautiful tonight and Plymouth with its torn buildings, gaunt and lonely, makes for a weird, surreal picture in the moonlight.

....

JULY 4, 1944: *This is getting monotonous, but for the sake of the record, it rained again today.*

The movie tonight was Around the World *with Kay Kayser. Crigler and I went for a long walk. The sun was still bright at 2130.*

It seems assured that we are leaving for somewhere on Thursday, but no official word.

I am reading Hans Zinsser's autobiography, As I Remember Him. *I enjoy it immensely.*

Fourth of July, the day commemorating our independence from Great Britain, has a renewed and happy significance to me at this time.

....

JULY 5, 1944: *Another Vicarage day: mail, walk, read, scuttlebutt. It was warm enough today to omit a top coat. First such day for a long time.*

There is a bombed church in Plymouth, St. Andrews, that is one of the most impressive sights I have seen. The roof has been torn off, but the heavy stone walls and Gothic arches remain. The windows are shattered, there are charred timbers piled in one corner, and two remaining chandeliers hang askew from the arches.

Carefully cut grass, broken only by tile crosswalks, form the floor. Pink climbing roses cling to the standing pillars. The pulpit is charred and broken but still used. There is a large gold cross over the altar. A sign just inside the doorway reads, "This place is none other than the house of the Lord. Services held from time to time depending upon the weather."

The sun filled the ruined church with a warm light as we stood in awed silence beneath the towering white arches. I looked toward the cross and to my mind came the familiar words, "In the cross of Christ I glory towering o'er the wrecks of time."

Midnight found me walking the streets through the ghostly, bombed-out buildings, searching for a taxicab.

....

JULY 6, 1944: *The long awaited news became official today. Tomorrow all of us remaining "docs" head back to the States. What wonderful news! How fortunate we have been! We have waited for this so long and have seen so many groups go, that when our orders actually appeared, we didn't quite explode, but we were glowing plenty hot on the inside.*

Lew Harmon, Crigler, and I went down to the local pub, just this side of Saltash Ferry, overlooking the river, where we drank brown ale, exchanged sea stories and speculated about our future. It was a fitting way to spend our last night in England. "Whither bound?" is the question on all of our minds.

....

JULY 7, 1944: *Today is the day! At 1300, after packing all our gear, we scrambled onto several trucks that transported us to Plymouth station, where we boarded the train for Rosneath, Scotland. The ride through the English countryside was, as usual, very beautiful. At Crewe, just this side of Liverpool, with a three-hour layover, we wandered around town, had a few ales and observed that people actually noticed us. We were getting into country where service men were not commonplace.*

The night trip to Glasgow, with five in a compartment, was rough. We slept in snatches and by morning felt beat out of shape and utterly trampled.

....

JULY 8, 1944: *Arrived in Glasgow 0900. We marched in a column through the main street to Queen's Street Station and boarded another train for Helensburgh,* *which is the boat landing for Rosneath. At Rosneath we learned that we would probably leave for the States on Tuesday. After eating lunch, Crigler and I obtained permission to go to Edinburgh. We boarded the ferry at 1620, the bus for Glasgow at 1720, and had dinner at the George Hotel. At 1935 we boarded the train for Edinburgh, to arrive about two hours later.*

We obtained rooms at the Scotia Hotel and then went to the American Red Cross to eat and dance until midnight. This town is beautiful and tomorrow should be a most worthwhile day. Right now we are plenty tired.

....

JULY 9, 1944: *The Scotia beds were very comfortable and both of us slept like rocks. "Bed and breakfast" cost ten pounds, six shillings apiece—so we ate breakfast at the Scotia. This was a typical war breakfast: porridge, one piece of sausage, one piece of bacon, one fried tomato, toast, marmalade, and tea.*

St. Giles' Church is the mother church of Presbyterianism, situated in the center of old Edinburgh along the Royal Mile. We attended 1100 services and were invited to sit in a "members-only" pew by a lovely lady, Mrs. Baird. The service was excellent including the sermon. It was all very simple.

Dinner at the American Red Cross was quite good: ham, potatoes, pastry. After dinner we visited briefly the Royal Infirmary Hospital of Edinburgh University; then, starting from the Red Cross, we made a walking tour of the city. Our guide was a venerable old man, Mr. Simpson, who showed us most of the important places in town in about two and a half hours.

We saw the cemetery where Hume is buried, the Holy Rood, the Palace, and walked the Royal Mile to Edinburgh Castle. Mary, Queen of Scots was the leading lady here.

A tea dance next occupied our time, then dinner with two A.A.C. Officers and a girl for each of us at the Royal British Restaurant. Here we had excellent Scotch whiskey and roast duck. From 2100 to 2300 there was another dance and with so many lovely Scottish girls present it was a pleasure.

....

JULY 10, 1944: *At 1100 we visited the Royal Infirmary again. This time, Colonel Stuart, Superintendent, showed us around. The hospital was huge, with over 2,500 beds and only 22 interns. Sir John Fraser is Surgeon in Chief. We ate lunch here* with one of the interns who found much to criticize about the set up. The beer at lunch was excellent.

After lunch, we visited medical bookshops, including the Livingston Publishing Company, where I purchased Surgery of Modern Warfare, by Bailey.

We had tea with Mrs. Baird and her two daughters-in-law. Both were beautiful with husbands in the service and each with one child.

After tea we boarded the train for Glasgow, then Hellensburgh, then the boat to Rosneath. The entire trip took four hours.

....

JULY 11, 1944: *Base 2, Rosneath is situated in lovely surroundings with all the Quonset huts in heavily wooded country reminding me of northern Minnesota. It is chilly and cloudy all day long, but the biggest disadvantage here is the presence of mice and bedbugs. Roberts was all bitten up by bedbugs, and the mice feasted on my cookies.*

We played basketball on an outdoor court this afternoon with Steiner, Yorkoff, Grainger, and Bradburn against Crigler, Moody, and me. We almost killed ourselves in our poor condition, but had great fun. Scuttlebutt again rampant. Hope we get some orders soon.

....

JULY 12, 1944: *Though the weather was cold and threatening, Moody, Crigler, and I started out this morning for Loch Lomond. We boarded a steamship at the western end of the lake, and cruised almost to the northeastern tip, an hour and a half trip. The water of Loch Lomond is brownish, but the surrounding hills and banks are truly "bonnie" with large growths of standing pine as well as a variety of leafy trees. After the boat trip we had tea and crumpets in a small town hotel and then hiked a mile to board the steamship for Dumbarton, then the base. Tonight we were told that we leave for the States either Friday or Saturday.*

....

JULY 14, 1944: *We learned today that we are definitely leaving Sunday on the* John Erickson, *a U.S. Army transport ship converted from the Swedish luxury liner, the* Kungsholm.

JULY 15, 1944: *In drizzling rain, Moody and I picked up our orders for the States. We later had dinner at the Castle, followed by the movie, Mine-sweeper.*

We returned early to our quarters because we have to be up at 0400. We listened to beautiful music on Yorkoff's radio until midnight, but all of us were so excited at the prospect of going home we couldn't get to sleep.

....

JULY 16, 1944: *At 0430, with dawn just breaking, we were rudely awakened by the Master at Arms. This was the day of days! We are all overjoyed. After a heavy breakfast and a two-hour anxious wait, the bus picked us up for the short trip to the pier and from there we ventured out into the harbor in small boats to find our transport. We zigzagged around and between hundreds of ships, and almost went crazy trying to guess which one was ours. After twenty minutes we pulled alongside the last ship in the harbor, a large two-stacker. Compared to our LST it looked tremendous! After we came aboard we were even more impressed with its immensity.*

Moody, Riley, MacPhail, and I were assigned a beautiful stateroom with a bath, two sinks, and three portholes. The room is large and undoubtedly first class during peace time.

Sunday dinner was a lovely dream. The dining room was beautiful and the service perfect. The dinner was out of this world with fruit cocktail, French onion soup, roast chicken, salad, olives, and peach pie à la mode for dessert. This was the best dinner I have had since joining the Navy.

We got underway at 2200, on our way to New York City!

....

JULY 17, 1944: *Day of days, a dream come true! Away from the British Isles for twelve hours and the sun is shining bright and warm. All rheumatic aches and pains from cold damp England were dissipated in the lovely warmth.*

Meals continued first class, but so much food. It is quite a job to negotiate three of those meals a day.

There are now forty-two ships in our convoy with a lot of escorts.

....

JULY 18, 1944: *This too-divine cruise continues with wonderful meals, movies, shuffle board, exercise, sunbathing, bridge, reading. All these make the days unbelievable! Weather still ideal.*

JULY 19, 1944: *More of the same. The bliss is becoming boredom. We are anxious to get home.*

A heavy wind has blown up quite a sea. An LST would be a bucking bronco out here now but the John Erickson *barely rolls.*

There are nine columns of ships across in this convoy, the lead ship in each being a beautiful transport. It is a striking picture to see the nine columns plowing ahead in even lines, almost like a neck-and-neck race.

....

JULY 20, 1944: *Today was like the others but much warmer. We should arrive in New York City one week from today.*

....

JULY 21- 22, 1944: *High winds and rough seas. The* John Erickson *is pitching heavily and we have slowed to between three and ten knots.*

....

JULY 23, 1944, SUNDAY: *Perfect calm today. Full steam ahead! Roast duckling for dinner. The joy of nearing home is overwhelming. I can't remember when I have been so happy.*

....

JULY 24, 1944: *Today, we approached the "grand banks" of Newfoundland with fog and clouds most of the day. The sea is almost like glass. What a thrill to be coming home.*

....

JULY 25, 1944: *We arrived in New York City Harbor on July 25. The Statue of Liberty was as thrilling to see as I had heard tell by returning Americans and immigrants as well. Staten Island and lower Brooklyn were beautiful sights. As we docked, an army band hailed us with "Stars and Stripes Forever," then a group of popular numbers. The American Red Cross gave us fresh cold milk, candy bars, and doughnuts. They also provided us with transportation to any place in town we wanted to go.*

My first action was to call home and it was wonderful to hear the dear familiar voices. I was fully aware of my extreme good fortune in having survived the war (so far) and in being back in the United States so soon after serving overseas. I thought about the thousands of young men who had been in battle for two years or more and were still engaged in the fighting. I was indeed fortunate and I knew it.

New York City was hot, but it was great to see the beautiful skyscrapers, the shop windows filled with worthwhile goods and real drug stores. My first glass of ice-cold beer (in contrast to the room temperature beer in England) at the Commodore Hotel bar was a treat I'll never forget.

....

JULY 26, 1944: *I left New York City for Boston and found it to be fresher and cooler than the "Big Apple."*

Tonight I met Olga Bogach (a dear friend I had met during my internship in Boston) in the lobby of the Touraine Hotel. She was her usual beautiful, bewitching, chic, charming, and laughing self.

We ate dinner at the "Hideaway," just off Boylston, then strolled through the Boston Commons and the Boston Garden. These places I have learned to love as dear old friends. How full and rich are the memories of the times spent in those enchanting surroundings. The Garden is my most favorite place. This night we sat at the edge of the lagoon with a beautiful star-filled sky above and the inky water at our feet. Lamplight, shining through leafy branches, reflections on the water, dark forms of ducks on the surface, the indistinct arch bridge, made this a fairyland that overwhelmed my senses and sent chills up and down my spine.

....

JULY 27, 1944: *We drove to Gloucester with Art and Millie Kane where we ate lobster and later waded in the pounding Atlantic surf. One whiff of the air in Gloucester loudly announces that this is a fishing village.*

....

JULY 28, 1944: *The day was spent revisiting my old stamping grounds, the Boston City Hospital. Here I enjoyed visits with Milton Anderson, Walter Long, Nancy Sheldon, William B. Castle, Maxwell Finland, Costello, Miss Maxon, and others. As I walked through the tunnels and visited the laboratories of this venerable old institution, I realized how rich my experience here had been. It was too brief, but I don't know where I could have learned more or been exposed to more fascinating clinical situations and sharper professors than here. I only wish it could have been longer.*

Tonight we had dinner at Olga's house in Brookline, where her folks put on a scrumptious feast: wine, beer, Scotch whiskey, chicken, ham, and for dessert, apple and blueberry pie. Later, Art Kane, his aunt and uncle, and Olga took me to the railroad station for my return to New York City.

....

JULY 29, 1944: *The five days in N.Y.C. prior to receiving orders were well spent. I saw several plays, visited the Scals in their three floor-apartment, danced at Delmonicos twice, met Crigler and his wife at the Café Rouge, and double-dated with Sinclair and his wife.*

Orders finally came for me to report to a recruiting and induction station in Buffalo, New York, to be preceded by a ten-day leave to go home. I took the first flight out of New York City, a night flight, and was mesmerized by the breathtaking beauty of the myriad Manhattan lights, forming fantastic patterns and fabulous designs befitting this city of gigantic proportions. Our plane glided smoothly down to the landing strip at Wold-Chamberlain Airport the following morning where Mother, Carol, Melba, Bud, Marcia, and Paul Lloyd were there to meet me. I was so thrilled at being back and seeing these dear loved ones that for awhile I couldn't even talk.

We had breakfast at Melba's house and then went to the lake. How beautiful old Lake Minnewashta is!

The ten days at home were spent swimming, sunbathing, visiting with friends and relatives, and touring the lake in the motorboat, reminiscing.

....

AUGUST 16, 1944: *The time went by incredibly fast and I boarded the plane for Buffalo, New York. The city was sweltering and after a few days at the Statler Hotel I was transferred to the University Club. This place reminded me of the Phi Rho Sigma fraternity house at the University of Minnesota, but was much larger and better equipped. Among other accoutrements, they had a very nice dining room and a bar. The members seemed generally quite old, but I did make some good friends during my stay. The meals were good, especially breakfast, served in a room with a fireplace and always the morning paper.*

My job at the induction station was to examine the hearts and lungs of new recruits. Listening to heart tones was always interesting to me, though attempting to differentiate a harmless functional murmur from a significant one, denoting underlying valvular disease or some esoteric congenital anomaly, was quite daunt-ing. Actually, the final decision in some cases was only a guess. My two civilian M.D. helpers were over seventy and both were hard of hearing. They were slow but faithful, especially old Dr. Resback. Once in a while I would be asked to help out in orthopedics.

Our induction team traveled to Rochester, New York, for a week each month, which broke the monotony. We also spent some time at the induction station in Syracuse, New York.

In Rochester most of us stayed at the Seneca Hotel. A Mrs. George Schlegel of Rochester provided all of us with complete basketball uniforms so we could enter a tournament at the YMCA. Ira Saposinct was a big-time promoter that worked for Mrs. Schlegel and swung the deal.

Fellow workers at the Rochester induction station were doctors: Vincent Leone, surgeon from Niagara Falls, a very friendly, capable man who never wanted to make any trouble; Ben Meyers, psychiatrist, very moody, unpredictable, but nevertheless friendly and kind; Joe Calgano, obstetrician, looked like Joe Stalin, always cheerful, but afflicted with asthma.

The most fun we had was playing basketball. We entered our team with our gold uniforms bearing the inscription "ARMY-NAVY" in bold letters on our shirts and jackets, into the "Y" league. Unfortunately, we never won a single game, but we always had a great time.

I'll never forget the guys who made up that team. Sgt. Anduck was built like a bull and ate like a horse. He was a fanatic on exercise, and on the court was always driving hard. Unfortunately, too often he would forget to dribble the ball and was called for traveling. Sgt. Lee Hoitink was tall, smooth, and a good ballplayer, but was out of practice. He would get the shots, but too often missed. He played center, wore contact lenses, and fought his heart out. Cpl. Ed Conan, thin as a rail, couldn't see without glasses, and was invariably in poor shape. He lacked strength, but had ability and was a scrapper. In addition to poor eyesight, he had flat feet. Pvt. Lou Klein was stubby and muscular but also had poor vision. He was another fighter who tried hard, but was always fouling. Pvt. Ed Weil was small, puny, and pale. He smoked cigars incessantly. He had lots and lots of heart, but just didn't have the strength or the stamina to go with it.

We didn't win a single regular game, mainly because we never had time to practice together. It was great fun, though, until I sustained a fracture-dislocation of my right index finger. This took me out of the last game before Christmas against the Crescents, which we lost miserably.

I met some wonderful people in Buffalo who were very kind to me and I will always remember. Could Mrs. Schlegel's money have been spent more wisely? Undoubtedly. Could it have been appreciated more? No way!

One of the most interesting experiences I had was going to work in December during one of Buffalo's worst blizzards, and they have a lot of them. This day, the whole town was tied up because most of the plows had been sent to Syracuse the week before to help them dig out of a previous storm. The Mayor urged everyone in non-essential occupations to remain at home because there was virtually no transportation. I knew I had 25 inductees to examine, so I started out hiking to the station and was shortly picked up by someone in a jeep. We managed to make it around stalled cars everywhere, and finally I reached my destination. The examinations were done in short order because everyone wanted to get out of there fast. The trip home was even more difficult with the snow continuing to fall. The bus driver of one of the city buses that got stuck in a huge snow drift asked all of the passengers to leave the bus, and to get behind it and push. When they finally got it moving, the bus driver kept going, leaving all the passengers fuming in the middle of the street. This episode made Time magazine the following week.

My return to the University Club was greeted by cheers and rewarded with a wonderfully hot Tom and Jerry. Most of the men at the club couldn't make it into work, so instead, they played cards, read yesterday's newspapers, and drank Tom and Jerrys.

....

DECEMBER 22, 1944: *Today my orders came. Again I experienced that peculiar, uncomfortable "gone" sensation that accompanies new orders. I am first to report to the Medical Supply Depot in Brooklyn, New York, then to Newport, Rhode Island, then to Wilmington, North Carolina, to help commission a new ship, the USS* Rankin *(AKA-103), an assault cargo ship. I am greatly relieved to learn that I won't be in a beach battalion or back aboard an LST. I will be paid seven dollars per diem until I board ship and still have the chance to visit home.*

I took the train to Minneapolis this very night, and had a wonderful Christmas at home with all the family. I made rounds at Swedish Hospital with Dad which was great fun, but I was plagued by the thought that our time together was so brief. We heard on the news that the Germans had broken through our lines in a new Belgian offensive and the entire war picture seemed to have gotten worse. The thought of all those young men suffering and dying on the frozen battlefields made it difficult to say "Merry Christmas."

....

JANUARY 1, 1945 TO JANUARY 25, 1945: *I boarded the train (Zephyr) for New York City, and the beginning of a new chapter in my naval career. A year ago I was heading for the Newport, Rhode Island, Navy Hospital.*

On this trip, between Cleveland and Buffalo, we were plunged into a severe blizzard. Our train was over seven hours late into Buffalo and we were informed that this was the worst storm in Buffalo history. Winds were clocked at over 75 miles per hour and you couldn't see fifty feet ahead of you.

I managed to make it again to the induction station to pick up my orders and then struggled to the University Club. There I saw many of my old pals.

That night I borrowed Jerry Bateman's car and in the face of the big bad storm, I cautiously drove the nine miles out Main Street to the home of a wonderful girl I had met a few weeks ago, Jane Sheeler. After wading in knee-deep snow across her large yard, I finally reached the door. There was a lovely warm glow inside, strengthened by hot Tom and Jerrys, the best I had ever tasted. It was a most pleasant evening.

The following day I left for New York City to arrive at about 11:30 PM. I had been invited to stay with the Scals, and was greeted by Mrs. Scal, who treated me to a large bowl of cornflakes, my favorite bedtime snack.

My days were spent at the Medical Supply Depot, checking material consigned to our ship. I didn't work too fast because I was hoping to stretch out my stay in New York City as long as possible. I finished the work in three weeks. The first and third weeks were spent with the Scals, and the second week I stayed at the Pennsylvania Hotel.

My entertainment schedule during this three week-sojourn was quite impressive as I tried to pack in as much of the wonderful New York offerings as I could. I saw two plays, Anna Lucosta, *and* Jacobowsky and the Colonel *and five grand operas,* Die Meister Singer, Lohengrin, Mignon, *with Rise Stevens and Ezio Pinza,* Lucia di Lammermoor, *with Patricia Munzel and Jan Pierce and* Don Giovonni, *with Pinza and Baccaloni. There were two operettas,* La Vie Parisienne, and Sing Out Sweet Land. *I also saw Sonja Heini's ice show,* Hollywood Review. *It was great!*

One Sunday, Skippy Ahlstrom, a good friend from Gustavus, and I attended Riverside Church together and enjoyed it very much.

I skated three times at Rockerfeller Center, which was fun, though too small a rink to really stretch out. Also, the background music was poor.

I attended a cocktail party at Schuster's (of Simon and Schuster) beautiful apartment and met his daughter, a very nice person.

At another party I met Eleanor Brisbane, the daughter of Reverend Arthur Brisbane of Riverside Church fame. Eleanor was very alert and charming, though on some crazy Hudnut diet. I had dinner at her place twice and both times the dinner was perfect, roast duck once and roast chicken with white wine the next.

For dessert they served my favorite, a mixture of chocolate and vanilla ice cream. I must have eaten eight dishes each time. Eleanor made me extremely nervous because she ate only oranges all the while I was stuffing myself. I am sure I made her nervous too, and maybe even a little depressed. Mrs. Brisbane, Eleanor's mother, was charming and her aunt, "Mrs. T," was a very dear old lady.

One night, during a soft snowfall, I wandered through Greenwich Village to call on Al Moody's cousin, Patricia Griffen. She was pretty and intellectually stimulating. She served Southern Comfort in her little basement apartment and we talked for about two hours. We then walked through the snow to a night club, The Vanguard, to see a floor show that was mediocre at best.

While at the Scals I read D.H. Lawrence's unexpurgated Lady Chatterly's Lover, *a hot number, but very well written.*

All these activities kept me chronically tired and though I disliked leaving New York City, the thought of getting some rest was a welcome one.

....

JANUARY 25, 1945: *I arrived in Boston in a snowstorm with a brutal wind and a temperature of 10 degrees below zero, the coldest day of the year. Olga met me at the good old Touraine Hotel and we spent the evening at the Arlington Avenue Officer's Club. It was great fun.*

That night I slept in Walter Long and George Maresch's room at the City Hospital. It was wonderful seeing those dear friends again.

JANUARY 26 TO FEBRUARY 6, 1945: *I ate breakfast in the old Boston City Hospital dining room I had learned to love and had a chance to visit many old friends, including Doctors Castle, Williams, Finland, Jackson, and Costello.*

From Boston I traveled by train to Newport, Rhode Island, and was assigned to the outpatient department of the Naval Hospital. I disliked the duty because it was dull, but one bright spot was meeting my new pharmacist mates, whom I liked very much. I also met some of the USS Rankin officers. They impressed me as being friendly and competent.

The regular mess at the hospital was pretty bad but I was shortly moved to Miantinomi Hall, where the food was marvelous.

FEBRUARY 6, 1945: *I was more than happy to receive my detachment orders to begin new duty in Charleston, South Carolina. The USS Rankin's commissioning date was set for February 24, 1945. I was elated to leave cold windy Newport and the dull routine of the outpatient department. The next day I started the trek to Charleston and new duty.*

FEBRUARY 10, 1945: *This morning we were awakened before dawn again, and all piled into the large Navy bus. After a big breakfast just outside the yard, Bob Tepper, executive officer, and I walked over to the hospital to see one of our officers, L. B. Foster, who had atypical pneumonia.*

At 1000 I met with my chief pharmacist mate, Richardson. We discussed our plans and examined our equipment. Both of us are thrilled with the possibilities afforded us by this job. We are united in striving to make our department the best.

Lunch was at the Officer's Club and after lunch I spent three hours reading medical literature in the hospital library.

The day was beautiful. Just crisp enough to be invigorating, but not cold. The sun shone all day.

I had supper at the Francis Marion Hotel, then went down to the Dock Street Theater and saw Kind Lady, starring Lillian Baland and John Holland. It was fairly well done.

Charleston streets are narrow and jammed, mainly with service men. All restaurants close at 11:30 PM even on Saturday. After stopping by the Hotel

Charleston Officer's Club for a short time, I hopped the bus and come back to our quarters to bring this diary up to date. It is truly a beautiful clear night.

....

FEBRUARY 11, 1945, SUNDAY: *This was a day well spent. On the King Street bus to town, I met balding Mr. Brunn, our chief warrant supply officer. We ate breakfast together at the Francis Marion Hotel, then went to St. Matthew's Lutheran Church. There we met Mrs. Muller and her daughter (about forty years old) and were invited to spend the day with them. We were treated to a delicious chicken dinner in their lovely home. The day was beautiful with a clear sky and a warm sun. After dinner we all piled into the Mullers' Packard and rode around Charleston. We saw the Battery with its beautiful Sea Walk, and Old Charleston's antebellum mansions. Out in the harbor could be seen Fort Sumter. We also saw Porgy's house and the courtyard of Porgy and Bess. He was an actual person who died not so long ago. Then there was the slave market, the old Huguenot Church (they do not believe there is a hell), John Caldwell Calhoun's grave, and St. Phillip's Episcopal Church. We drove across Memorial Bridge to the mainland, where the original Charleston was founded. There was no town here now, but the forest with hanging Spanish moss was exotic and beautiful. It was interesting to learn that all the "real" and old Charleston was south of Broad Street at the Battery. These people would rarely associate socially with anyone above Broad Street.*

Around 6:00 PM we stopped by the C.P.O. club for a short time, then went back to Mullers' home for a light snack. We left there around 9:15 PM,walked through the park, then to our "home" in the Citadel to hit the sack.

....

FEBRUARY 12, 1945: *You would never know that it was Lincoln's birthday today by the attitude of the people in this town. It was just another day in Charleston, and you get the feeling that most of the folks here think that it was a shame he wasn't shot earlier.*

This was the hottest day so far. It was as hot as a day in June back home. I visited Foster this morning, read medical literature in the hospital library, met with Hayden and Richardson at the ship, and then had lunch at the Officer's Club with Tepper, Modell, Price, and Forest. After lunch I read some more at the hospital, put in for a seven-day leave while back at the ship, then rode over to the Citadel, the

Francis Marion Hotel, and the Yacht Club. The tour was concluded with a walk along the historic Battery and then back to the Citadel to bed.

The work on the ship seems to be progressing nicely, though slow. I feel a new thrill every time I think of the great responsibility of my job. It's going to be fun!

....

FEBRUARY 13, 1945: *Seven day leave granted today! I'm going to Florida to see the folks. Great day!*

....

FEBRUARY 14 TO FEBRUARY 21, 1945: *I left Charleston at 2:35 AM on an Eastern airlines plane and was the only passenger on board. We touched down in Jacksonville at 5:00 AM and one and one-half hours later took off for West Palm Beach to arrive there at 9:00 AM. Due to some misunderstanding, Mother and Dad went to the railroad station instead of the airport to meet me and that took awhile to straighten out. I finally took a cab to the R.R. station and met them there. Later we drove over to Palm Beach. We walked along Worth Avenue and I marveled at the contrast between Palm Beach and Plymouth, England. I couldn't believe how much beautiful merchandise there was for sale and how expensive it was. I returned later that night to spend a little time at the Taboo night club, the Alibi, and the Mont-Marte. It was a beautiful night.*

The week sped by and I will never forget the wonderful time we had; swimming in the ocean, eating out at fabulous restaurants such as the Brazilian Court, the La Chaumière, a French sidewalk café, and the swank Everglades Club, where we heard a lecture by John Mason Brown, drama critic. He was clever, but given to exaggerations, superlatives, and verbosity. I will remember the extravagant Everglades Club much longer than his speech.

Knowing how woefully inadequate my surgical knowledge was, Dad gave me some good advice and a few wonderful tips, including how to do a side-to-side intestinal anastomosis using two socks and a needle and thread. At least I got the idea. During the week we saw the movie, The Thin Man Goes Home, *and on Sunday, we attended church services at the Royal Poinciana Chapel, where we heard Dr. Charlton preach a sermon entitled, "The Way to God."*

News highlights are encouraging. We have taken Bataan and are continuing our air assault on Tokyo.

FEBRUARY 21, 1945: *Bad weather delayed my plane and I was notified that I had no seat from Jacksonville to Charleston. Good old faithful Mother and Dad saw me off. It was hard to say goodbye; they had been so wonderful.*

The ride to Jacksonville was rough. Having been bounced by the airline, I took the train (The Champion) at 2:55 PM. It was crowded, but the trip to Charleston wasn't half bad. I arrived at 8:55 PM washed up and hit the hay.

....

FEBRUARY 22, 1945: *Washington's birthday was regally observed here in Charleston. Such a contrast to poor old Abe's.*

This was a red-letter day of accomplishment for me. I left for the Navy Yard at 7:30 AM to visit the ship, next ate breakfast at the Melrose, then stopped by the Ship's Service to see where a certain beautiful girl worked and, ostensibly, to check the price of suitcases. Then I walked to the Administration Building to turn in my leave papers, then to the hospital to check on Foster. Next I took the station wagon all the way down town to Clyde Mallory Docks where I planned strategy with Chief Richardson. I then walked over to Geraldine Parker's house, met her formally, confirmed my date, then walked her to the broadcasting studios at the Dock Street Theater. I hiked back to the Fort Sumter Hotel, caught the 12:00 noon station-wagon back to the Navy Yard. Lunch at the Melrose. Following lunch I sauntered to Ship's Service for a milkshake; mainly, however, to see the beautiful girl. Fortunately we met right in the hall. I introduced myself (again today I introduce myself), invited her for a coke, which she accepted. So we "coked" and were joined by Cotsirelos and his wife, Terry. I was lucky enough to get a date for tomorrow noon and Sunday. She seems like a real winner: Sylvia Barfield, American Red Cross.

But the day is still young. After that delightful tête-à-tête, I trudged to the hospital and visited with Foster and Earp. I checked Foster's chest X-ray, which was okay. I then walked the two miles from the hospital to the ship, and met with Stokes and Tackaberry, two of my pharmacist mates. We discussed plans for our sick bay. I started to read my week's mail accumulation but had to quit to catch the 5:00 PM bus to the Citadel. A quick wash-up and then down to the Battery. Tepper and I then whirled away to pick up our dates and go over to the East Bay Yacht Club for cocktails and dinner. Gerry had a play rehearsal which I walked her to, watched it, then walked her home. We chatted with her mother and aunt for over an hour, and at midnight I caught a taxi back to the Citadel. My legs are screaming. Goodnight!

FEBRUARY 23, 1945: *Breakfast and lunch with Sylvia. She is beautiful!*

The Marines are suffering terrible losses on Iwo Jima, over 90 casualties per hour. Total now is over 5,700. Representatives Rankin and Hook had a fist fight in the House of Representatives today over the CIO-PAC. The big Western Allied offensive has just started. How soon will it all be over?

The sick bay setup aboard ship looks wonderful. I've never been as enthusiastic about anything before as I am about this job. Tomorrow we commission.

Ernie Brunn and I had dinner at Muller's home with the Mullers and Mary Cuttino. The food was delicious and the company charming, except I hate their attitude towards Negroes. They still look upon a Negro as a beast of burden, and now someone to be feared.

Charleston's weather is brisk and fresh. Peach and apple blossoms are in full bloom and many other flowers and leaves are venturing forth. It's like Minnesota in May.

....

FEBRUARY 24, 1945: *Today the USS* Rankin *was commissioned. We were awakened at 0615 by the usual cheerful voice over the loudspeaker, "Rise and shine!" Just before the ceremony, Sylvia and I met at the Melrose Cafe for breakfast. The commissioning program was impressive with about 60 guests present. After the program the guests roamed about the ship until 1000. Mrs. Parker and Mrs. Gundrum were my guests.*

There was an air of excitement and anticipation on board today. Everyone seems happy and busy. We filled the fuel tanks early and began loading medical supplies on board this afternoon. There were a lot of them. We kept busy cleaning the sick bay until 1600 when I saw Sylvia again. Tepper, Price, and I had dinner at the Officer's Club. This evening I packed away my clothes.

....

FEBRUARY 25, 1945: *This was a busy day for everyone aboard ship. We all turned to and scrubbed shelves and drawers and unpacked our non-medical supplies. We checked them all and then stowed them away.*

The ship took on ammunition until 1915 tonight. The moon was full and Sylvia and I went to dinner at the Officer's Club, then for a stroll.

FEBRUARY 26, 1945: *At 0800 the USS* Rankin *steamed seven miles down the Cooper River to Clyde Mallory Docks, just a mile north of Fort Sumter. The big monster slipped noiselessly and speedily through the muddy water. Additional supplies were loaded aboard, including the balance of our medical supplies, which was a prodigious load in itself. The operating room and the sick bay are stacked to the ceiling with huge boxes. This afternoon I saw Sylvia again. She's awfully nice!*

This evening the corpsmen and I checked and stored medical supplies until 2100. I'm beat!

....

FEBRUARY 27, 1945: *Loading continued all day today. The "Medical Department" opened crates and checked off scads of beautiful equipment. There doesn't seem to be sufficient room for all the supplies, but we'll have to find room somewhere. Went out with Sylvia again tonight. Full moon. She's a sweet girl.*

....

FEBRUARY 28, 1945: *Another busy day. We admitted our first patient into sick bay today, our own Chief Pharmacist Mate Richardson. He fractured his right great toe when a 175-pound packing case fell on it. Also today the first surgery was performed in the O.R.; I lanced a boil! Shortly thereafter a boy whose scalp was lacerated by a swinging boom came in for suturing. There were about 25 men in for sick call this morning. Instruments were sterilized in the autoclave today for the first time.*

Tonight a beautiful moon shines down on a fatigued Rankin *crew.*

....

MARCH 1, 1945: *We were "de-magnetized" today at the degaussing dock. All clocks and watches were sent ashore during the process.*

This was another busy day during which all first aid boxes, stretchers and other emergency equipment were placed around the ship.

Officer's Club for dinner with Sylvia.

....

MARCH 2, 1945: *Today was warm and lovely. The USS* Rankin *cruised leisurely under the Cooper River Bridge, then turned around and came back again, just to* *get her picture taken. Then it was out to sea for a trial run. The guns were tested and all went well.*

We were still busy in sick bay sorting material, completing records, etc. I gave one arsenic injection today and incised a perirectal abscess.

....

MARCH 3, 1945: *It was as warm as a day in June back home. Today the welders came aboard to change some of our doors and shelves. They messed up our beautiful hospital and now we have to start all over again. The Chief and I walked all over the ship and placed first aid kits close to battle dressing stations.*

....

MARCH 4, 1945: *This was a record breaker for work. Two boys were admitted to sick bay, one with a temperature of 104 degrees Fahrenheit and one with gastro-enteritis. We are still getting our supplies in order, and what a job! Chief R. finally completed his cough syrup itemization. With the patients, their records, the storage and dispersing details, it's tough and tedious. Fortunately, work agrees with me.*

....

MARCH 5, 1945: *This morning all officers met in the ward room for a talk by the Captain entitled, "The Mission of Our Ship." It was rather thrilling to hear the ship's Captain stress the importance of education. We are going to have a series of lectures by different officers on their departments.*

All three patients were better this morning. Another was admitted today with acute tonsillitis. It's a busy time. Tomorrow we leave for Norfolk and we have so much to do.

Saw Sylvia tonight. Sylvia—Charleston. Two names that go together. Fog settled in heavy tonight.

....

MARCH 6, 1945: *The struggle to complete our Medical Department continued again today. I managed to sneak off the ship long enough to mail a suitcase to Dad. As I walked back to the ship in the warm spring air with fresh flowers blooming everywhere, I thought how much I will miss this when the sea becomes my home.*

After lunch we were tugged from our mooring and pushed out into the Cooper River. The wind was strong which made for moderate seas. We secured all our gear. As soon as we left sheltered waters, the ship began to roll, much slower and easier than the LST, but definitely a roll.

Another sailor was admitted to sick bay today with "cat" (catarrhal) fever. Temp 103.6 degrees F.

Sleeping athwart ship made me feel as though I was standing on my head one minute and on my feet the next. The night was filled with sounds of crashing and banging as loose equipment rattled back and forth.

....

MARCH 7, 1945: *I'm no sailor. The ship is rolling quite heavily and I've got that old feeling, only this time I'm not violently sick. I haven't vomited all day. However, I do feel nauseated, have a headache, and have no ambition. Also no appetite. It's extremely unpleasant.*

All patients have normal temperatures this morning which makes me happy. We are still getting ready for inspection. How I yearn for the good old U.S. and I haven't even left yet.

....

MARCH 8, 1945: *We arrived in Norfolk harbor about 0930. It was good to see land and feel a steady ship even after such a short time. We expected inspectors today but they never arrived. Instead, the Captain and all department heads rode a small-boat into shore where we met with various "shake-down" officials. I saw Jack Herman who is on the AKA-84, the* Waukashaw. *They have had more trouble than we. Their drinking water became contaminated with sewage by some odd mistake, and 11 men were admitted to their sick bay with acute gastroenteritis. In addition they had one severe head injury. We've been lucky. All our patients but one have normal temperatures tonight.*

....

MARCH 9, 1945: *The long-feared inspection occurred today and it was surprisingly benign. We did all right too—"Four-0!" We were "well organized." The entire ship received a high rating. We admitted a sailor with chronic otitis media tonight and worked on lab forms and hospital record sheets. The Chief mixed up some* *sulfur ointment and Stokes prepared a few stains. I checked with engineer Modell, who helped get our condenser going. It produced crystal clear water.*

....

MARCH 10, 1945: *It was very spring-like here today, and I rode into the Naval Operating Base, Norfolk in one of our LCVPs. It was a typical Navy base, but the Officer's Club was better than average. I also visited the Aircraft Carrier, CV-36, the* Entiatem. *It was tremendous!*

I spent the evening making up a laboratory record sheet for our clinical chart, visiting patients, and discussing our setup with Chief Richardson. I met Lt. j.g. Falk, whose father is president of Baxter Pharmaceutical Company.

....

MARCH 11, 1945: *We had a field day in sick bay today. The small boats, 26 of them, were lowered for practice. The sea was rough and they hung dangerously, swinging from huge booms. One boy was caught in the bite of the line as a small boat was dropping down to the water. He was thrown to the deck, and would have been pulled through the chock hole if he hadn't disengaged himself at just the last moment. His ankle looked as though it was fractured, but there was no displacement. Our X-ray machine has not been delivered as yet so we couldn't visualize the ankle bones, and we were too far out to sea to take him in. I put his leg in plaster and there was some excitement as we madly initiated our plaster setup. Almost simultaneously with the above accident, a boom with a small boat attached broke loose, crashed to the deck, and missed one sailor by six inches. He would have been crushed. The small boat then bounced off the side of the ship and plunged beneath the surface. It was then cut free from the broken boom and allowed to sink.*

There were several other injuries and two medical admissions: acute tonsillitis and acute gonorrhea. At 1930, as we were moving back to anchorage off Hampton Roads, the ship suddenly "backed down" (reversed gear). We missed an ammunition ship (AE-13) by 30 feet. Wow!

....

MARCH 12, 1945: *Dad's birthday. The AE-13 sent a message today, "Pilot will come aboard shortly," which was meant as a dirty crack, because of our near miss.*

This morning we steamed into Chesapeake Bay, about 48 miles from Hampton Roads, to run the degaussing range.

Fortunately, there were no injuries, because our beds are full. To make room for one medical admission we had to discharge the sailor with gonorrhea. He seemed to be cured after only 22 hours of treatment with the wonder drug, penicillin. There have been a number of bad throats lately.

....

MARCH 13, 1945: *Chesapeake Bay was beautiful today with blue skies, a soft breeze, and a bright sun. The gunnery department held forth with all guns blasting at flying sleeves and surface targets. It all made quite a racket but their accuracy was excellent.*

I lectured to three different groups on first aid, and the stretcher bearers practiced casualty handling. Just after I went to bed, Stokes told me we had a case of measles aboard. I checked it out and sure enough, the sailor had German measles. We will now have to practice contagion techniques.

....

MARCH 14, 1945: *The German measles case is blossoming full today. I hope it isn't the beginning of an epidemic.*

All guns were used again today for target practice, drones being the targets. Our gunners were hot and knocked down two drones. Only four have been knocked down all season. The shake-down control officer said we did better than any other AKA-or APA and also better than a lot of new cruisers and destroyers. That's comforting news.

It was a beautiful day, fresh, but pleasantly warm. Sunlight streamed through the port into our operating room. I love our little hospital.

We changed the cast on Haluska. His leg looked quite good. One patient has a temperature of 104 degrees F. Probably "cat" fever.

....

MARCH 15, 1945: *We are anchored just off Annapolis way up Chesapeake Bay where Maryland can be seen to the west and Delaware to the east. A heavy fog blanketed the Bay, delaying our getting under way until 1300. All patients in sick bay were feeling good tonight. Saw a lousy movie in the mess hall: Abbott and Costello in* Lost in a Harem. *Sick call was characterized by petty problems: a boil, crabs, plantar warts, balanitis, and athlete's foot.*

MARCH 16, 1945: *Pay day today, so no one showed up for sick call. With liberty looming, everyone will stay well until it's time to work again. Strange beings, we humans.*

The big event today was refueling at sea. A sleek, swift destroyer escort drew up alongside; we passed her the fuel hoses fore and aft and shortly the job was done.

The AKA-102 passed us heading out to sea, loaded to the gills. We dropped our hook just off Charles City. It's been a balmy day.

....

MARCH 17, 1945: *We were assigned a battle problem today with this scenario: a bomb hit in the No. 5 hold, several near misses and deck-strafing by enemy planes. After successful management of the "attack," we steamed into the Portsmouth Navy Yard and tied up alongside the AKA-84. It's a hot, sweaty day. The Navy Yard foreman and staff came aboard to see what kind of repairs and changes needed to be done. Everyone haggled for their projects as the foreman attempted to hold down on the list.*

....

MARCH 18, 1945: *The morning was spent at the Norfolk Navy Dispensary with the sailor who had fractured his ankle. X-rays showed a bimalleolar fracture of the ankle in excellent position. There was so much swelling from extravasation of blood present that I decided to transfer him to the Naval Hospital.*

The afternoon passed, dull and barren, evening the same. We are painting directional signs about the ship.

....

MARCH 19, 1945: *This morning I brought four of our sick sailors over to the U.S.N. Hospital, Portsmouth, for diagnosis and treatment. The hospital is huge and in beautiful surroundings.*

The movie camera and Kodak came today, and they are really nice. Chief Richardson went home for a 48-hour leave. We are down to two sick sailors in our sick bay, having transferred the diagnostic problems.

Tonight, Captain Price, Executive Officer Tepper and I went to the Naval Operating Base in Norfolk to attend our ship's enlisted men's party. Only a few officers were present.

It's now 0030. The yard workers still swarm all over the ship, chipping, welding, and painting. It's a beehive of activity. At 1200, when the quitting time horn blows, the workers dash down the gangplank in a mad rush.

I visited the cruiser Duluth *and the LST-659. The cruiser was nice, but the LST gave me the willies.*

Had dinner at the Officer's Club with Tepper and Chamberlain. Very good.

....

MARCH 21, 1945: *The ship is again "assailed" by the yard workers. I would never have believed that a ship could get messed up in such a hurry. The operating room looks like it had been hit by a tornado. They did some nice things, though, like building us developing tanks and a laboratory tray.*

....

MARCH 22, 1945: *It turned bitter cold today, dark, gloomy, and windy. The* Rankin *moved from Portsmouth Navy Yard to Norfolk for loading. It is rumored that we will load light here and then take off for somewhere.*

The day was spent cleaning up the mess left by the workmen. There were three admissions to sick bay today: chronic prostatitis, acute gonorrhea, and cellulitis of the right leg.

....

MARCH 23, 1945: *Spring smiled on Norfolk today. I took two neuropsychiatric patients to the Portsmouth Navy Hospital. On the way I picked up our yellow fever vaccine at Portsmouth Navy Yard. When I arrived back at the ship, the sick bay was as clean as a pin. The corpsmen had put in a good day.*

Tonight, Bud Chamberlain, Bill Wells, Jack Herman, his wife, Sue, and I had dinner together at the Officer's Club. It was delightful.

....

MARCH 24, 1945: *We were medical guard ship today and received a number of ailing sailors from other ships. I felt lousy from the night before but managed to struggle through the day. I transferred two additional psychoneurotic patients to the hospital.*

Received word that we get underway tomorrow at 1600. One hundred fifty sacks of mail were brought aboard for delivery somewhere. We are going through the big ditch (Panama Canal), but after that, where? No one knows yet, at least aboard this ship.

....

MARCH 25, 1945, SUNDAY: *This was the big day! At 1600 the tugs pushed us out into the Elizabeth River. Then, under our own power, we steamed out into the Atlantic, Panama-bound.*

The weather was beautiful. We spent the day getting secured for sea, painting first aid boxes, making splint sets, preparing procaine solutions, planning inoculations, and autoclaving instruments.

The moon was almost full tonight, the air cool and fresh, and the sea calm. I hope this lasts.

....

MARCH 26, 1945: *The ocean is turquoise and as we moved into the Gulf Stream, the water temperature rose from 42 to 68 degrees F. This was a warm but pleasant day, though most of my time was spent below decks working in the sick bay. We are between Charleston and Wilmington.*

....

MARCH 27, 1945: *The coast of Florida will be 130 miles to our west, all day. I've never seen such blue water. Seeing my first flying fish this cruise was like seeing the first robin of spring.*

The medical department administered 63 inoculations today. It went smoothly. Considering how calm the ocean appears to be, this ship sure rolls a lot.

....

MARCH 28, 1945: *Around 1492, Columbus sailed through this area headed the other way. San Salvador, his first stop, was off our starboard beam, about 18 miles. It could barely be seen with the naked eye.*

Numerous flying fish were seen today.

I treated the Captain's sore toe today, and he invited me to dinner. We had chicken giblets, soup, and an orange custard with strawberries. He is indeed a fine fellow.

The moon is full tonight, and a strong wind is blowing. The sea looks like a seething bubbling cauldron of molten metal. We pass within sight of Cuba at 0200. I'm afraid I'll miss it.

....

MARCH 29, 1945: *We slipped past Jamaica today and are now in the Caribbean. It's rough today, remindful of LST days. I hate this athwart ship bunk. All my blood and guts are driven up into my head when the ship rolls. Our FPO (Fleet Post Office) address was changed to San Francisco today.*

....

MARCH 30, 1945: *Month's end brings more work in the form of reports to the Navy Medical Department. I had a busy day with several difficult diagnostic problems, letter writing and, of course, the never-ending reports. The wind has died down, but the swells are terrific. It's getting hotter.*

....

MARCH 31, 1945: *This birthday was spent almost entirely going through the Panama Canal. It was a relief to get inside the breakwater and find an end to the incessant rolling.*

The day was hot, relieved only by a cool breeze from the Caribbean. Donkeys pulled us through Gatun Locks, then under our own power we steamed through the great "artificial" Gatun Lake. At the far end our engines conked out and we were left stranded, utterly helpless. After an hour, with engines repaired, we were under way again. Now the Canal narrowed to only two ships wide. Two more locks and we were in Balboa Harbor.

After a quick dinner, six of us went over to Panama City. It was a typical tropical town with plenty of "spirits" of all kinds, jewelry, wrist watches, and leather goods. We went to the Hotel International, then to Happy Land for a tropical floor show.

....

APRIL 1, 1945, EASTER SUNDAY: *The day started hot and my head is pounding. I got up for breakfast, walked to the Navy Chapel for Easter Service. The thin-walled screened building and the hot humid atmosphere were in marked contrast to the church in Southampton where I attended services one year ago.*

The Chaplain was dressed in white. He looked good, but that's all. His sermon was poor: too long, too wordy, too dull, and poorly planned.

Sunday dinner was delicious with chicken and all the trimmings.

We got underway at 1400 today, bound for San Francisco. Panama Bay is as calm as a mill pond. I've never seen a rippleless ocean. Saw a whale this afternoon.

....

APRIL 2, 1945: *Learned today that the whale I saw yesterday was really a "Blackfish," which is actually a species of whale, so I guess I really did see a whale.*

The ocean remained perfectly calm all day with huge but almost imperceptible swells rolling the ship. Aside from the heat, I like the Pacific better than the Atlantic, at least so far.

This morning there was a simulated attack upon our ship with bomb hits, fires, and torpedoes striking everywhere. The corpsmen and the stretcher bearers were running like mad trying to bring in the casualties. In the midst of the confusion the following announcement was blared over the loudspeakers, "The ship is sinking, all hands abandon ship!" It was so real I almost jumped over the side.

....

APRIL 3, 1945: *A cooling breeze roughed the ocean's surface and formed the first waves I've seen on the Pacific. We cut through a school of gamboling porpoises this morning. They are fluid motion and beautiful.*

Sick call was busy with several boils and sundry other minor ailments.

We are running alone tonight, and all our running lights are on. The phosphorescent water illuminates the crest of every wave. Tonight we are just off the coast of Mexico.

....

APRIL 4, 1945: *The waves tired and the Pacific is once again calm. It is a vast undulating sheet of water.*

I attempted lancing an abscessed jaw, but the man fainted on the table so I had to delay the job until morning. He passed out just after I had injected the local anesthetic which caused me to think he may have had an allergic reaction to procaine. The O.R. was very warm, however, and I believe that was the major factor.

I spent the majority of the day reading up on dental pathology and treatment. It is very warm tonight. We are almost opposite Acapulco, Mexico.

....

APRIL 5, 1945: *The sailor's jaw was better this morning, but there was still a good-sized swelling, so I injected the procaine again, this time with no untoward reaction. I then incised deep into the swelling but didn't find any pus, which was a disappointment.*

This afternoon I opened a cold abscess on a penis, cause unknown, though we are doing every test in our repertory.

It's getting cooler as we sail north.

....

APRIL 6, 1945: *This day was largely devoted to "Captain's" inspection. The Captain and department heads went through every hold and storage space on the ship. The inspection took four hours, and was very tiresome. It did, however, afford me an opportunity to get to know the ship.*

....

APRIL 7, 1945: *It's getting cooler every day and tonight it's very chilly. We are off the coast of Southern California.*

This morning was spent in the second phase of Captain's inspection, personnel and living compartments. We drew a blood Kahn on all symptomatic sailors this afternoon. It's been a beautiful day.

....

APRIL 8, 1945, SUNDAY: *It was downright cold today though the afternoon sun warmed things up a lot.*

This morning I did a spinal tap for a suspected case of meningitis. The fluid was negative for cells or organisms, which was a relief.

Tonight I was ordered to execute three parakeets that had been smuggled aboard by a couple of enlisted men. These birds were so pretty and tame, I hated to be the executioner, but there was no choice. I put them in a jar containing chloroform and after I was sure they were dead, I committed them to burial at sea. Their owners were very sad and I'm afraid I'm the villain in their eyes.

APRIL 9, 1945: *When I awoke this morning I found we were in the center of a storm. The sky was clear but the wind velocity was about 30 to 35 knots. We are headed into the wind and the ship is pitching and plunging. The spray dashes over the conning tower. It was a dreary tiresome day. I hate a rough sea.*

....

APRIL 10, 1945: *The sea raged all through the day, but somehow it didn't seem as rough. Either I was becoming more accustomed to it, or the fact we were very near San Francisco helped me to ignore it. Mountains could be seen along the California coast this afternoon. They seem huge and forbidding.*

The day was spent writing up records for five men who are to be transferred to the Naval Hospital.

I learned tonight that I am no longer on a watch and rate "every night liberty." What a break!

....

APRIL 11, 1945: *Way before sunrise, Bud Chamberlain and I crawled out of our sacks to watch our entrance into San Francisco. It was still dark when we stumbled up the ladder to the bridge. Far in the distance we could see the blinking street lights of early morning San Francisco.*

Day dawned slowly, and soon, in the distance, could be seen the great, beloved Golden Gate Bridge. The sun rose behind it so it did not have the burnished gold appearance given by the setting sun. Sunrise then painted the surrounding hills in multi-colored hues that canvas could never portray.

A pilot steered the ship under the Golden Gate Bridge, then the San Francisco Bay Bridge, unerringly to Pier 90, our loading dock.

The Americans are only 57 miles from Berlin tonight and are moving fast. That war cannot last much longer.

After a busy day and a delicious chicken dinner, Bud and I "did the town." We went first to the Chinese "Forbidden City," then to the Pago-Pago in the old International Settlement District (the old Barbary Coast). We then stopped at Monas, renowned as a lesbian hangout. To us it seemed weird to see all the "men" in double-breasted suits.

APRIL 12, 1945: *"ROOSEVELT IS DEAD!" screamed the morning headlines. This shocking news rocked the entire city, but wasn't brought to my attention until around 1500. The Chief and I had been busy in sick bay all day when Carper, yeoman first class, stopped by the door and asked if we knew that Roosevelt had died. I couldn't believe it! It was just too incredible. At least three times I said, "Carper, you're kidding us, that can't be true." The tone of his voice and his serious look told me that he wasn't kidding. After the first sudden shock wore off and while I felt rather weak, as one does following this kind of disturbing news, my next thought was: Truman would become President of the United States! That was almost as incredible as Roosevelt's death! How can easy-going, mild-mannered politician Harry S. Truman carry our terrific load at the conference table with the likes of Churchill and Stalin? He was the Vice President chosen because he would lose fewer votes than some of the others who might have been better qualified. Obviously, it was never intended that he should become President. Amidst my mixed emotions ran a strong element of anger and resentment toward Roosevelt and the Democratic Party for not providing the country with someone capable of leading us in just this eventuality. I never voted for Roosevelt in either election because I thought he was hypocritical, talking peace and non-involvement on the one hand, and preparing for war on the other. After Pearl Harbor, however, his stature improved, in my opinion, and I felt he was beginning to show signs of greatness. He will be remembered as a master salesman, showman, fireside chatman and politician, and now a great Commander in Chief. With Roosevelt gone there is a spooky void that I hope will be filled by a Congress that will roll up its sleeves, forget inter-party bickering, and get down to work. Someone has to steer the "Ship of State" because I don't think Truman is up to the job. Time will tell. I hope I'm wrong in my assessment of our Vice President.*

The San Francisco conference of the United Nations is apparently going to be held as scheduled.

But life must go on. Soon the aura of astonishment was smothered in pressing little tasks that were my responsibility, and the world-shaking news had to be relegated to the back burner. When the news first broke, there was a momentary flutter of excitement and activity among the men "topside," but soon they were back to their regular jobs—mending lines, scraping paint, and scrubbing the decks. Their lives went on as if nothing had happened. The yard workers were also back working as before. I heard one of them call over to another, "Did ya hear that Roosevelt just kicked the bucket?" "Yea," responded the other. That was all.

In downtown San Francisco there was a subdued atmosphere. The headlines on every corner proclaimed the news in six inch type: ROOSEVELT IS DEAD! What will the morrow bring?

....

APRIL 13, 1945: *All the Allied world mourns the death of our "beloved" President. That is the sentiment of the day. All radio time is devoted either to news about Roosevelt or to religious or classical music. Truman's first act as President was to announce that the United Nations conference in San Francisco would go ahead as planned. He set tomorrow as a day of mourning for the President. To reporters his words were, "Pray for me now, boys. I feel as though the sun, the moon, and all the planets had fallen on me." Maybe this quiet mild-mannered little fellow will do better than most people anticipate. He should be given every possible chance to do so.*

One of our armies is only 45 miles from Berlin. Patton and the Russians are only 90 miles apart. Vienna has fallen to the Allies.

Chief Richardson fractured his jaw about a month ago and because of increasing pain was sent into the hospital this morning.

I visited my lifelong friend and next-door neighbor, George Garske, and his beautiful wife, Beth, in Vallejo this afternoon. Their new baby is very pretty. We attended a wedding on Mare Island at St. Peter's Chapel which was small, quiet, and very sweet.

I called Mother and Dad tonight. It was wonderful to hear their dear voices.

....

APRIL 14, 1945: *This was an unusual Saturday in San Francisco. The stores were closed all day and only a few renegade bars were open. People in larger than usual crowds were seen wandering aimlessly about the town with no apparent destination in mind.*

Along with all the news about Roosevelt's funeral, the papers and radio have devoted much time building up Truman. The thought occurred to me that his weakness may prove to be our strength. Roosevelt so overshadowed Congress, it seemed to consist only of a group of non-entities. Truman liked being a senator, was well-liked, and with his apparent inadequacy for the Presidency may draw heavily upon Congress for help and guidance and would thereby strengthen both the legislative and the executive branches of government.

Tonight I walked around Nob Hill. Beautiful night.

....

APRIL 15, 1945, SUNDAY: *This was not one of my better days. After a rather uninteresting morning, I jammed into the 1530 bus to downtown San Francisco. There I met Christiansen, and we proceeded to "do the town." We went through China Town, then to the "Top of the Mark," then the Cirque Room at the Fairmont Hotel, then to the Macombo for dinner and a good floor show. We should have gone home after the floor show, but instead we cruised through about seven other cocktail lounges until utterly fatigued. We had become overstuffed at the night-life buffet, and had no one to blame but ourselves.*

....

APRIL 16, 1945: *All the boats were loaded aboard this morning and we are to be prepared for sea at 1200 tomorrow. This afternoon Hurd, White, and I went to Stanford University in Palo Alto where we met three girls. The campus was different-looking (different from any I had seen before), with low, tan buildings. The trees and flowers were beautiful. The girls were fair and I am sure very intelligent. We ate dinner at Dinah's Shanty. It was delicious with mint juleps to start and fresh strawberry sundaes to conclude.*

We then took a taxi to another dance spot which was fun. The girls were then taken back to their dormitory, and properly kissed goodnight. We next boarded a bus that barely crawled, back to San Francisco. At the bus station we stocked up on magazines for the long boring days ahead.

We just now heard the news that Nuremberg fell!

....

APRIL 17, 1945: *This morning I went into San Francisco, purchased some film developer solution and other photographic equipment, some books, and had a glass of orange juice. This town is so fresh and lovely.*

We got underway at 1800 today. The ship was grounded for a short while, but tugs helped push us into deep water. As we pulled away from San Francisco my heart was heavy because I knew our return would be a long time away. The city was shrouded in darkness, with a few lights beginning to twinkle. The Golden Gate Bridge slowly faded from view as darkness and distance closed in. We are steaming full speed ahead to our next destination, Hawaii.

....

APRIL 18, 1945: *The ship rolled quite wildly all day long and I was just on the border of being seasick. I could eat a little, but felt nauseated most of the day. Toward evening I felt better.*

I saw the movie, Keep Your Powder Dry, *starring Lana Turner. It was terrible. The sea is quieter and more peaceful now.*

....

APRIL 19, 1945: *The calm water today is in marked contrast to the wild ocean of yesterday. I prefer it this way.*

We did a lot of work today, but much remains to be done. I wrote an article for our newspaper entitled "The Black Death," which was about the bubonic plague.

Ernie Pyle was killed yesterday on Okinawa; machine gun bullet through the left temple. He was an excellent war correspondent who constantly exposed himself to danger. Nimitz reports more casualties at Okinawa than all previous Pacific battles combined.

....

APRIL 20, 1945: *The calm continues. Admitted three men to sick bay. I'm learning about X-ray. Bud and I are learning the Morse code. Each day gets warmer.*

....

APRIL 22, 1945, SUNDAY: *The day was pleasant but rougher than before. There were scattered showers. Church services were conducted by Christiansen in the swaying mess hall to a congregation of about sixty. We sang some good old hymns. Chris gave a peachy (excellent) sermon.*

The afternoon was spent writing letters, reading, and lolling about the ship. We had a chicken dinner with strawberry sundaes for dessert.

APRIL 23, 1945: *At 1400 we docked at Hilo, Hawaii. The island was mountainous and covered with tropical vegetation. The climate seems ideal. I stayed aboard tonight. One of my corpsmen was given a* lei *made of fresh cinnamon tree blossoms by one of the Hawaiian girls.*

The Russians are in the center of Berlin and our forces have almost met. The American Army has been held back for political reasons, or we would have been there by now or earlier. The San Francisco Conference (United Nations) on world security started today.

....

APRIL 24, 1945: *After rushing through sick call, I joined 93 other shipmates for an island tour by bus. The journey started at 1000, and aside from forgetting our sandwiches on the pier, the day was extremely pleasant. We saw several volcanoes that were not active at this time, one of them being Mauna Loa. The vegetation was lush, except near the volcanoes. Flowers were everywhere in profusion and the fragrance was almost intoxicating.*

At lunch time we stopped at the Volcano House Hotel, but unfortunately, too late for food. Like flies on a honey jar, the men swarmed into the bar and almost swamped it. The universal drink was rum and Coca-Cola at forty cents a glass.

There were two charming and beautiful American girls in the hotel lounge that I managed to meet, so Win Hurd and I remained behind when the tour got underway. The girls were Muriel Heath and Estelle Castleberry, both originally from California and now in the Hawaiian Civil Service. It was truly pleasant to be listening to Russ Morgan's smooth band while conversing with these two lovely damsels in such gorgeous surroundings. But like so many enjoyable experiences, it ended too soon. The last bus left at 1600 and Hilo, being 30 miles away, was too far to walk. So we left, but not without regrets.

Several of us, White, Tepper, Chamberlain, Hurd, Modell, and I ate dinner at the Mauna Loa Hotel. The setting was beautiful. After dinner Bud and I walked around town. The night was gorgeous, something out of a dream world. The moon was full and there were a few white fleecy clouds. There wasn't a breeze and yet it felt pleasantly cool. Both of us were almost overwhelmed by the beauty of the night. At 2200 we reported back to the ship. It had been a perfect day.

Today the Russians and the Americans met below Berlin. The Third Army is driving towards Berchtesgaden, 165 miles away.

APRIL 25, 1945: *Our scheduled departure to get underway at 1600 was delayed a day but we moved to an anchorage in the center of the harbor to prepare for tomorrow's journey to "wherever."*

We arose early to a morning of unparalleled beauty to make "getting underway" reports. The sun, just rising, brightened the green hills and a fresh new-mown hay aroma filled the air. The white top of Mauna Loa could be seen for a short time this morning, but then disappeared behind clouds.

Soon the skies clouded over and while on the way into shore in a small boat it began to pour. I bought a grass skirt for Marcia Swanson, my niece.

Just before dinner, Earl Newton, Bill Barwick, and I went to Coconut Island for a swim. It was wonderful, so refreshing!

Back at the ship, chow was poor—hot dogs, but the movie in the mess hall, My Reputation, *with Barbara Stanwyck and George Brent, was excellent. Bud and I are still learning Morse code.*

The British entered Bremen. The Germans are retreating across the Po Valley in Italy.

....

APRIL 26, 1945: *It was hot but beautiful today. Mauna Kea was out in all her splendor. I picked up some photo paper in Hilo today, went for a walk, and had a malted milk. Later back at the ship, we all went swimming. It was a strange sight to see all the guys, bare naked, diving over the side. At 1300 I gave a lecture to 130 men. At 1700 we got underway for landing practice.*

....

APRIL 27, 1945: *We joined eight APAs (transport ship attack) today and maneuvered all day under a hot Pacific sun. Tonight, by light of a full moon, convoy tactics were continued. We came within thirty feet of colliding with the ship in front of us when the entire convoy stopped, except the Rankin. We were so close, the men on our bow could easily converse with the sailors on their fan-tail. In the breathless, tense moments just before the expected collision, one of the sailors on the stern of the ship about to be rammed anxiously called over, "Hey, is there any one over there from Ohio?"*

No one knows what's on the program tomorrow. Not another close one, I hope.

APRIL 28, 1945: *An intensive six-day training session started today. Our boats could be lowered in about 45 minutes. The ocean was calm and a beautiful blue. We are anchored just off the beach at Maui. The boys are improving and nothing exciting happened, which is good. There are now 16 ships in our convoy, including four AKAs (cargo ship attack).*

False rumors announced Nazi Germany's surrender. It can't be too much longer.

....

APRIL 29, 1945: *The day was tedious and rather unpleasant for me. I admitted one sailor with pneumonia and lanced an ear with suppurative otitis media. An accident case with minor injuries was treated and released. I also learned X-ray settings.*

The ship lowered all boats in 29 minutes. We towed, and were towed. Tonight we are cruising under a waning full moon.

Munich was taken and Berlin almost.

....

APRIL 30, 1945: *At 0830 we were "attacked" and men were being "killed" and "wounded" all around. We certainly got a workout.*

A questionable fracture forced me to use the X-ray machine. The entire after-noon and evening was spent just getting organized. Over three hours was spent cooling the solutions. Finally, the X-ray taken, though over-exposed, was really quite good. There was a questionable chip fracture of the 5th metatarsal of the foot.

In a second exciting episode of the day, Seaman Maziar broke a large varicos-ity in his calf and blood was squirting out all over the deck as he rushed into sick bay. He responded well to treatment (elevation of the leg and pressure), but Jones, the lad with the fractured foot, almost fainted at the sight of all that blood.

General Quarters was sounded at 2100, occasioned by a night-fighter "attack." It lasted until 2300. No casualties. I'm tired and ready to crash.

....

MAY 1, 1945: Lei *day in Hawaii. The entire forenoon, up to 1400, was spent getting repeat X-rays of Jones' foot. I wasn't satisfied with our first attempt. It's such a nui-sance to pour five gallons of hypo and developer in and out of the tanks every time* they are used. They have to be cooled to 68 degrees from 80 degrees, which requires many pails of ice. The plates today turned out fine, and definitely ruled out fracture.

There was another "battle" problem for us at 1430 today with seven wounded. G.Q. again tonight at 2100.

Hitler was reported killed and Mussolini as well. Germany is being cut to ribbons but won't give up. It can't last much longer.

....

MAY 2, 1945: *The exercise today is "smoke making." It was an easier day.* Here Come the Waves *was the movie. The mess hall is an oven. We are rolling a little tonight. I'm learning all the signal flags and pennants.*

....

MAY 3, 1945: *H-hour of today's operation was to be at 1300 with support fire, live bombing, etc. A few low level bombers "attacked" our ship, but the whole affair was rather dull. I guess we have to be thankful that it wasn't real.*

It was calm with clear skies, a hot sun, and ever so blue water. Germany is tottering and surrender is expected momentarily. German troops in Italy surrendered unconditionally. Berlin surrendered. Hitler was reported "killed in action," and Mussolini was shot by partisans and buried in a potter's field. These men were uncontrollable meteors who blazed brightly for awhile but have now been ignominiously snuffed out. The amount of pain and suffering they have caused throughout the world will be felt for centuries.

....

MAY 4, 1945: *We were "attacked" at dawn by drones and several of them were shot down. A battle problem today presented us with several "wounded" and many "dead." Submarines "attacked" this afternoon and again tonight.*

The Germans have surrendered in Denmark, Holland, and Northwest Germany.

....

MAY 5, 1945: *For two hours this morning our guns chattered and roared with murderous intent at the elusive "sleeve" which always slipped by.*

Just after lunch we steamed through the open submarine nets into Pearl Harbor. The sun was merciless as it beat down on the flying bridge. On the right was Hickham Field. It was difficult to appreciate that just over three years ago this place was a flaming hell.

There were plenty of ships around, especially AKAs and APAs. We tied up next to the AKA-8.

Hammontu, one of our sailors, had been having stomach cramps all day and by 1900, when I first saw him, had the unmistakable signs of acute appendicitis. I visited the doctor next door and, because he had had surgical experience, we transferred the patient to his ship, the AKA-8. At 2200 we operated and found a red hot appendix. The operation took one hour but went fine. I returned to our ship at midnight and read all my mail. It has been a good day.

....

MAY 6, 1945: *This was a full but unsettling day. Several of us had snacks at the Officer's Club, then went in to Waikiki. The Royal Hawaiian Hotel is now the home of the submariners. Blue jacket laundry hangs out to dry on the beautiful patios and verandas. Literally thousands of sailors loll about on its spacious lawns and its lobby. The place has never served a more worthwhile purpose, though its pristine charm is gone. Like MacArthur, I am sure it will return.*

The famed Waikiki Beach was jammed with military personnel, and the strung-out barbed wire made a very surreal picture.

We returned through Honolulu to the Club. Here I met Clem Halupka, my former roommate, who told me that the LST-6, my old ship of the Normandy invasion, had been sunk! This was a terrible shock to me because I had so many good friends aboard. He had no details, but he thought it probably struck a mine in the Channel.

We then visited the Naval Hospital, saw a number of interesting cases, and returned to the ship.

....

MAY 7, 1945: *"GERMANY QUITS!" Again, world-shaking news was brought to the Chief and me as we were quietly planning the day in our midget office. It chilled me, made me choke up inside, and brought tears to my eyes. Thank God, that one is over!*

The whole future looks different now. We can see the end, though everyone knows getting there will be bloody.

I met Guy Lalone, an old friend from Washburn High School, at the Officer's Club. His ship was sunk off Okinawa. "Those suicide planes are really tough out there," Guy remarked, grimly. He should know.

....

MAY 8, 1945: *On May 9, at 0231 (1231 here) all hostilities ceased in Europe. It is difficult to comprehend the significance of this wonderful news even though it came as no great surprise. What impact will this have on the countries of Europe and of Russia, that have been virtually bled dry, and on the war in the Pacific? The road back will be long and arduous in all belligerent countries, but at least now it will be with hope. It can't help but have a favorable impact for us in the Pacific.*

I sweated the bus trip to Honolulu, ate lunch at the Blaisdale Hotel, then went to Waikiki Beach. The beach stretches out beautifully and the water is so shallow in places that you can wade out for almost a mile. The ocean was as warm as a tub bath, but not very clean. In fact there were even bits of garbage floating around in some areas. The coral bottom was very rough in spots. It was a thrilling sight to see the outrigger canoes speed onto the beach just ahead of a big wave.

Dinner at the Kau Kau Korner was terrible. Flies dominated the scene.

The tenor of the people here following the VE day announcement has been one of sobriety and prayerfulness. All bars and nightclubs are closed. The people I talked to said they didn't want to celebrate until after Japan has been defeated.

Hammontu (appendectomy) was hoisted back by stretcher from the AKA-8. He's doing well.

....

MAY 9, 1945: *I stayed aboard ship all day. Quite pleasant but unexciting. Tonight the movie was topside. It was quite a sight to see the audience perched up on the gun tubs, directors, etc. The theater was great, but the movie,* The Very Thought of You *was only fair, at best.*

....

MAY 10, 1945: *Just after lunch I took the small boat into Fleet Landing, where I picked up the bus to Honolulu. The afternoon and evening were spent at Moody's place in Monoa Valley. It was beautiful and so quiet. The trees and other vegetation were exotic, at least to my eyes. There were mango trees, avocado trees, guava trees, and banana tree orchards, just like our apple orchards back home.*

MAY 11, 1945: *The morning was a rat race with one thousand little things to do. I received a letter from Representative Rankin (indirectly) requesting a physical examination on one of his constituent's sons aboard our ship. "The boy has headaches, backaches, and is not able." Then the crowning statement: "Don't forget that President Roosevelt died of head trouble." (This was an enclosed letter from the boy's mother.)*

I attended a medical conference meeting at Aiea Heights Hospital—"Allergy in the South Pacific." It was quite dull and I couldn't help sleeping through a lot of it.

The movie tonight, Carolina Moon, *with Kay Kyser was entertaining.*

....

MAY 12, 1945: *With all the exotic enchantment of the island so close at hand, I spent the entire day aboard ship. Strange behavior!*

The day was fairly profitable because I learned more about the management of syphilis, and new information about the treatment of certain battle casualties. We were informed today that navy casualties at Okinawa have exceeded 6,500, with suicide planes a continuing threat.

....

MAY 13, 1945, SUNDAY: *This seemed less like Sunday than any other I have ever spent. The sick bay is now full with sailors afflicted with one of the following problems: third degree burn (leg), catarrhal fever, pneumonia, cellulitis of the leg with possible osteomyelitis, post-appendectomy, recurrent gonorrhea, and one sailor with a four-plus Wasserman that will require treatment.*

After lunch I went swimming at the Officer's Club, then saw the movie, Clock, *with Brent and Damico at the Submarine Base.*

The Marines have entered Naha, Okinawa, after bloody fighting.

....

MAY 14, 1945: *Last night a few of the chiefs got drunk aboard ship, had a brawl, and one of them was sacked. Now they are all restricted. I spent half the morning examining the chiefs for the presence of intoxication.*

I did a spinal tap on Dennison and had occasion to use the fluoroscope today for the first time. We are down to five in the sick bay now.

MAY 15, 1945: *The entire day was spent taking and developing six X-ray pictures. The solutions and water had to be carried from the ship's refrigerators to the dark room, then the cassettes loaded, the pictures taken, developed, dried, viewed, and finally recorded. There was one jaw fracture and one case of probable active tuberculosis. A questionable case of osteomyelitis appeared to be normal on the X-ray.*

....

MAY 16, 1945: *The sailor with the fractured jaw (Henning) was transferred to Base Hospital No. 8. At Base Hospital No. 10, Aiea, the radiologist interpreted the chest X-ray I had taken as bronchopneumonia. He said that technically it was a very good plate. Lunch with the medical officers was quite enjoyable. This evening we had dinner at the Officer's Club and later saw a movie on the ship,* Guest in the House.

....

MAY 17, 1945: *Sick call, writing up records, and checking dental appointments occupied the morning. Foster and I went to the Hotel Moana in Waikiki for dinner. The dining room and the environs were very lovely and the food was delicious.*

Tomorrow we get underway for Honolulu. What's up? My guess is that we are going there to load up for a trip west.

....

MAY 18, 1945: *My guess was right; it's west in three to four days and we'll be carrying a 5,000 ton load of ammunition! Special frames and padding are being built in the holds right now prior to loading the ammo. Train cars loaded with large caliber army shells (105s and 88s) wait patiently on the dock. Smoking is prohibited except in certain areas. Special guards are assigned just to monitor smoking. We apparently travel alone. The ship is abuzz with rumors and dry wit. We are now an ammunition ship without the safety advantages of a standard ammunition transport. Our holds have no cooling or humidifying units, no elaborate sprinkling systems, no special compartmentalization, and no dedicated fire-fighting equipment. The crew has had no training in this kind of work. It's going to be a very ticklish and tense trip.*

We inoculated 320 men this morning, but were interrupted by an accident. A sailor fell from a suspended small boat 13 feet to the steel deck below. He was lucky and only fractured a bone in his ankle, the talus. He could have easily fractured his skull. We transferred him anyway.

....

MAY 19, 1945: *It was a welcome relief to get off the ship. After lunch at the Hotel Blaisdell, I went swimming at Waikiki. There were the usual crowds but the water was lovely and the sun nice and warm.*

Supper tonight at Moody's was delicious with roast lamb, peas, potatoes, and plenty of fresh milk. Jimmy, Jackie, and Mrs. Moody were most hospitable.

After dinner I listened to Schubert's "Unfinished Symphony," read awhile and then went to bed. The bedroom was large and a cool breeze through the windows made it ideal for sleeping. The rustle of the leaves outside, the entire atmosphere, reminded me of Lake Minnewashta.

....

MAY 20, 1945: *When I awoke this morning, the warm sun filtered through the thick foliage outside my window, making bright patterns on the floor.*

Mrs. Moody fixed old-fashioned waffles for my breakfast before I said goodbye.

The block walk to the bus was delightful. The temperature was perfect, the trees, shrubs, and flowers were indescribably beautiful. Lush green lawns extended right up to the street, there being no sidewalks. Houses were spanking clean and summery and the palm trees rose stately and exotic against the clear blue sky. It was with little joy that I returned to the ship.

I was told upon my arrival that a full load of 8-inch shells, 2,400 lbs. of explosives, dropped two decks to the hold below and didn't explode (obviously). There were tons more in the same hold. Everyone present when it happened almost died of a stroke or heart attack.

Our load has been increased from 5,000 to 6,500 tons. I guess 1,500 tons more or less wouldn't make any difference if we took a hit.

....

MAY 21, 1945: *Ammunition is being loaded at all hatches, day and night. There are all types and sizes: 8-inch and 5-inch mortar shells, Howitzers, smoke shells, powder in boxes and fuses. The ship sinks further in the water as the load increases.*

We completed all our shots today.

MAY 22, 1945: *Loading continues. The men are becoming nervous and jittery. Willis, seaman first-class, had a hysterical fit in sick bay today. Every one is edgy.*

I went swimming today, and later met my roommate and dear friend, Bud Chamberlain, at the Royal Hawaiian Hotel. After dinner we walked along the beach in front of the Moana Hotel and then cut inland for about two miles. The weather is perfect and the scenery gorgeous.

The earring rage is in full bloom. The men puncture their left ear with a needle, place a thread through the hole for a few days, then insert the post of a cheap brass-alloy earring. The first ear lobe infection reported to sick bay tonight.

....

MAY 23, 1945: *The day was unpleasant. Loading goes on and we are approaching a full load. I have much to learn.*

....

MAY 24, 1945: *We are at last fully loaded. The ship is way down in the water, 25 feet fore and 26 feet aft. We have yet to take on fuel, water, and our small boats.*

I took a taxi trip through Pali Gap to the other side of the island. It was beautiful there and much quieter. I met a Mrs. Craig who invited me to swim at her place next time I come over.

Bumped into Win Hurd and Cal Fairborne at P.Y. Chongs. The steaks were the best I have had in years.

Tomorrow we get under way for the fuel docks, then west to the Orient. Hope it is in a convoy.

....

MAY 25, 1945: *To the people of Honolulu this was just another beautiful morning, but for us it was very special. For four hours we took on fuel oil, then loaded on our small boats, and at 1800 we left Honolulu Harbor for points west. Waikiki Beach, The Royal Hawaiian and the Moana Hotels, and then Diamond Head slowly receded in the distance as we steamed ahead. The breeze on the flying bridge was good and fresh. It was pleasant to be under way again and I felt a joy in my heart. The loudspeaker announced to eager listeners, "We are headed for the forward area and our first stop will be Ulithi in the Carolines."*

We are traveling alone—no convoy and no escort.

MAY 26, 1945: *Long lazy undulations are all that disturb the Pacific's serenity. At quarters the Captain exhorted all hands to be extremely vigilant on our important and hazardous mission.*

Sick call consisted only of injecting a few varicosities and starting penicillin therapy on one chief with latent syphilis.

Recognition pictures for rapid identification of Japanese aircraft were presented to the crew this afternoon.

Full moon tonight. Peace and beauty enfold our destruction-loaded ship as we move silently and alone toward the Carolines.

....

MAY 27, 1945, SUNDAY: *Church service was packed. Foster played a trumpet solo, "Rock of Ages," Christiansen led devotions, and the Captain gave the sermon. We swayed as we sang. It was a "moving" experience, in more ways than one.*

Clocks were set back one hour, making the day unbelievably long. Chicken dinner was superb.

Lectured to corpsmen for over an hour on anatomy.

I made some changes in my battle plan. Time is growing short.

....

MAY 28, 1945: *Today I felt that inward, unexplainable, driving urge to get ready– to get prepared for action.*

We inoculated the entire crew with cholera vaccine.

Lectured on first aid to stretcher bearers and repair parties, then to the officers. There is so much to cover and to do before we're ready to handle multiple casualties.

The Japs are attacking our shipping heavily off Okinawa, sinking one ship and damaging twelve. Seventy-seven Jap planes were knocked down.

Rumor is rife that we are going to Okinawa. Only the Captain, the Executive Officer, and the Navigator know for sure and so far they aren't talking.

....

MAY 29, 1945: *At 1800 we cross the International Date Line, the 180th meridian, which means we skip tomorrow, and there won't be a May 30 for us. More lectures to officers and men today. All went quite well.*

We are now taking inventory of all supplies, which is a drag.

The Japs claim to have sunk one battleship and two cruisers in their kamikaze *attacks at Okinawa. We are about 1,600 miles from Pearl Harbor and over 3,000 miles from San Francisco. This is a big puddle.*

....

MAY 31, 1945: *No Memorial Day for us—we just skipped it.*

The Pacific stretches on forever: sky, clouds, sun, and water. At night, millions of stars. The Southern Cross rises as we move south. It's getting warm and muggy.

....

JUNE 1, 1945: *For what is so hot as a day in June in the South Pacific?*

We had quite a scare today. After lunch General Quarters sounded. "This is no drill!" We were checking our instruments, so none were sterile. Hurriedly, we selected a set and threw it in the sterilizer.

Men were speeding through the passageways and up the ladders as they had never done before. Faces were set. This was the real thing! An unidentified plane was picked up at 26 miles and was moving in fast. Because there was no I.F.F. (identification friendly) it was called a "bogey" (a Jap plane). It was only during the last few minutes that it was identified as friendly. When the "All Clear!" was sounded we all breathed a sigh of relief.

....

JUNE 2, 1945: *The heat is becoming more intense and even when we are lying quietly in bed the sweat flows freely. The "cold" water in the shower is actually hot enough to burn.*

Like two thieves, Bud and I quietly slipped into the wardroom to fill our thermos jugs with cold water. It seems almost impossible to quench our thirst.

The men's quarters are much hotter than ours. Many sleep topside where it is quite a bit cooler.

We passed within sight of Eniwetok in the Marshalls this afternoon. Time for preparation prior to anticipated action grows short. Much remains to be done.

....

JUNE 3, 1945, SUNDAY: *Another hour was added to this afternoon, making it a long, drawn-out day.*

Church service wasn't quite as good today, though the reading of the 23rd Psalm gave me chills and brought tears to my eyes.

I lectured to the corpsmen this afternoon on advanced first aid.

Two merchant ships were visible on the horizon today and we also saw a plane, a Coronado. Today was Father's Day and I often thought of dear old Dad.

Every day it grows hotter and many officers are now sleeping topside.

....

JUNE 4, 1945: *Tonight we are only about 550 miles from Ulithi and it is getting hotter by the hour. My skin is constantly water-logged with perspiration.*

We are slowly reaching completion of our battle preparation. Today we set up the receiving station in the troop officer's compartment.

The battle drill this morning was very realistic.

....

JUNE 5, 1945: *We typed blood and checked Kahns on twelve men today to be used as blood donors if needed; another step toward complete preparedness. A rain squall cooled the ship considerably.*

....

JUNE 6, 1945: *Under a merciless sun, on sparkling deep blue water, we steamed slowly into the coral-rimmed lagoon known as Ulithi. At least 150 ships: tankers, oilers, LSTs, and others were already there at anchor.*

A year ago today, on the opposite side of the earth, under more strained conditions, I was steaming into Normandy on the LST-6. I was lucky that time and I hope my luck holds out on this coming adventure. Tomorrow we fuel, then get underway for some battle zone, probably Okinawa. Last year I read about the invasion of Normandy in Time *magazine (Pony Edition) before it came off. Tonight I'll read about Okinawa in my latest* Time *and then get into it. I like to check up on these events before getting involved!*

....

JUNE 7, 1945: *It was a clear, fresh, "blue-eyed" day. We took on fuel at 1530, following which the Captain invited all department heads to meet in his cabin. Here we learned that our destination was to be Okinawa. The Captain earnestly* *informed us that it would be far from a pleasure cruise. We are to travel in the company of one tanker carrying high octane aviation gasoline, with one destroyer escort. Exactly what harbor in Okinawa and how we are to unload will be divulged by dispatch soon. Our expected time of arrival will be Sunday, June 10. We are gathering up the loose ends in sick bay and are finally getting in pretty good shape.*

Saw a lousy movie in the mess hall tonight, Flesh and Fantasy. *I disliked it immensely. The mess hall was terribly hot and humid. Never again!*

....

JUNE 8, 1945: *A fresh, cool breeze brought welcome relief from the past week's heat. Blue, frothy waves slapped against our gray hull. We are heading north.*

The day passed uneventfully but I kept very busy checking a questionable case of secondary syphilis.

The last Jap-held airfield fell to the Yanks today.

Suicide planes have taken a heavy toll at Okinawa; 44 destroyers and 8 AKAs were sunk and many others sunk or severely damaged. This was information that we obtained from the tanker that refueled us yesterday.

Our spirits are high, however, and we all expect a rather easy time of it. At least that's the feeling on the surface.

....

JUNE 9, 1945: *We were so busy in sick bay that we hardly had time to contemplate the significance of our nearness to Okinawa and Japan. I was bogged down with the problem of making a differential diagnosis between late recurring secondary lues and an urticarial reaction to penicillin in one of the sailors. The corpsmen were making last minute preparations for casualty handling.*

Tonight I prepared a lecture on ether, chloroform, and spinal anesthesia for tomorrow.

The Chief and I went through most of the ship on a "sanitation" tour and were well pleased with what we found.

The Japs are squeezed into a 22-square-mile area in southern Okinawa. There was a 67-plane Jap raid on our shipping reported this morning; two ships were damaged. We will arrive in Okinawa harbor on Monday instead of Sunday as originally planned.

JUNE 10, 1945, SUNDAY: *Today was like every other day, except there was that expectant, somewhat foreboding feeling shared by all of us as we realized we were drawing close to our objective and the ubiquitous* kamikaze *planes. Right now we are less than one hundred miles from Okinawa and should arrive at about 0700 tomorrow morning. We will "put in" forty miles above Naha on the west coast. At 0600 we pass within 12 miles of the Jap-held southern tip. Radio reported two Jap planes about 60 miles away this afternoon. We don't know what to expect. I'm not worried, oddly enough, but am very alert and expectant wondering what will happen tomorrow, or even tonight and those long days after.*

We sterilized all surgical linens and instruments today, and last-minute details were ironed out. I finished my lecture on anesthesia and I think we are now fairly well prepared. The ship moves inexorably on toward the hot zone. What will the morrow bring?

....

JUNE 11, 1945: *All our worry was in vain. The day was docile and unexciting. As we rounded Okinawa's southern tip, we saw, heard, and actually felt the great guns of the cruisers and battleships as they pounded the 15,000 remaining Japs who were trapped in a 19-square-mile area. The cold-blooded slaughter chilled me even though they were our hated enemy. We wedged gently through scores of all manner of ships to a point seven miles above Naha and dropped our anchor about one mile off shore.*

A red alert sounded about 1900 but the Jap planes turned back when they were about 13 miles away.

A typhoon from the northwest is heading our way and tomorrow we are going to move out of the harbor to ride it out, away from all these ships to avoid the chance of a collision.

The U.S. Navy and Army seem to have everything under control around here except for the kamikaze *raids.*

The LST-930 with Elroy Peterson and Ted Watson is only a few ships away.

....

JUNE 12, 1945: *The typhoon changed course and missed us. Very considerate! Red letter day today. Visited Ted and Pete on the 930. Bill Devney, another medi-*

cal school classmate and good friend, then appeared, followed by Al Olson and
Al Harwood. What a day! We went into the beach, then came back to the 930 for
lunch. We talked and laughed, migrated into the beach again and laughed and
talked some more. We hiked around a bit, then came back to the 103 where we had
dinner. The boys thought our layout was wonderful. Before our visit ended, we
discovered that the 930 was underway and we had to step on it to catch her.

Air alert tonight, but no planes seen.

*We started to unload ammunition tonight into DUKWs, (also called Ducks) to
be hauled into the beach. It will be about a two-week deal.*

....

JUNE 13, 1945: *Slowly, but with dogged persistence, the DUKWs, like a group of
water beetles, carried our ammunition from ship to shore. They could carry only a
small quantity each trip, but with 35 of them scooting back and forth they kept it
moving steadily.*

*The day crept by. Mr. Tackaberry, Field Director, visited us from the beach
today and said that the island was virtually secured. There have been no air raids
so far today.*

....

JUNE 14, 1945: *Lew Christiansen, Captain, Medical Corps, U.S. Army, a classmate
of mine, came aboard today to visit his brother, Vince. He looked thin and tired.
He has had amebic dysentery for several weeks. "There are 10,000 Japs left on the
island to be killed or captured," Lew stated. "It will take another week at least."*

*This morning we sent a big box of apples, oranges, and eggs with Mr.
Tackaberry for the boys "up front."*

*The unloading creeps on, seemingly imperceptibly, but apparently at a satis-
factory rate.*

*No air alerts, but the moon is filling which enhances our chance of being
a night-time target.*

....

JUNE 15, 1945: *Pete and Ted spent most of the day aboard. It was great fun chat-
ting about old times back home while we basked in the warm Okinawa sunshine.*

Mr. Tackaberry and Junior brought back some souvenirs for Bud and me:

trays, vases, dishes, and Jap gas-masks. Their stories sound incredible but are true. This morning they shouldered carbines and went hunting Japs, much as we go hunting quail. They didn't bag any, but they picked up some interesting personal effects from the numerous dead Japs. The bulldozer grave-digger is way behind the killing. Foul-smelling, bloated bodies litter the ground.

The Red Cross, just secured back in Naha, was again ordered into the front area which probably means they anticipate more fighting there.

Two red alerts halted unloading for about an hour tonight. The smoke-makers created a London fog effect over the entire harbor.

A quarter moon shone unusually bright and we seemed so huge and so exposed. But the night passed quietly with nary a plane.

....

JUNE 16, 1945: Visited Ted and Pete on the LST-930 and we had a lot of fun playing volley ball.

At 0400 there was an air raid on the harbor and I saw my first Jap plane. It was high off our stern and shore batteries knocked it down. Two more torpedo bombers were shot down by our planes.

When the camouflage smoke cleared away, we saw our smoke-making boats circling the wrong ship. They got razzed by our crew.

The moon is even brighter tonight.

....

JUNE 17, 1945, SUNDAY: An air raid at 0300 tumbled all of us out of our sacks again. An urgent voice over the P.A. system called out "Flash Red! Flash Red! Walk, don't run to your general quarter stations! Make smoke! Make smoke!" All lights are extinguished, the ventilating system is stopped. The ship becomes stifling and smoke-filled, illuminated only by red battle-lanterns. Men sprawl around passageways, many of them too sleepy to care.

Outside the smoke is so dense you can see but a few feet ahead. Being so well hidden brings comfort, but not without plenty of discomfort.

The Japs didn't come close, at least to us, but one of their suicide boats sank an escort vessel.

After the excitement quieted down and we had some sleep, I spent much of the day developing films (not X-ray). I am the ship's photographer.

The Japs flew over at 2130 and dropped bombs on Yon Ton Airfield which is in sight of our ship on a clear day. Smoke again covered all. These raids are becoming very annoying, but it could be a lot worse so we really can't complain.

....

JUNE 18, 1945: *Flash Red again, this time from 0230 to 0345 . One Jap plane flew right over us, but kept on going. We couldn't see him for smoke. At 0400 another Flash Red, but this time it was a false alarm.*

Lt. Wilbur, U.S. Army, gave me a Japanese anatomy book, which represented a common ground between the enemy and us. The very thought of them studying the same thing I studied gave me a real thrill. There are little or no hatreds in music, art, or medicine between warring peoples, probably because these disciplines are less politicized and tend to deal with broader, internationally acceptable themes.

At 2000 a Flash Blue indicated that there were Jap planes 18 miles away, but not moving in our direction.

We were 60 percent unloaded at 1200 today.

....

JUNE 19, 1945: *The Japs didn't return, giving us all a good night's sleep. Howie Johnson, my cousin Miriam's husband, came aboard this noon. He looked a bit drawn and tired with an atabrine-yellowish color. He now wears a mustache. It was very pleasant and worthwhile talking with him. He seems satisfied with his duty.*

Flash Red at 2200. Very short G.Q.

We are now 70 percent unloaded.

....

JUNE 20, 1945: *The day was too rough to unload, so we just bounced around on the end of the anchor chain to wait for quieter seas.*

Flash Red at 2100, but the enemy planes never came close.

....

JUNE 21, 1945: *This morning, Mr. Bender showed unmistakable signs of appendicitis. We transferred him by LCVP through rather rough seas one and a half miles to the hospital ship,* Samaritan.

Dr. Nelson did the operation, with me as his first assistant in one of the Samaritan's *lovely, large, and cool operating rooms. The appendix was long and* inflamed with a large quantity of sero-purulent fluid in the adjacent abdominal cavity. There was no perforation. "Chips" Bender came through fine.

Flash Red at 1900. Japs sank one LSM, one DD, and damaged two AVs about thirteen miles from here.

Flash Red at 2300 lasted until 0300 this morning. There were twenty-two raids. Two ships were sunk, but none within thirteen miles.

....

JUNE 22, 1945: *Flash Red at 0700 this morning that lasted for about one hour. One plane came within three miles.*

Flash Red again for about an hour. One "bogey" came within seven miles of us, but there were over twelve raids this morning with five to twenty planes in each, in an adjacent area. Our location was not attacked, but the bogeys were all around.

I slept this afternoon and at 2330 there was another Flash Red for one hour. There were a number of planes about nine miles away.

....

JUNE 23, 1945: *Quiet day. Unloading has reached its final stages. Visited Bender. He looked fine.*

Full moon tonight with cool breezes. Okinawa was secured yesterday by U.S. forces, and Japanese soldiers are surrendering by the thousands!

....

JUNE 24, 1945, SUNDAY: *Fortunately we completed unloading last night, for today the sea is rough. We moved anchorage to the outer edge of the transport area where we are to await formation of the next convoy.*

The day dragged. I finished Forever Amber and found it repetitious, dull, and poorly written. The ending left me flat.

Flash Red at 2230. One bogey was shot down about 40 miles from here and another came within four miles.

The burning question now is, what will be our next destination? We live from one guess to another.

....

JUNE 25, 1945: *Visited Ted and Pete on the LST-930 this afternoon. They are going to Leyte on the 27th. So far no orders for us.*

Flash Red at 2245 tonight. About 12 different raids occurred. Four enemy planes passed overhead at different times. Several bombs were dropped. The moon was full and a stiff breeze prevented good smoke coverage. The raid lasted until about 0300.

Communications Officer Frank Schiel and Supply Officer Bud Chamberlain on duty topside reported that one of the kamikaze *planes flew so low over our deck that they could have reached up and touched the wheels. The plane crashed in the water less than 100 yards from our ship but fortunately didn't explode. The pilot was rescued and held in our brig. It was a wild night!*

....

JUNE 26, 1945: *Everyone was tired today. Mail arrived which was wonderful and lifted everyone's spirits.*

Went on a wild goose chase to remove a steel splinter from the eye of a merchant mariner. After searching for quite a while, I determined that he didn't have any foreign body in the eye, but a scratched cornea which can be very painful.

Learned today that a suicide plane crashed right next to ACG, Control Ship. That was the explosion we heard last night and thought was a bomb.

....

JUNE 27, 1945: *Pete and Ted visited today. They should be leaving soon. We had a good discussion of group medicine.*

Printed photographs this afternoon. We shifted berths. Rumored that we leave tomorrow. Red alert at 2400.

....

JUNE 28, 1945: *At 1230 we weighed anchor. Our destination, Saipan. There are eight transports and four escorts in our convoy.*

The day has been beautiful and it's a great feeling to be underway again. We passed within 500 yards of a floating mine. The DD detonated it.

....

JUNE 29, 1945: *Quiet, uneventful day. Blue skies, blue water. Played bridge and went to bed.*

JUNE 30, 1945: *Another blue-eyed day at sea. Uneventful. I am growing accustomed to simple pleasures and find myself enjoying reading, conversing, playing bridge, and of course, eating.*

....

JULY 1, 1945: *Pleasant, cruiser-type holiday routine made this day most enjoyable. I read some psychiatry this morning and* Of Human Bondage *this afternoon. I also had time for a sunbath, a nap, and bridge before bed. The sea was blue and quiet with fleecy clouds and a bright sun.*

....

JULY 2, 1945: *Arrived at Saipan today. It's extremely hot, without a breeze. Underway tomorrow.*

....

JULY 3, 1945: *Departed Saipan, bound for San Francisco!*
The "Suicide Cliffs" are at the north end of Saipan. There are still Jap snipers in the hills. Four were reported shot last night.
Long columns of B-29's were seen taking off for targets in Japan. We travel unescorted.

....

JULY 4, 1945: *The day passed quietly with calm seas and a cool breeze. In preparation for the "Big City," I brushed and aired my "blues."*
Red hot bridge tournaments tonight as we got "underway."

....

JULY 5, 1945: *The day's activities consisted of playing bridge, reading* The Way of All Flesh, *a few chapters in* Psychiatry, *writing two letters, listening to a lecture on ship nomenclature, and eating three meals. Still smooth sailing.*

....

JULY 6, 1945: *Another uneventful day. A light rain cooled off the ship.*

JULY 7, 1945: *The day dragged. Inspection this morning. I inspected the engine room, of all things. It wasn't my call. I tried to prepare a sermon for tomorrow on "Faith."*

....

JULY 8, 1945, SUNDAY: *I gave the sermon today that I spent quite a bit of time on yesterday. It took me about 10 minutes to do it and it seemed to be quite well received. Perhaps what they liked was its brevity.*

Yankee from Olympus, by Bowen, is an interesting book. One feels very humble when contemplating the achievements of the two Holmeses, father and son.

Played bridge and had a good exercise session. We're heading north and it's getting cooler.

....

JULY 9, 1945: *Charley, George, Warner, "Ski," and I played kitten-ball in the No. 4 hold. It was fun.*

....

JULY 10, 1945: *My appetite for reading is increasing daily; I cannot read enough. I feel almost as if I have been starved. These long dull days may serve a purpose and the time must not be wasted. I am getting too old to waste a lot of time.*

....

JULY 10, 1945: *We passed the 180th today so we get two July 10's. The Pacific was a mill pond all day, though we did pass through several showers. A song fest in the mess hall tonight was a lot of fun.*

....

JULY 11, 1945: *We reached the halfway mark today. The pleasant calm continues. Days are not tedious now because reading has become such a pleasure. Writing is fun too.*

....

JULY 12, 1945: *Organic chemistry and psychiatry have engaged my more serious attention and the morning was spent embarking on those formidable seas. At 1500, Mr. Damico lectured on the 40-mm gun.*

At 1600, physical exercises. The improved body tone and general sense of well-being make this arduous process worthwhile.

I wrote a letter to Carol and Morley, faintly philosophical, feeble exposition, but a start.

Benjamin Franklin *by Van Doren is my light reading. After 68 pages I was tired, not of the book, because I am enjoying it a lot, but just fatigue. After a cup of delicious hot tea with two pieces of hot buttered toast, my strength, hope, and well-being were restored.*

Before retiring I ventured out on the deck, finding more repose for my soul. A new moon hung low over the horizon and the sky was packed with stars. The ship was a black shadow against the deep blue of the night.

During the 20 minutes before the moon sank from sight, I relived the basic outline of my life, attempting to perceive what it was about and who I really was. I am convinced of one thing and that is when the war is over I'm going to take a residency in surgery so I will never have to feel this inadequate again. In trying to analyze my deficiencies, I concluded that my reading had been inadequate in both quantity and scope, and the realm of love and romance was an uncharted sea. The night was worth the day.

....

JULY 13, 1945: *Organic chemistry proves to be quite interesting and* Ben Franklin *amazes me. I've begun the study of words today.*

Played bridge tonight and won $1.60.

Little things have a delicious flavor in a restricted life of this sort, such as eating a bit of toast with tea, standing on the flying bridge at night, playing a few hands of bridge, and reading. These have much greater pleasure here than at home.

....

JULY 14, 1945: *Each day is more enjoyable than the one before. I'm beginning to like this life so much I feel almost inclined to make the sea my vocation. This is a strange, and I'm sure, transient state of mind. I don't quite know where it is coming from. Whether it's the cooler weather, the exercises, or just part of a cycle, I feel so much more ambitious and filled with a zest for living and learning, I hardly seem the same person.*

Today I became acutely aware of the pleasure derived from giving. I spent quite some time visiting with Mr. Modell, who was sick, and cheered him up. Then

I played bridge, taking Mr. Brunn, the worst player, as my partner, making him feel good. Then I visited my corpsmen and helped lift their spirits. Lastly I gave some of my magazines to the stewards who had nothing to read, for which they were profoundly grateful.

I was savoring the warm glow of self-satisfaction derived from my generosity when further self-analysis stripped the unselfishness from every act: 1) I had to visit Mr. Modell, my patient; 2) Mr. Brunn was the last available partner for bridge, and it was either play with him or not at all; 3) I visited sick bay because it was exactly what I felt like doing. The corpsmen just happened to be there and our conversation was lively; 4) I didn't give the magazines to the stewards, I loaned them, and I was very careful to place my name in the corner and also impress on them the importance of returning them. One was an old Colliers *and other an old* Saturday Evening Post.

On later reflection, it became apparent to me that my giving was bare. How easily we can delude ourselves.

Captain's inspection with everyone in dress blues made the ship look real "Navy" and sharp.

....

JULY 15, 1945, SUNDAY: *Attended church service today with our executive officer giving the sermon entitled, "Tolerance." I then did two spinal taps down in sick bay, took a sun bath, read* Benjamin Franklin *and one chapter of organic chemistry, played two rubbers of bridge (won $1.45), exercised for an hour, and then wrote a letter to brother Paul.*

Tonight we travel with running lights. We're getting close.

....

JULY 16, 1945: *A department meeting on repairs and liberty in San Francisco, plus a talk on "Naval Leadership" by the Captain, occupied most of the afternoon. The day was otherwise rather barren.*

....

JULY 17, 1945: *The "Rankin Follies" had its debut tonight. The humor was rough and bawdy. Hula dancers with deck swabs for hair, well-filled brassieres, and grass* skirts were a scream. The pie-eating contest was gross and the poem I wrote was presented disadvantageously.

The excitement of the evening was almost too much for me. I feel wrought up; I'm used to a well-oiled rut.

....

JULY 18, 1945: *Tonight I showed a movie,* Sex Hygiene, *on venereal disease prevention, preceded by a short talk on related subjects. The mess hall was packed. The topic was obviously timely, inasmuch as the ship's store sold over four gross (576) pkgs. of rubber condoms last week. San Francisco women beware! These men have blood in their eyes and come well armed.*

Following the sex movie, 'H' Division celebrated Junior Tackaberry's birthday with a surprise party in our office. There was a huge cake with pink and white frosting of at least one inch thickness, a gallon of pineapple ice cream and excellent coffee. The party was delightful; thoroughly enjoyed by all. Stories and funny jokes were told and interesting incidents related. I told about several of my experiences at the Boston City Hospital which amused the boys a great deal. I left the party at 2200 to finish Benjamin Franklin *tonight.*

....

JULY 19, 1945: *The day was brisk and exhilarating. The sea was perfectly calm, the sky cloudless with bright sunshine. Our ship glided effortlessly over shimmering blue water.*

The moon is almost full and the night is cold, dark, and beautiful.

....

JULY 20, 1945: *When I arrived on deck this morning we were already deep in San Francisco Bay, with the anchor poised for lowering. Our anchorage is located in the center of the Bay just south of the gigantic Bay Bridge, the old Fleet Anchorage.*

The day was brisk and breezy and the bright morning sun, chasing away the last remaining fog, gave promise of a warm, pleasant day. I was again impressed with the clean, bright appearance of the city and also the blueness of the sky.

Having received a promotion, I added a stripe to my uniform; now full Lieutenant.

Liberty commenced at 1300 today and I was in the first wave of boats to hit the beach. After the long confinement on board ship, we all tried to do as much as possible in the short time we had in this wonderful city. First came Kellys by the water front, next the Orchid Room at the St. Francis Hotel, then the "Snake Pit" at the Sir Francis Drake Hotel, then the Cirque Room at the Fairmont Hotel, then dinner at Kit Carsons, then the Officer's Club dance at the Fairmont, then the Top of the Mark, the Zebra Room, the Snake Pit again, then to bed at the St. Francis.

It was just too much crammed into too short a time. It now seems like a blurred hodgepodge.

The view of San Francisco from the Top of the Mark is indeed beautiful. Amber lights on the bridge interspersed with white lights give the appearance of a sparkling necklace.

Bed was welcome, but having to get up at 0530 to catch the 0630 boat back to the ship was no fun. The 0630 boat left early causing me to miss it, necessitating waiting over an hour at Fleet Landing for the next one. I had no coat and it was cold and raw. A heavy fog covered the Bay.

By the time I arrived back at the ship, I was tired and half-frozen. The entire experience was more pain than pleasure, but the change after 57 days aboard ship was indeed welcome.

....

JULY 21, 1945: *I slept in this morning. After arranging for a new corpsman at the Federal Building, I went to my room at the St. Francis and slept until 1800 when I got ready for my date with Muriel. I walked up and down at least four large hills, a distance of some two miles, to meet her. We ate dinner at Alfeos on Powell Street, both of us having squab which was very tasty. Later we danced at the St. Francis. After walking Muriel home, and then walking for what seemed to be miles in the cold early Sunday morning fog to Fleet Landing, I caught the 0330 boat to the ship.*

....

JULY 22, 1945, SUNDAY: *I slept most of the day. Dinner was tops: fruit cocktail, roast chicken, fresh milk, and corn on the cob.*

At 1330, "Anchors Aweigh." We're off for Seattle!

As we steamed under the Golden Gate Bridge, onlookers above waved cheery farewells. A high wind whistled and sang through the lines. The sea looked angry,

*but the roll felt soothing. It was comforting to get away from the noise, the compli-
cations, and the struggles of a civilized community.*

*The two days in San Francisco were too strenuous. It was like bolting your food
and suffering indigestion. When will I ever learn?*

....

July 23, 1945: *A blustery, cold morning that chilled the marrow, mellowed
gradually into a lovely calm evening.*

*Darkness came late and with it a full moon and a cloudless sky. Smooth, but-
tery swells were all that marred an otherwise mirror surface. Moon beams created
dancing, sparkling sequins in a bright, golden path to the distant horizon. Stars
faded in the light of this night.*

*Myriads of small, black fish, swimming in closely packed schools on the water's
surface, formed large, dark, ominous shadows. At first they were mistaken for logs,
submarines or just flotsam. The ship changed course to avoid them until their true
nature was appreciated. Many whales were seen today and the air is laden with a
fish-like, Gloucester odor.*

....

July 24, 1945: *We have been traveling close to the rugged Oregon coast all day.
These waters abound with fish and sea ducks.*

Saw God is My Co-Pilot *in the mess hall. The movie was good, but the theater
is the worst in the world.*

....

July 25, 1945: *The trip through Juan de Fuca Strait and Puget Sound was
beautiful, reminding me of northern Minnesota. Tall dark pines, rugged cliffs, and
endless hills with the pleasant odor of spruce and pine made for a happy journey.*

*At the end of one limb of the Sound, after several hours, we reached Seattle.
The city looked hilly but very pretty, extending down to the water's edge.*

We were towed in to dry dock almost at once and at 0730 liberty began.

*The evening started at the Marine Room, Hotel Olympia, then moved to the
Officer's Club for dancing and singing. Later, Bud Chamberlain and I went over to
Nina and Mary Winslow's house for toast, eggs, and milk.*

*Bud and I stayed at the Hotel Olympia, arose dead tired at 0630, and stumbled
back to the ship.*

JULY 26, 1945: *Tired, grim, I set about the business of transferring one of our sick stewards to the hospital. This occupied the morning. Bud and I then went to town in his borrowed truck. We ate dinner at the Olympia Grill, then saw* Valley of Decision *with Greer Garson. Fine picture. In the Marine Room, I talked to Chesty Hoyt who had been "kamikazied" at Okinawa.*

After some trouble starting the truck we came back to the Rankin *at 1220. All the paint has been sandblasted from the hull, and we now refer to her as the "naked lady." She will get a wash down, then a coat of hot plastic. The old girl really looks huge, a monster, bared to her bottom.*

....

JULY 27, 1945: *We left dry dock this morning. Tugs towed us through the Washington Canal locks, then to the Lake Union dry docks for the second stage of our repair.*

Lillian Heggem and I went to dinner at the "Little Bit of Sweden," then danced at the Officer's Club. She is a very lovely girl.

....

JULY 28, 1945, SUNDAY: *The day was dark, cold, and raw. Bob White and I visited the home of Phyllis Ross on Lake Washington. It was a lovely place and the afternoon was quite enjoyable, but the girls seemed so lonesome that it was kind of sad.*

We ate dinner at the Officer's Club, met two rather peculiar girls, left them, and went back to the ship.

....

JULY 29, 1945: *John Proc and I played golf at the University of Washington's golf course. The weather was perfect and the course beautiful. My score was not good but I did have a lot of fun anyway. Mrs. Roning and Mrs. Armstrong took us with them to dinner and then drove us back to the ship. I'm going to bed early tonight.*

....

JULY 30, 1945: *Though I have never taken much stock in clairvoyance, or extra-sensory perception, today I believe I experienced one, or both of the above. While* shopping in town I developed a peculiar, dissatisfied feeling I couldn't shake nor explain. I soon realized it was an urge to go back to the ship and yet it was not logical to do so because I was on liberty and covered. Try as I may, I couldn't shake the feeling and several times I tried getting a taxi, but no luck. I was miserable and couldn't understand why. Then I met Charlie W. and the feeling gradually disappeared as we got busy doing other things.

Later, when I came back to the ship the Officer of the Day told me that one of the sailors became terribly ill that afternoon and was taken to the hospital by ambulance. It was at the same time I had the peculiar feeling. Now was this pure coincidence or clairvoyance? I guess I'll never know. Fortunately, everything turned out all right.

....

AUGUST 1, 1945: *I visited the Naval Hospital to see the sick sailor and then went out with Lillian, Mabel, and Bob. We saw two lousy movies,* Nob Hill *and* Within These Walls. *Both were hideous, boring, feeble and endless. The evening was unpleasant for all.*

....

AUGUST 2, 1945: *Tom Hall and I spent most of the day together. I took him through the ship, then we visited the Marine Room, after which we had an excellent dinner at the Athletic Club. It was fun just talking and I now feel much less dissatisfied and depressed.*

....

AUGUST 3, 1945: *Phyllis Ross came to dinner with Bob White. He had the duty, so she and I, with Bob's good wishes, went out. We spent the evening at the Athletic Club, then drove out to her home. Here, overlooking beautiful Lake Washington, we enjoyed a nightcap and then turned in to our respective bedrooms.*

....

AUGUST 4, 1945: *Morning came too soon and I just barely made it back to the ship in time for a quick breakfast before quarters.*

Bud Chamberlain, Leoni, Jimmy, Lillian, and I had dinner at the Athletic Club. Then Lillian and I went to the dance. This night life is beginning to wear me out.

....

AUGUST 5, 1945, SUNDAY: *I arose fatigued but managed to grind out Dennison's transfer write-up and then go to church. Bud took Brunn and me to University Lutheran in his open jeep.*

Bob White and I spent the day at Phyllis Ross' home. It was warm and beautiful. We swam, sunbathed, had a fine dinner, went for a speed-boat ride, then came back to the ship. Every one was so good to us. I called the folks, then met the Jack Maulders and Ethel Sweeney from Brooklyn.

....

AUGUST 6, 1945: *The U.S. dropped an atom bomb on Japan! It is said to have 2,000 times more explosive force than TNT and is equivalent to 20,000 tons of bombs, or the load carried by 2,000 Superfort planes, or seven times the explosive force than that which literally destroyed Halifax in 1918.*

This is our response to Japan's rejection of the Potsdam Ultimatum. It should shorten the war, but the potential of this new destructive force is terrifying.

I spent a quiet day shopping for our next trip out to sea. I picked up a copy of Time *magazine, some books, and a pair of sweat pants. I then had a chocolate malted milk and later a beer before going back to the ship. I stayed aboard tonight.*

....

AUGUST 7, 1945: *We moved from Lake Union to Pier 91. Liberty commenced after all ammunition and stores were loaded aboard, which was not until 2200. Hurd, Gardenier, Fairborne, Doty, and I took shore-leave together. Because of the late start we had to make the rounds rather rapidly and moved from the Marine Room, which closed early, to the New China Cafe and finally the Flying Tigers. We were joined by others of both sexes and all were in a celebratory mood. By 0530 we were somewhat fatigued and went back to the ship in time for breakfast.*

....

AUGUST 8, 1945: *Russia declares war on Japan! We all have the attitude that the war is virtually over and will end soon. Drills seem stupid. All preparation now is anti-climactic.*

I slept most of the morning. We left Seattle at 1100 and are underway for Lacoda, Oregon on the Columbia River, between Portland and Astoria. It's cold and foggy.

....

AUGUST 9, 1945: *Through heavy fog we reached the Columbia River and after a few hours delay, with the fog gradually lifting, we proceeded slowly up the large tortuous waterway. Fishing boats were numerous and the surrounding country was rugged and beautiful with heavy growths of pine and fir, and mountains in the distance. Along the river were sawmills and fish houses. After 45 miles we reached our destination which was actually only an ammunition dump with the nearest town five miles away. This time we will carry navy "ammo" (for the invasion of Japan.)*

I was called out to see a boy who was injured in a camp about two miles away. Transported by jeep, I found that he was not seriously hurt, only bruised. After checking him over, I had a midnight dinner with a few of the officers.

....

AUGUST 10, 1945: *Japan surrenders! This world-shaking news was heard over the radio just before breakfast. Apparently a second atomic bomb was dropped somewhere in Japan yesterday. Though not totally unexpected, it was still incomprehensible. There was no riotous cheering. Although the announcement was not official, i.e., not from Washington D.C., it sounded like the real thing, coming from Japan, Stockholm, and Berne. I'm sure it's true. Thank God!*

Our loading has been temporarily discontinued pending a possible change in orders. I hope they cancel the load because it's made up of heavy duty ammunition: 14-inch powder shells, torpedo war-heads and 20- and 40-mm shells.

Well over half of our ship's personnel went on liberty, the town being Longview, Washington. It is a clean and neat little town with lots of pretty women. I had a bad cold so could only observe, prompting me to return to the ship early.

....

AUGUST 11, 1945: *Tense excitement prevails as surrender terms are being mulled and disputed. China and Russia do not wish to allow the Emperor to remain. The U.S. has offered a counter-proposal to Japan which would make the Emperor a mouthpiece or figurehead for an American director. Later the people of Japan can decide whether they wish to retain the Emperor as a nominal religious head. This* *counter-proposal was approved by all Allied nations and has been sent to Tokyo from Switzerland. The Japanese are expected to accept. Official surrender is not expected until Sunday night or Monday.*

All ammunition loading has been suspended and the large freight cars have been taken away. We are about one-quarter filled and are waiting for orders before continuing, which apparently awaits Japan's decision.

All the boys went to a party in Longview. My cold kept me aboard. Here are the books I read over the past year.

1.	ONE MORE SPRING	GEORGE NATHAN
2.	FOREVER AMBER	WINDSOR
3.	STRANGE WOMAN	WILLIAMS
4.	BATTLE REPORT-PACIFIC	KELLEY
5.	GAZING INTO MY EIGHT-BALL	EARL WILSON
6.	OF HUMAN BONDAGE	MAUGHAM
7.	THE WAY OF ALL FLESH	BUTLER
8.	YANKEE FROM OLYMPUS	BOWEN
9.	FLOWERING OF NEW ENGLAND	VAN WYCK BROOKS
10.	BENJAMIN FRANKLIN	CARL VAN DOREN
11.	AMERICA UNLIMITED	ERIC JOHNSTON
12.	THE PHILOSOPHY OF SPINOZA	RATNER
13.	FAITH, REASON AND CIVILIZATION	LASKI
14.	WRITERS, HELP YOURSELVES	MILDRED REID
15.	HISTORY OF THE FAR EAST IN MODERN TIMES	VINACKE
16.	BAREFOOT BOY WITH CHEEK	MAX SCHULMAN
17.	THE CITADEL	CRONIN
18.	RABBLE IN ARMS	ROBERTS
19.	THOREAU	CANBY
20.	MAGIC MOUNTAIN	THOMAS MANN
21.	KITTY FOYL	MORLEY

My least favorite was Forever Amber *and my most favorite,* Magic Mountain. *All of them were worth reading. Time for bed.*

AUGUST 12, 1945: *All day the entire world breathlessly awaited Japan's answer. A false surrender report was made through the U.P. around 1800 but was soon retracted. It was enough, though, to send most cities into gala, sometimes wild, but premature victory celebrations.*

The war is still going on. Word from Japan is expected tomorrow.

Jim Damico and I went to Portland today. It is about 55 miles away and our means of transportation varied. We crossed the Columbia River by small boat to Oak Point, then a truck to Kelso, then hitchhiked to Portland's outskirts, then hitched another ride to the Portland Hotel. Time required was two and one-half hours.

We visited the Officer's Club and then the Actor's Club. We took a bus to Vancouver and hitched a ride back to Kelso. After stopping by our mutual room at the Hotel Monticello, I took the bus back to Oak Point and the boat back to the Rankin. In bed by 2400.

Still no official word from Japan.

....

AUGUST 13, 1945: *The suspense continues with no official proclamation. We are still expectantly awaiting further orders.*

"Ski" and I went into Longview tonight and met five girls with a car. We went riding for awhile, then to a Mrs. Howard's home for food and a party. There was some imbalance here with five gals, Billy, Barbara, Dena, Sally and Ella, and only three men, Barwich, Ski, and me. We danced with all five of them and had a wonderful time, not getting back to the ship until 0515.

....

AUGUST 14, 1945: *Japan surrenders unconditionally! This soul-stirring news flashed on the radio at about 1630 today. It was impossible to fully comprehend its total significance, but it struck all of us as unbelievably wonderful! The entire war is really over! We had expected this outcome during the past few days, but its official announcement was still a dynamic and earth-shaking event.*

Warner, Bud, Ski, and I went to Longview to witness the victory jubilation. We arrived at about 1930 and the streets were already littered with confetti, torn bits of paper and white ribbons of toilet paper thrown down from second and third floors of buildings. Sidewalks were crowded with cheering inhabitants and cars jammed the main street. The principal expression of the overwhelming elation was the raucous honking of auto horns at about one-minute intervals.

The armed personnel of all branches that happened to be present were much quieter than the civilians. Most of them stood in the background and simply watched with amused interest the wildly shouting and honking townspeople.

At the Monticello Hotel all uniformed personnel were invited to room 206 for refreshments, which turned out to be Scotch whiskey, bourbon, gin, rye, and mix. The place was jampacked with partially and completely intoxicated sailors, officers, and civilians. The only place I could find even stand-up room was in the lavatory and I did my celebrating there.

That too became so crowded, we left with the five girls we were with the night before and moved around the town from one house to the next celebrating the gala day.

....

AUGUST 15, 1945: *It wasn't all a dream. Peace is actually here! Except for a few trouble spots, the formal war is over. China seems now to be embroiled in a civil war and fighting continues in a few far-flung battle grounds where the Japs haven't gotten the word that the war is over, or are so fanatic they refuse to stop fighting, despite the war's official end. But the truth is "The War Is Over!" What a wonderful thought!*

Already, demobilization plans are in progress and 1.5 million men are expected to be discharged from the Navy in 12 to 18 months. According to the Navy point system, I should be out by 1950, but medical doctors are not included anyway, so I have no idea how long my "hitch" will be.

I certainly have a lot to be thankful for; that I'm alive, for starters. Stayed aboard tonight.

....

AUGUST 16, 1945: *The Russians and the Japs are still fighting in Manchuria. MacArthur is giving the Japanese envoy a little more time to straighten out his home difficulties before demanding his presence in the formal signing of the surrender terms.*

I played six holes at the Longview Country Club. (Game called due to darkness.) There I met Lt. Eslick, U.S. Public Health Service. We had dinner at the Club together, then picked up Billy Bonham (one of the five) and went to the Elk's Club. Later, Billy took me back to the Rankin.

AUGUST 17, 1945: *At 1300 the C-Bs started to unload our ammunition. There are only 900 tons, so we expect to be unloaded by tomorrow night.*

I went out with Billy again tonight.

....

AUGUST 18, 1945: *Six of us officers from the ship played basketball at the Longview YMCA this afternoon and almost knocked ourselves out.*

I had dinner with Pat, Billy, and her mother, Mrs. Bonham, at the Hotel Monticello. They treated me to a filet mignon dinner. It was terrific. Everyone has been so kind and generous.

Ski, Meyers, Dena, Barbara, Billy, and I then went to the Country Club. We danced until 2430, then went on a picnic. We built a huge fire in the center of a clearing, surrounded by tall pines. The air was brisk and the sky loaded with a billion stars.

....

AUGUST 19, 1945, SUNDAY: *The day was perfect with a warm sun and invigorating air. This morning I strolled along the road to the ammunition dumps and absorbed the day's loveliness.*

At 1630 we got underway for Manila, empty, and have no idea what our job is going to be. After moving past Astoria, 45 miles from Beaver, we reached the open sea and the Rankin *is rolling.*

....

AUGUST 20, 1945: *Our first day at sea, after our pleasant visit, proved to be identical to all the rest. It will take a little time to readjust to sea life after shore leave. We all wonder how long it will be before we come back. Next time, I hope it's for good.*

....

AUGUST 21, 1945: *Brother Paul's birthday today, but I am in no position to send him my greetings.*

A boy with tapeworm infestation reported to sick bay today. He has had symptoms for three years but has done nothing about it.

The sea is quite rough today. Life goes on about the same.

AUGUST 22, 1945: *The new basketball court in the No. 4 Hold was inaugurated today. The play was sloppy but some of the men showed real talent. We started treatment on the tapeworm victim today and hope it works because we have only one course of therapy.*

I am struggling through The Philosophy of Spinoza *and find some of it evades my comprehension. The portions that I could grasp were so pithy and filled with wisdom that the book is well worth the effort. I would have gotten a lot more out of it if I had a broader background in philosophy terminology.*

....

AUGUST 23, 1945: *Overnight, the weather changed from cool and cloudy to warm and clear. It is a typical calm, sun-shiny Pacific today. I was busy with basketball, bridge, and reading. Time passes quite rapidly now.*

....

AUGUST 24, 1945: *Smooth sailing. Basketball has been a great innovation.*

....

AUGUST 25, 1945: *The Captain held personnel inspection today with everyone in their dress whites standing under a blue sky.*

Played basketball twice today. We won our first game from the Gunnery Dept., 26 to 5.

I am still struggling with The Philosophy of Spinoza. *I thought one aspect of his philosophy seemed inconsistent, but it could be that I didn't understand it.*

....

AUGUST 26, 1945, SUNDAY: *An all-day holiday routine was all that made this day any different from the rest of the week. Even our little Sunday service was not held today.*

I read, slept, played basketball, read some more and now, fatigued, it's bed again.

....

AUGUST 27, 1945: *We are passing south of Midway tonight. Only two weeks more to Manila.*

The basketball court rolled with the ship in the moderately heavy sea, lending a peculiar new sensation to the game.

Ernie and I won a couple of dollars apiece playing bridge tonight.

....

AUGUST 29, 1945: *Crossed the 180th today, hence skipped Aug. 28. Every day gets warmer. Basketball is really a hot game now.*

We are heading toward a storm.

....

AUGUST 30, 1945: *Gave examinations to the corpsmen today and all were promoted one rate. We had a little party in celebration, with fancy cake, strawberry ice cream, and lemonade.*

Watched a basketball game tonight. In spite of the hot court, the boys played like mad.

....

AUGUST 31, 1945: *On and on we sail. It seems endless. What an immense body of water, the Pacific.*

Venereal disease victims of the Longview-Kelso exposure are beginning to file in. Since arriving in Seattle, we have had over 14 cases of gonorrhea.

We played basketball against the "5" division tonight and won 27 to 19. The court was stifling.

....

SEPTEMBER 1, 1945: *Our present position is 10 degrees latitude, and 160 degrees longitude. We are very close to Eniwetok. From now on it's due west. With a tail wind and a bright sun, the day was a scorcher.*

Inspection today of personnel and materiel dragged on for hours.

In spite of the heat, twelve of us crawled down the ladder two decks to the basketball court and played a strenuous game. Sweat poured from all of us and the ball became so wet we could hardly hold on to it, but what fun!

The initial elements of the occupation forces moved into Japan yesterday and follow-up groups continue to land without event. The Japs are acting the part of a vanquished nation with great finesse and ability, according to news reports.

September 2, 1945, Sunday: *Aboard the battleship* Missouri *in Tokyo Bay at 1030, Tokyo time, the formal surrender of the Japanese Empire took place. At our location it was 1200. We listened to the surrender broadcast as we ate our Sunday dinner. Reception was quite poor but we were able to hear the concluding statements and were profoundly moved by the great reality that "peace had finally come to all the world." We were told by the radio announcer that the sun, which had been under the clouds all day, burst forth in a blaze of glory right after the document was signed. Heady stuff!*

Every day gets hotter. We played basketball again and I almost passed out.

....

September 3, 1945: *We are deep in the Carolines, approaching Ulithi. Clouds, a few showers, and a freshening wind made this day cooler than the few preceding scorchers.*

Tonight, our team, Officer's Blue, beat the 'N' Division 18 to 15. At the half we were trailing 15 to 6 but then we began to fight. The last half was a terrific battle. There was great satisfaction in winning because they were so confident of victory.

....

September 4, 1945: *It poured all day, making it much cooler. Tonight, we are passing north of Ulithi.*

Censorship has been lifted so we can now write anything we wish.

....

September 5, 1945: *Three floating objects, closely resembling mines, were sighted by lookouts this forenoon. G.Q. was sounded and the gunners had a field day. Two of the three "mines" were sunk, and they went down without a sputter. The ominous looking spheres were probably net buoys that had drifted away.*

The much-vaunted Officer's Blue team was royally trimmed tonight by a smart, scrappy little team, the LCMs. They out-played, out-smarted and out-fought us all the way. Bud Chamberlain's finger was badly infected, so after the game I incised it.

We are just north of Palau tonight. It is still quite cool.

SEPTEMBER 6, 1945: *Dark and rainy all day. Played basketball and tonight I'm dead tired. Opened Bud's finger wider tonight. It's a stubborn infection but the finger looks better. We arrive at Tacloban, Leyte Gulf, tomorrow.*

....

SEPTEMBER 7, 1945: *We are crossing the Sulu Sea, having bypassed Tacloban. It's dark, cool, and windy. The surrounding Philippine Islands are mountainous, green-clad, and dark under the overcast sky. The rainy season has just begun.*

....

SEPTEMBER 8, 1945: *Through Mindoro Straits into the South China Sea, we are now, after 19 days, only 8 hours from Manila. My reaction to concluding this long journey is neutral. I feel very little excitement or anticipation in finally reaching our destination, except that it brings us closer to our return. Manila happens to be at the wrong end of the trip. My heart is back in the States more than ever before.*

The order discontinuing the black-out at night came through today. It is wonderful to be able to keep the portholes open whenever you wish.

We played what is probably our last basketball game for a long while this afternoon. It was great fun.

....

SEPTEMBER 9, 1945: *With a tropical downpour obscuring vision we inched slowly past famed Corregidor into Manila Bay. It was only January of this year that MacArthur made good on his promise, "I shall return!" and landed his troops at Lingayen Gulf, and the end of February that Manila was completely liberated from Japan. Luzon was still a battleground in certain isolated strongholds less than a month ago.*

The ugly black and rusting hulks of sunken ships scattered throughout Manila Bay reflect the terrible sea and air war that raged here during the past several years. From one position, without the aid of binoculars, I counted 12 sunken ships. These are but a small percentage of all the ships of both sides that have been lost here. The bay is currently packed with functioning American ships, the majority of them being AKAs, APAs and Liberties.

Manila sounds like a bad deal for liberty, with malaria, dysentery, leprosy, venereal disease (90 percent of pick-ups and 100 percent of prostitutes), contaminated food and water, and poisoned liquor.

···

SEPTEMBER 10, 1945: *A rough sea prevented anyone from going ashore today. It also tossed a small boatman into the water, lacerating his right armpit. Our surgical team had its first major "surgical experience" tonight. The operation went well.*
Later, played basketball, bridge, and bed.

···

SEPTEMBER 11, 1945: *The wind abated enough to allow refueling at a neighboring tanker. Most of the warm day was spent reading medical literature. No mail yet. I visited the medical officer on AGC-11 tonight. First time off the ship in 22 days.*

···

SEPTEMBER 12, 1945: *On calm seas under cloudless skies, the USS* Rankin's *"liberty party," including the doctor, churned into a shambled Manila. Our LCVP carried us past numerous gutted and sunken ships, down the rubble-bordered Pasig River, right into the torn-up heart of town. Destruction here was even greater than in Plymouth or Southampton. The only buildings that remained standing were burned-out skeletons, walls without roofs.*

Time had not permitted extensive cleaning and filth was everywhere. Odors of rotting flesh, garbage, sewage, and horse manure filled the air. The streets were narrow, crooked, and dusty. Small makeshift shops, concession stands, photostudios, stores made of sheet-tin or discarded lumber were built in the skeleton buildings which lined most of the streets. Prices were astronomical: ice cream, $1.00 a dish, a cheap watch, $100, one roll of film, $2.50, slippers, $7.50, one quart of "Imperial" whisky, $32.50. We were told that most of the "spirits" of any kind were grossly contaminated and watered down.

Pitiful people scratched through the ruins in search of firewood or metal. Most were poorly dressed and seemed so discouraged.

The heat, the dust, the odor, the absence of safe places to eat or drink, the depressed atmosphere, and the tomb-like ambiance caused me to return early to the ship.

Our basketball team played against the team on the CVE-29, the Sante, *on their beautiful hangar deck court. We lost 25 to 26.*

SEPTEMBER 14, 1945: *At 0810 we got underway for Subic Bay. Going through the channel between Corregidor and Bataan brought to my mind the terrible pounding Corregidor received in 1942 before its capitulation, and the miserable treatment suffered by our soldiers in the Bataan "Death March." It filled me with awe and admiration for their courage.*

Corregidor was larger, greener, and less craggy than I had anticipated. On the Manila side the slope is quite gentle. Only portions of buildings remained.

Bataan was green and mountainous. The jungle looked impenetrable. Our LCMs and maintenance crews were left at Subic Bay, and by 1830 we were under way again, this time for Lingayen Gulf.

....

SEPTEMBER 16, 1945, SUNDAY: *Loading operations began today. High octane gasoline was the first cargo to come aboard.*

A sailor from an LCFF was brought to sick bay, very drunk. He had consumed half a bottle of island whiskey. After an hour in a deep coma he began to come around.

Sunset tonight was one of the most beautiful I have ever seen.

....

SEPTEMBER 17, 1945: *Removed a lipoma from Chief Baumer's head this morning. The operation was more difficult than I had anticipated, being deeper and more vascular. The procedure took about one hour and I thoroughly enjoyed doing it.*

This evening the medical department celebrated Corpsman Ed White's birthday. The operating room table was set up with all the goodies and two bulbs were unscrewed from the operating light for low-light atmosphere. For refreshment, we had grape juice and apple pie à la mode.

....

SEPTEMBER 18, 1945: *Trucks, jeeps, tractors, and gasoline were carefully loaded aboard and we are now 50 percent loaded. I developed films this afternoon and played bridge tonight. Still no mail.*

....

SEPTEMBER 19, 1945: *At last a letter. It was from Mother and I sure loved it.*

An epidemic of virus pneumonia in the 35th Battalion has caused loading operations to cease on all ships in Lingayen Gulf, except ours. We are about 70 percent full so it was decided that in our case the loading would be pushed to completion.

....

SEPTEMBER 21, 1945: *The rough, green-clad hills surrounding Lingayen Gulf are beautiful. Some achieve mountainous proportions and their tops are usually smothered by clouds. Occasionally a dark gray rain cloud envelops all the hills as though it had been applied by some giant putty knife and then it bursts in a torrential downpour. The rain falls in gushes.*

....

SEPTEMBER 22, 1945: *Seven months ago, MacArthur's troops hit the beach of Lingayen Gulf.*

Several of us walked inland to see how the people lived. Houses were made of different materials: grass, cardboard, canvas, or in a few cases, wood. Doors and windows were open and the farm animals, pigs, water buffalo, chickens, and dogs, lived under the huts. Children, hardly old enough to walk, were taking care of children who were too small to walk. The women wore long, wrap-around dresses, carried everything on their heads, and smoked long, black Manila cigars. From the large number of children all over the place, you know these folks are very prolific. The youngsters amuse themselves with very simple games and activities.

They play one game similar to "jacks" but have no ball, and no jacks. They use pebbles instead. Their toys are crude. "Cars" or "trucks" have can covers for wheels. There were no beggars here as were so numerous in Manila.

The small boats beached for us at 1700 and after wading through water up to our ankles and getting soaked by spray on the trip back, we arrived just in time for supper, wet but hungry. The movie tonight was Star Spangled Rhythm. *Not bad.*

Full moon tonight.

....

SEPTEMBER 23, 1945, SUNDAY: *Nothing about today even remotely resembled the Sabbath. Aside from reading a few verses in the Gospel of Luke, I spent the whole day printing pictures.*

Watched a movie topside about saboteurs, the title of which I didn't get, starring Pat O'Brien. It was a bit outdated, coming after war's end, but still engrossing.

The moon came up midway through the movie, painting such beautiful colors on the clouds that I couldn't avoid being distracted.

Letters from Melba, Mother, Carol, and Olga came today. They were wonderful. Melba's new baby boy is named John Bradley.

....

SEPTEMBER 24, 1945: *We visited a native family and gave them some medications for their baby whose scalp was grossly infected. They were very appreciative.*

Bud and I then struck out for San Fabian some five miles away. We hitched a jeep ride and were there in about 15 minutes. The town was quite large and most of the houses were of the straw-and-stilts variety. All the larger and more permanent dwellings had been destroyed during San Fabian's "liberation" by the Japs last February.

Interesting sights were these: the marketplace where raw caribou meat in large chunks lay on open tables under millions of flies, the Catholic Church which was partially demolished but still being used, the two school houses where smiling dark-eyed girls and boys sang songs and learned English and arithmetic, the municipal hospital made of bamboo with army cots for beds and where a pitifully emaciated four-year-old girl suffered with bronchopneumonia. Outside and all around were many caribou, wallowing in the mud.

....

SEPTEMBER 25, 1945: *Our back-mail finally came and was it welcome!*

The Task Force Commander hatched the brilliant idea that all ships in the gulf would have to chlorinate their water supply. This order came after ten days in this area and two days prior to our departure. He based this decision on his stated conjecture that the tide was "running slow." That determination was made by simply looking over the side of the ship, which was a useless exercise. This must either have been an order from headquarters, or otherwise he was just in a bad mood. In any event, it caused me to spend the entire afternoon working out the details for fresh water chlorination.

....

SEPTEMBER 26, 1945: *Bud, George, Art, and I hitchhiked to Dagupin, a fairly large town about 20 miles south. Dagupin had been almost completely destroyed in MacArthur's drive to Manila. Small grass-thatched stores had mushroomed up* and now lined both sides of the main street where all the stores were located for at least a mile.

This was the hottest day I've experienced in the Pacific and the road was so dusty at times it was impossible to see six feet ahead.

Coming back out to the ship in the small boat, a fresh breeze whipped up new waves and we all got soaked.

A shower before dinner was indeed a pleasure.

....

SEPTEMBER 27, 1945: *Today, and for the next several days, our departure was delayed because of a typhoon along the route.*

....

SEPTEMBER 30, 1945, SUNDAY: *I preached the sermon at church service today on the "The Good Samaritan," the subject being "giving."*

We heard by dispatch that the typhoon wreaked havoc on a convoy bound for Okinawa from Leyte and six or seven ships were lost. We have much to be thankful for.

....

OCTOBER 1, 1945: *At last! Underway for Japan!*

Very soon after leaving the sheltering bay, we ran into rough seas. The Rankin, *again, rolled like a drunken sailor and I felt like one. To complete a miserable night, a sailor developed appendicitis and one of the soldiers was afflicted with atabrine poisoning. It's too rough to even consider doing an appendectomy, so I'm treating that problem conservatively: ice packs to the right lower quadrant and penicillin. The atabrine case required sedation.*

I'm seasick myself. Goodnight!

....

OCTOBER 2, 1945: *The night might just as well have been spent in a cocktail shaker. Fortunately, in spite of the rolling, pitching ship, my seasickness disappeared upon arising.*

The sailor with appendicitis showed definite localization to his right lower abdomen this morning, but I'm going to adhere to a conservative plan of therapy because it's just too rough to attempt an appendectomy, especially because it would be my first one. Even on terra firma, for me, it would be a harrowing experience and for the patient, a hazardous one as well!

Captain Price offered to change course to see if that would reduce some of the pitching and yawing so I could do the appendectomy, but I convinced him to "stay the course." To do otherwise wouldn't help that much. I couldn't tell him that the real reason I didn't want to operate was because of my own inexperience. I didn't want to undermine the confidence that he and all of the crew enjoyed because they had a "real doc" aboard.

The atabrine poisoning case is much better. At least he is rational. The day was spent closely checking Riddle (appendicitis). He showed improvement by nightfall, so present management will be continued. The seas have calmed a good deal, but a healthy roll continues. This situation is not very pleasant.

....

OCTOBER 3, 1945: *Weather reports indicate a storm north of us and a typhoon, southeast, moving toward us. If the typhoon does not change course, we could get to Japan before it catches us. Riddle's appendicitis attack has subsided. Lucky for both of us. I felt tired, weak, and unsettled all day.*

....

OCTOBER 4, 1945: *The next three days were spent reversing our direction to try to avoid the storm. It was terribly rough but we dodged the most violent center of the typhoon. By October 6, the ocean finally calmed down. We are just cruising around now in a holding pattern, because we are not due to land in Japan until tomorrow morning.*

....

OCTOBER 7, 1945, SUNDAY: *We arrived in Wakayama harbor, Honshu, Japan, this morning. Nineteen transports, led by a destroyer escort, solemnly steamed, single file, into the harbor.*

The surrounding country is rocky and mountainous. A sprawling power plant with some 20 to 30 smoke stacks lies in partial ruin right on the shore's edge. The town beyond looks like a skeleton town through the glasses. The day was raw and dark with heavy clouds and a cold drizzling rain. Thank God that we come as an occupying force and not an invading one.

OCTOBER 8, 1945: *I spent the entire day aboard the hospital ship* Consolation *where I transferred Riddle for an interval appendectomy. Later in the afternoon I attended a medical conference on beriberi, as seen in over a thousand repatriated Allied prisoners of war. Very interesting.*

Just as we were about to leave the Consolation *to return to the* Rankin, *a thick haze and driving rain struck the harbor and we couldn't even signal our ship. Much later and well after dark, we were taken home in a whale boat from the hospital ship. It took over an hour to find the* Rankin *in the maze of ships that cluttered the pitch-black harbor.*

·····································

OCTOBER 9, 1945: *Another typhoon struck Okinawa, damaged a great number of ships in the harbor, and is headed our way. It is a cold, dark, and rainy day.*

·····································

OCTOBER 10, 1945: *The typhoon arrived on schedule, with winds between thirty and sixty knots and waves thirty feet high. Both anchors have been lowered and the screw has been set at 27 turns. The height of the storm should be reached in three to six hours, when its center is expected to pass 50 miles south of us.*

The ship isn't pitching nearly as much as it did on our trip from Lingayen Gulf. Aside from the roaring noise and pounding surf, it seems rather quiet in my room. It's a very tough night for the anchor detail.

·····································

OCTOBER 11, 1945: *The typhoon took an unexpected turn and passed 125 miles inland from us, resulting in an uneventful night. This afternoon the winds died down, the sea quieted, and the sun came out gloriously, just before it disappeared below the horizon.*

·····································

OCTOBER 12, 1945: *At 0800 I took the long boat ride into the beach. In this area there was little war damage. There were numerous small souvenir shops all along the winding road that led to Wakayama. Everything was clean and orderly. Many of the houses were well built and beautiful, with surrounding gardens and hedges. The merchandise was of high quality: lacquerware, swords, parasols, kimonos,* dishes etc. and could be purchased for a few packs of cigarettes. Cigarettes were of much more value than yen.

The people were very friendly and seemed to enjoy our presence. Only the Japanese soldiers were glum and seemed to be mad about something. (I wonder what!) Babies were cute and were carried like papooses. There was no apparent starvation or disease; nothing like the sad situation we observed in Manila.

I bought a few souvenirs, took some pictures, and returned to the ship at 1200. Choppy waves breaking over the bow soaked us all. Cold, wet, but invigorated by the mere change of scenery, I dragged myself up the debarkation ladder onto the deck. It was a worthwhile day.

....

OCTOBER 14, 1945, SUNDAY: *I spent most of the day in Wakayama. Bud, Meyers, and I walked miles bargaining, buying, sightseeing. I bartered three packs of cigarettes, four cigars, one Hershey bar, two folders of matches, two packages of gum, and 150 yen ($10) for the following: one small silk kimono, one silk Japanese flag, one candy dish, three saki-dish-and-rice-bowl combinations, one lacquer bowl of beautiful design, one silk handkerchief, chop sticks, two fans, three lacquer saki dishes, joss sticks, post cards, and a Japanese magazine. Commerce at any level is a fundamental fact of life.*

....

OCTOBER 15, 1945: *I printed pictures most of the day and they weren't bad. It will be fun to look at them again some day when I'm old and gray.*

The boys who had liberty today said that they were all searched for cigarettes, now considered contraband and illegal for barter. Hundreds of cartons were confiscated. Men had hidden them in strange places: in canteen covers, down their pants legs with two cartons tied together inside socks, one down each leg, inside hats, shirts, sleeves, etc. George Cotsirilos and Warner managed to get by with three cartons apiece at morning liberty and they repeated the procedure in the afternoon. In an attempt to appear perfectly innocent, George bravely jumped from the small boat to the pier, tripped on the top step, and fell flat on his face at the feet of two MPs, the cigarettes, hidden under his hat, flying before him. He got razzed plenty by his buddies, but no fines nor jail time to my knowledge.

OCTOBER 16 TO OCTOBER 19, 1945: *During this four-day period we made several shopping forays into Wakayama and one memorable trip into Wakanura, a town about five or six miles from Wakayama, which I will relate in more detail shortly. The tight prohibition against bartering cigarettes had been relaxed and the Shore Patrol and MPs looked the other way when these transactions occurred. Consequently, all hands are shopping madly and prices are skyrocketing, following the dictates of a market economy. Every house has become a shop and the locals bargain shrewdly.*

An officer's club has been set up in a building high on a hill overlooking the harbor, which I believe had been a geisha house. In any event, geisha girls served as waitresses and occasionally provided Japanese entertainment which was very proper in every respect (dancing, singing, tea ceremony). This was no bawdy house. The view from here over the harbor, loaded with ships, was breathtaking.

....

OCTOBER 20, 1945: *The day was spent attempting to diagnose a very peculiar condition in a sailor by name of Hepler. His symptoms included abdominal pain, fever, diarrhea, anorexia, and a macular-papular red rash involving his trunk, thighs, and genitalia. His temperature ranged from 103 to 104 degrees Fahrenheit, pulse 105 to 110, WBC 7,500 with 50 percent PMNs and 50 percent lymphocytes, half of them large and half small. Stool and urine studies were essentially normal. Among the possible diagnoses were Sonne dysentery (atypical), amebic dysentery, infectious mononucleosis, Tsutsugamuchi disease, malaria, trench fever, and gastrointestinal allergy. Because of our limited diagnostic facilities, we transferred Hepler to a hospital ship on the following day.*

....

OCTOBER 22, 1945: *Today, George, Oscar, and I took the small boat to the Army Pier, which was only a mile from the center of Wakayama. I carried a modest trading ration of one carton of cigarettes, five candy bars, and three packages of gum. Oscar and George were loaded with over two cartons of cigarettes each, candy bars and gum. The day was cool but a bright sun reminded me of Indian summer in Minnesota. We walked briskly for about one-half mile and were then picked up by an army truck going into the center of town.*

The town was utterly destroyed. Buildings had been leveled and nothing was left standing except for a large public library which, oddly, had only a few windows broken. There were a few charred trees standing, some new telephone poles, and a number of recently thrown together tin huts and shops. This destruction was much worse than that in Manila. There, at least the skeleton of buildings remained. Here there was nothing. The bricks, tile, and cement of buildings had been pulverized and the steel girders were twisted, bent, and rusting. Never had the terrible destructive power of modern war been so graphically burned into my consciousness as witnessing this sight! The bombed towns I saw in England didn't have anywhere near this much destruction. We just stared at it all, speechless.

After adjusting to the shock of seeing this town, we decided to hike to the adjacent town of Wakanura, about five miles away. When we reached the main road to Wakanura, a Shore Patrol sentry stopped us and said we were out of bounds. We would have to go back and go around by boat. This was impossible, because there were no boats. Shortly after we left the SP we were approached by a young Japanese soldier named Kittyama who wanted "cigaretto." He spoke a little English and we learned that he was 18 years old and had been a Zero pilot during the war. We conveyed to him the idea that we wanted to get to Wakanura, but to avoid all the SPs and MPs. He agreed, so off we went on one of the longest, most circuitous hikes I have ever experienced. We followed paths through the ruined city, then twisted and turned through numerous cultivated fields and back alleys of small villages. After two hours over a distance of five or six miles, we suddenly arrived in the center of Wakanura. We traded our contraband for a few souvenirs and made it back to the harbor and the Rankin via the approved route. It was an exciting day.

....

OCTOBER 26, 1945: *After two and a half days of delay, we got underway for Nagoya. We are the fifth ship in a single column of 16 ships that extends 21 miles from beginning to end. Our destination is 250 miles away and we expect to arrive at about 1200 tomorrow.*

....

OCTOBER 27, 1945: *On this clear bright day our long line of ships wove a serpentine path through the mine fields into Nagoya. We were one of the first ships to dock and after much maneuvering, finally tied up to Pier No. 5. The water front, aside from a dry dock, was almost untouched. Deeper inland, however, we could see through binoculars that Nagoya had been quite thoroughly blasted.*

On a short walk into town tonight, Earp and I saw several small campfires around which were huddled, side by side, American soldiers and Japanese waterfront workers. It was an amazing picture. I wondered how they managed to communicate.

....

OCTOBER 28, 1945, SUNDAY: *The day was jumbled and hectic and only tonight did I realize it was Sunday. This afternoon I left the ship and strolled around the dockyard environs for about an hour. As far as I could see, wherever I walked, was destruction. Few houses or buildings were spared. Small shacks had been built since the bombings, but there were no substantial buildings to be seen except on the waterfront. Small vegetable gardens were planted everywhere amid the debris and all of them stunk horrifically, having been recently fertilized with human excrement. There were no shops selling souvenirs as in Wakanura, and trading was on a minor scale. Soldiers were beginning to trade cigarettes, candy, and C-rations for yen. Here the Japanese paid 30 yen for cigarettes and 20 yen for a small C-ration can. For the most part, though, the Japanese here seemed quite awed and subdued and have not yet begun to exploit their new lucrative market as they had in Wakayama.*

....

OCTOBER 29, 1945: *Immediately following lunch, several of us started out on a long jeep ride around Nagoya. It was a warm spring-like day and riding to town was extremely pleasant. Seeing the town was a different story.*

The city was almost completely destroyed, except for the center of the downtown district and the geisha houses. How they managed to escape the bombings is beyond me. Pure chance, I guess. I bought a glass fish in one of the department stores that had just begun to sell to occupation troops.

Outside of town, we saw long processions of people on foot, carrying large bundles, or walking with a horse-drawn cart containing all their belongings. They were coming back from the hills where they had hidden to escape the bombings.

....

OCTOBER 30, 1945: *We learned today that the* Rankin *will be attached to COMPHIBPAC for permanent post-war duty.*

Shortly after receiving the bad news of long-term Pacific duty, we were ecstatic to hear that we are going back to the United States. After the Captain made that announcement over the loudspeakers, resounding cheers shook the ship. I hope this last order will not be changed.

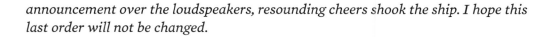

NOVEMBER 2, 1945: *We are underway for Samar, Philippines, with 300 additional passengers. We are packed to the rafters.*

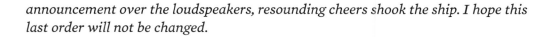

NOVEMBER 4, 1945, SUNDAY: *Today, I conducted Divine Service in the mess hall at 0945. With passengers and crew combined, approximately 50 sailors were present. There were another 50 or so sleeping in their bunks immediately alongside the mess deck, but they cannot be counted because they were present only of necessity and heard none of the "goings on" despite their proximity. It was a little disturbing at first to commence the program with all the bare, sleeping bodies around, but soon they were forgotten and the service went on without a hitch.*

The subject of my sermon was "Men Talk, They Do Not Act," taken from an oration given by Francis Gamelin at Gustavus in 1938. I finished with Carl Sandburg's great poem, "Prayers of Steel," the poem ending with the powerful plea, "Let me be the great nail holding a skyscraper together through blue nights into white stars." We sang several good old fashioned hymns, including "The Old Rugged Cross." I led the singing and fortunately I got on the right pitch, though the tempo dragged too much. We'll do better next time. I don't know if my sermon put anyone to sleep, but at least it didn't awaken any of the sleeping sailors.

Heavy tail winds still prod us toward Samar. We are yawing and rolling with abandon. All my distaste for life at sea crystallized today and I knew it would be a long trip home.

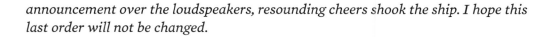

NOVEMBER 7, 1945: *We arrived in Samar this morning. Our mail was distributed and I read the disturbing news that Dad had been operated on and had suffered a relapse. Fortunately, the last letter reported that he was feeling much better. He is very anxious that I return and help out at the hospital and in the office. I would certainly be of more service there than here, especially now that the war is over. I don't want to jeopardize my navy record, but intend to do what is required regardless.*

NOVEMBER 8, 1945: *We finished loading today and will get underway for San Francisco at 0830 tomorrow.*

....

NOVEMBER 9, 1945: *I finished reading* Magic Mountain *tonight and am trying to comprehend all its significance, which is a big task. I learned more new words from this book than from any other I can remember.*

....

NOVEMBER 10, 1945: *I received the wonderful news today, that upon arrival in the United States, I am to report to the nearest naval base for further assignment. This is undoubtedly my last navy cruise. Hooray!*

....

NOVEMBER 11, 1945, SUNDAY: *Church services today were held in an improved atmosphere. The Captain ordered all the sleeping sailors in the bordering bunks to arise and either listen or leave. I don't think many of them hung around, but we did have approximately sixty sailors in attendance. Foster accompanied all the hymns on the trumpet and things went along quite smoothly. My sermon topic was the Biblical injunction, "Seek ye first the Kingdom of God." It covered individual applications of the above and then expanded into international behavior. I roped in Ben Franklin, John Foster Dulles, and concluded with the atomic bomb. There being no collection, l am sure the congregation felt they got their money's worth.*

....

NOVEMBER 12 TO 18, 1945: *Rough seas dominated this period of time as we progressed steadily, at eight knots, eastward toward San Francisco. The pitching, yawing, and rolling made doing anything, except lying in your bunk, difficult. When the ship rises on a huge wave crest and then crashes into the trough it shudders from stem to stern and feels as though it's going to split apart. In this miserable situation, time seems to have stopped and getting to our destination, an eternity.*

At night a waxing moon silvered the churning sea and made the split waves look like ploughed snow. Finally the wind died, but the sea remained very much alive. Huge swells now create the sensation of going up and down large hills. Every so often the ship literally drops off the top of one of the greater swells and lands with a resounding thwack in the valley beneath; then an avalanche of white foam spews out from either side.

Gradually the ocean flattened out and gave the feeling of traveling over rolling midwestern prairies. How I wish that were true!

....

NOVEMBER 18, 1945, SUNDAY: *There will be two Sundays the 18th, back to back, because early tomorrow we pass the 180th. We are now better than halfway back and with the wind, current, and 90 turns of the screw in our favor, we are doing about 400 miles a day.*

Church service this morning went well. My sermon was not that great, but the hymns went smoothly. Foster now plays the entire hymn through before we sing, which improved the singing immensely. The sermon title today was "Religion, Bulwark in a World of Change." The audience was a little larger this week but only two officers attended. No one fell asleep, which is something.

It's getting cooler and the sea has smoothed considerably. I spent the rest of this day writing my discharge letter, preparing photographic solutions, reading, and playing bridge.

....

NOVEMBER 19, 1945: *We are now only five days from San Francisco and the wind is beginning to build up again, with a freezing cold rain. The ever-compliant ocean is obeying the fierce winds and the Rankin is again beginning to roll madly. Oh, for the life of a sailor!*

....

NOVEMBER 21, 1945: *We've changed course a bit and are now paralleling the waves which results in maximum roll; by actual measurement, 29 degrees. Chairs, books, dishes were dashed about the ship like flying ten-pins. With each roll there is a crashing and banging that sounds as though the dear old Rankin's insides were being dashed to bits. It's impossible to sleep except in snatches.*

....

NOVEMBER 22, 1945: *Today we celebrated Thanksgiving and with only two more days to go, we have much to be thankful for. The dinner was outstanding.*

We had turkey with all the trimmings and pie à la mode with chocolate ice cream. The sailors had the same menu as the officers, but in addition, they had nut cups, free cigarettes, and cigars. It was indeed a contented ship that ploughed its way towards the Golden City by the Bay.

....

NOVEMBER 23, 1945: *As if to punish us for our unmistakable urge to abandon the ship and the sea, high winds overtook us again and the Rankin behaved like a wayward canoe caught in gargantuan rapids. The constant swing and sway of the ship, with attendant crashing and banging of interior furnishings, became utterly nervewracking. There is no rest or sleep even in the sack, which is a tragic situation.*

We are now so close to San Francisco, that flocks of sea gulls are circling around us and radio reception has become crystal clear.

....

NOVEMBER 25, 1945, SUNDAY: *The great city came into view. Oh, what joy! A large yacht, loaded with young ladies and a WAC Band, met us just past the Golden Gate bridge. On the side of the yacht was a large sign, "WELCOME HOME!" and all the girls waved and cheered madly. We didn't know what to do exactly, but we loved it and every sailor had a grin a mile wide. There were other "Welcome Home" and "Well Done" signs around the bay and a navy band serenaded us as we docked at Pier 7. All the passengers and the high point sailors then disembarked, and my replacement doctor came aboard. I was ecstatic and found it almost impossible to keep my feet on the ground.*

....

DECEMBER 3, 1945: *I reported to the Commandant of the 12th Naval District and was told that orders for my next assignment should arrive in a week to ten days. What that assignment might be he didn't have a clue, or so he said. Nothing to do but wait and see and have a good time until new orders arrive. I submitted a request for early discharge, so I can help Dad out at home. I won't hear about that for at least a month.*

DECEMBER 8, 1945: *I've had a great time in San Francisco with new and old friends: attending the San Francisco Symphony several times, visiting Golden Gate Park, and attending the horse races. Pierre Montieux was the Orchestra Conductor and I heard Horowitz play Rachmaninoff's Piano Concerto No. 3 at one of the concerts.*

....

DECEMBER 9, 1945: *I boarded the good old* Rankin *for the last time. It had been moved from Pier 7 to an anchorage way out in the bay. I said goodbye to old friends who were still aboard, and though I did have some nostalgic feelings as I hiked around the deck, I was very happy that I would not be taking the next cruise.*

....

DECEMBER 15, 1945: *My new orders arrived! My next assignment will be as a medical officer at the U.S. Naval Training School in Del Monte, California. I have no idea what this duty will be, but the location sounds great and I am sure that whatever problems it might present will not be as bad as going back to sea.*

....

DECEMBER 19, 1945: *After five hours' sleep and with great anticipation, I took the bus to Del Monte. The Naval Training School is located in the posh old Del Monte Hotel, close to Monterey and Carmel. There is an 18-hole, regulation length, golf course immediately adjacent to the hotel, as well as a swimming pool.*

I was given a tour of the sick bay and the outpatient facility by the senior medical officer, Dr. Splichel. Everything was so sparkling white and in such a gorgeous setting, that I could hardly believe it was true. There are two of us medical officers, one chief corpsman, Bill Gleason, and several other lower ranked corpsmen.

The unmarried officers were assigned to a lovely large home on the compound called "Boy's Town." There are about eight of us who live in Boy's Town and there is plenty of room for everyone. We will do some of our own cooking on a cooperative basis, but will have help with day-to-day cooking, dishes, and housecleaning.

Our responsibility is to provide medical care to the entire student body, the faculty, and all their resident families. During the war this training station had been a very large and important school, but with the war winding down and now over, there is a significant cutback in class size, with a corresponding decrease in the volume of our patient load.

My tour of duty at Del Monte lasted until September, 1946, and was such a wonderful experience that I felt guilty every time I picked up my paycheck. My request for early discharge was turned down, but Dad was feeling better and back to working full-time at the hospital, with good help, so the urgency of my return home was gone.

I returned to Minneapolis in October, 1946, where, on rounds at the Swedish Hospital, I met and fell in love with a lovely laboratory technologist, Evodia Marie Larson. We were married on November 13, 1948.

Although I was granted major surgical privileges at the Swedish Hospital on a preceptorship basis, after brother Paul returned from his service as a medical officer in the U.S. Army in 1950, I fulfilled the second part of my dream, which was to become a proficient, Board-Certified surgeon. I began a four-year surgical residency at the U.S. Veteran's Hospital, a division of the University of Minnesota, where I received a Master of Science degree in surgery and certification by the American Board of Surgery in 1954.

REFLECTION

....

To provide a more intimate and personal view of WWII not possible in an historical overview, as presented here, I strongly recommend two books to the reader: *Our War for the World: A Memoir of the Life and Death on the Front Lines in WWII* by Brendon Phibbs, Combat Surgeon for the Twelfth Armored Division of the Seventh Army, and *The Boy's Crusade: The American Infantry in Northwestern Europe 1944–1945* by Paul Fussell, WWII army officer and post-war professor of literature at the University of Pennsylvania. These books decry the romanticizing of war that appears in so many books and the media. The books vividly describe the pain, fear, and suffering of the infantry in the battle across France and Germany after D-Day. Fussell's concern is mostly for the adolescent boys *(the children's crusade)* that made up so much of the army, especially as replacements.

One of Phibbs' many gripping passages relating his medic experience reads as follows:

> I'd been looking out across the field when the first shell exploded next to one of our half-tracks and I'd run out across the field to the shouts of "Medic!" A wounded man was lying across an aid man's knees. His face was streaming red and I foolishly concentrated on it, mopping blood with an aid packet, looking for lacerations, ignoring the frantic stammering of the aid man. Finally he connected his words. "He ain't got no back of his head, Major. It's all tore off at the back." As we turned the boy over his brains slid out on my lap and he died with a couple of gurgles. The occiput was torn off as neatly as if a neurosurgeon had been sawing and chiseling.

> The sound of the next shell ripping the air in our direction sent us flat: I sprinted in bursts back to the command post, diving under tanks between explosions, furious, raging with impatience to get to a radio to call appropriate authorities to deal with the criminals who had just torn the boy's skull off.

When I reflect on my WWII experience I realize how fortunate I was that my tour of duty was free of any of the harrowing, miserable, and painful experiences of the foot soldier, the marine, the bomber, or fighter pilot, or the prisoner of war. I had good food, good quarters, and I never had to worry about hand-to-hand combat, trench-foot, jungle-rot, or a malfunctioning parachute.

Aboard ship my fears were mostly psychological—the uncomfortable concern of not being qualified to do the surgery that I was expected to do, the dread of the ship taking a hit by a torpedo, bomb, *kamikaze*, or mine, or breaking apart in typhoon seas. Any of the above would be followed by the chilling embrace of the cold black ocean. These were not constant fears but they assailed my mind whenever the action heated up. I found it important to get busy with the routine tasks at hand and not to dwell on what horrible event might happen in the next week, the next day, or the next minute. All of us aboard ship learned to function normally despite our fears. As I touched on earlier, the perception and anticipation of danger was often more frightening and disabling than the actual event itself.

Ernie Pyle, killed at Okinawa, described the haunting fear he felt from time to time during his coverage of the war in one of his nationally syndicated newspaper columns in 1944:

> My own devastating sense of fear and depression, of which I have spoken before, disappeared the moment we were underway. As I write this, the old familiar crack and roar of big guns is all around us, and the beach is a great brown haze of smoke and dust, and we know that bombers will be over us tonight. Yet all that haunting premonition, that soul-consuming dread is gone, and the war is prosaic to me again. And I believe that is true of everyone aboard, even those who have never been in combat before.

Lt. General George Patton, addressing his troops just before their debarkation from England to France in the summer of 1944, had this to say about fear:

> Yes, every man is scared in his first battle. If he says he's not he's a liar. Some men are cowards but they fight the same as the brave men or they get the hell slammed out of them, watching men fight who are just as scared as they are. The real hero is the man who fights even though he is scared. Some men get over their fright in a minute under fire. For some, it takes an hour. For some, it takes days. But a real man will never let his fear of death overpower his honor, his sense of duty to his country, and his innate manhood.

One other intriguing and baffling aspect of the war was trying to make sense out of why, in the heat of battle, a few servicemen were miraculously spared death or serious injury, when many others were not. These miraculous events did not, obviously, happen only to the virtuous. Consider Hitler's escape from death when the bomb exploded near to where he sat. Goebbels exploited that event, as noted earlier, attributing Hitler's salvation to God's will. If the will of the Almighty could be discerned by mere mortals, it seems to me that Goebbels would be among the last to be privy to it. It is impossible to attribute the sparing of Hitler's life or the deaths of good men like Bonhoeffer, Delp, Simon Buckner Jr., or Ernie Pyle to the will of God. Although miraculous escapes from death have occurred, such as when dog tags or a small family Bible deflected a bullet or piece of shrapnel, I believe these are by chance and not by divine intervention.

On the other hand, there can be no denying the power of prayer and faith in God when you consider the numerous accounts from downed pilots, prisoners of war, and sailors adrift at sea who ardently attribute their survival to their faith in God. How many times have we heard it said by these survivors, "If it hadn't been for my faith in God, I never would have made it." Miracles abound in mystery.

Looking ahead, the United States, as the world's most powerful nation, has an obligation to oppose wherever possible, crimes against humanity such as terrorism, genocide, and "ethnic cleansing." Obviously, all peaceful means to prevent or abort these inhumane practices must first be exhausted. The problem with using military force as a tool of diplomacy is that it does nothing to correct the deep-seated animosities and prejudices that often extend back for centuries; it kills too many people, reduces the chastised country to third-world status, costs all the belligerents a fortune, and creates new animosities against the policing countries. The only consistent beneficiary is the "military–industrial complex." New tools of social and religious education must be applied by indigenous leaders over the long term or these ugly war-breeding inhumanities will arise again and again.

Shortly after the Sept. 11, 2001 (Twin Towers) disaster, the United States found it in the best interest of our country to strike at Osama Bin Laden's al Queda terrorist cells in Afghanistan, taking down the cruel obsessive-compulsive Taliban rule in that country and establishing a new interim democratic government in Kabul, the capital city. Legitimate elections in October, 2004, have now created a fledgling democracy with a newly elected president, Karzai, and a governing body.

In March, 2003, a coalition of countries—the United States, Britain, Australia, Spain, and Poland—invaded Iraq in a preemptive and controversial strike in spite of a negative vote by the United Nations. The wisdom and ultimate effectiveness of this action remains to be seen. The hope is, of course, that Iraq, with our help, can build an effective army and police force that can protect the new democratic government, the Iraqi people, and make possible our early departure. The Iraqi government's impact on the war, terrorism, roadside, and suicide bombings, after more than two years in power and four years of fighting, however, has been disappointing.

We obviously can't be the police force for the entire world. All international peace-keeping with military action against terrorist cells and large scale humanitarian crimes should be handled, whenever possible, through the United Nations, as ineffectual as that organization often is, or NATO.

World Wars I and II, though considered phases of a single war by many historians, were separated by a period of 21 years. The world has now had almost 60 years of relative peace since the end of WWII, punctuated by a number of lesser but by no means inconsequential wars: Korea, Vietnam, Desert Storm, Yugoslavia, Afghanistan, Iraq, and the overarching war on terror. The potential for WWIII, as horrible as that possibility is to contemplate, is pervasive, with seeds of conflict scattered all over the world: the Israeli-Palestine imbroglio, the religious and cultural cleavage between the Middle East Muslim world and the Western Christian world, the dependency of all industrialized nations on oil, the China-Taiwan standoff, the animosity between India and Pakistan regarding Kashmir, and the unfathomable, totally unpredictable behavior of North Korea and Iran, to name some of the most troubling hot spots. Up until now, at least, nuclear war has been held in abeyance by the deterring MAD (mutual assured destruction) balance of power.

Harvard historian Samuel P. Huntington, in his book *Clash of Civilizations and the Remaking of World Order,* stresses the importance of nurturing the commonalities within the different civilizations. "In the emerging era, clashes of civilizations are the greatest threat to world peace, and an international order based on civilizations is the surest safeguard against world war."

While pursuing laudable goals of commonalities—educational exchanges, religious tolerance, and cultural appreciation—the Western World, particularly the United States, must buttress its diplomacy with effective international intelligence, and most importantly, a powerful, but rational military capability. We have learned from two world wars that isolationism, coupled with disarmament and wishful thinking, is a recipe for disaster.

REQUIEM FOR THREE SHIPS

....

T HE FATE OF THE THREE SHIPS ON WHICH I SAW SERVICE DURING WWII, the LST-52, LST-6, and the AKA-103 (USS *Rankin*) has been of great interest to me. Fortunately, through the National LST organization, to which I belong, and from a friend and shipmate of mine on the USS *Rankin*, Communications Officer, Lieutenant j.g. Frank Schiel, I was able to learn what happened to each of these ships.

"LST-52: During WWII, LST-52 was assigned to the European Theater and participated in the Normandy invasion from 6 to 25 June, 1944. Immediately following the war, she was assigned to occupation duty in the Far East during the fall of 1945 and January, 1946. She was decommissioned on 29 August, 1946 and sunk as a target on 19 April, 1948. Her name was struck from the Navy list on 30 April, 1948. LST-52 earned one battle star for WWII service."

LST-6: During WWII, LST-6 was assigned to the European Theater and participated in the following operations:

Sicilian occupation—July, 1943.

Salerno landings—September, 1943.

Invasion of Normandy—June 6, 1944.

On 17 November, 1944, she was mined (struck a mine) and sunk in six fathoms (36 feet) of water while en route from Rouen, France, to Portland, England. She was struck from the Navy list on 22 December, 1944. LST-6 earned three battle stars for WWII service."

I have never been able to learn if there were any survivors. This tragic accident occurred only four months after I left the ship.

AKA-103 (USS *Rankin*): An Associated Press news release in the Fort Myers paper on July 24, 1988, was sent to me by Frank Schiel. The gist of the article was that naval architect, Charles Petzold, of Stuart, Florida, who had designed the *Rankin* in 1944 and had followed its career during the war years, learned to his amazement, that on July 26, 1988, his creation, the *USS Rankin,* was going to be sunk seven miles off the shore of Stuart, his hometown, to be part of an artificial reef. "It's crazy! It really is crazy! I can't believe how that thing is following me, Petzold exclaimed. "I did a double-take, I'll tell you. Here it is, all these years later."

In its new role, the 43-year-old ship will be a fish magnet, attracting fish to its shelter and its plant-encrusted steel much like natural coral reefs. Fishermen and divers alike are expected to troop to the old transport vessel, and scuba diving will be allowed beginning Monday."

I can't imagine what it would be like for me to dive down to see and feel that proud old ship, that once vibrant mass of steel now moldering, dead in the deep. No matter how much I hated some of my days on the *Rankin,* especially when the ocean was rough, I still feel a warm fondness for the ship that was home to me for so many months and which held together during the most violent of storms when it seemed certain that it would break apart. Most importantly, through it all, the dear old *Rankin* had the good grace to never get hit. It deserves the most beautiful coral the ocean can provide.

The AKA-103 earned one battle star during WWII for its service as an ammunition transport during the invasion of Okinawa, and two battle stars after WWII for its role in the Korean conflict and the Cuban Missile Crisis.

Maps

....

ALL MAPS ADAPTED FROM *A WORLD AT ARMS* BY GERHARD
WEINBERG—REPRINTED WITH PERMISSION OF CAMBRIDGE
UNIVERSITY PRESS, JULY 15, 2000.

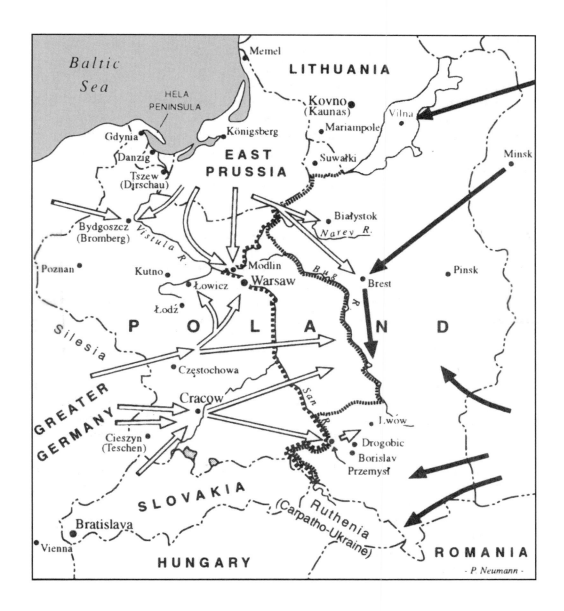

MAP 1. THE 1939 INVASION AND PARTITION OF POLAND BY GERMANY (WHITE ARROWS) AND RUSSIA (BLACK ARROWS). Poland didn't have a chance despite the declaration of war against the invading countries by England and France.

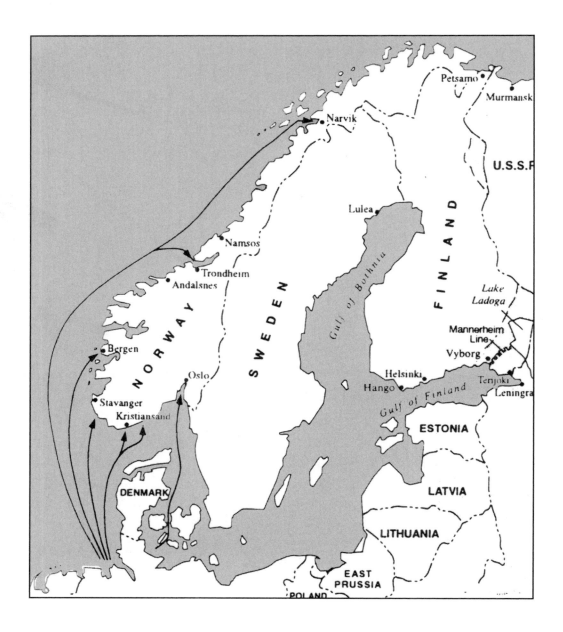

MAP 2. SCANDINAVIAN COUNTRIES. Norway and Denmark fell to Germany in 1940. Sweden's neutrality was respected in return for vital steel products.

MAP 3. WESTERN EUROPE. Here, in 1940, Germany drove across Holland and Belgium, then rolled through France, almost unopposed. Here also is the site of the Normandy invasion of 1944.

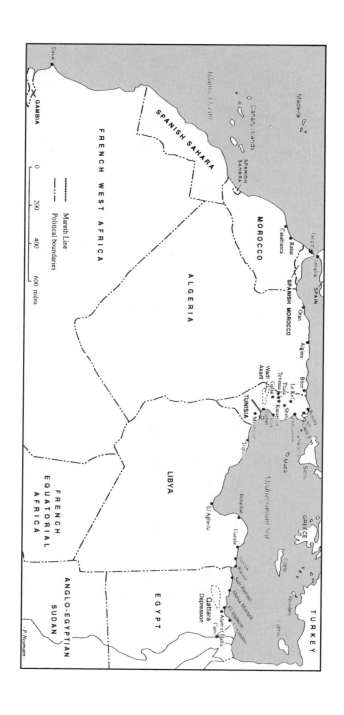

MAP 4. NORTH AFRICA, 1942–1943. General Erwin Rommel's *Africa Corps* was sent to North Africa by Hitler to rescue the Italian Army, to dislodge the British from Egypt, and to protect the "soft underbelly" of Europe.

NORMANDY TO OKINAWA

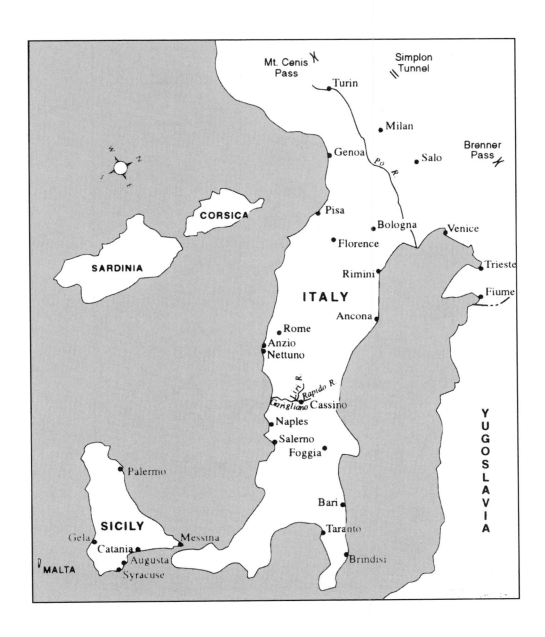

MAP 5. SICILY AND ITALY, 1943 TO 1945. Even though the Italians surrendered in 1943, the battle up the Italian peninsula was slow and bloody.

**MAP 6. USSR AND GERMAN LINES OF BATTLE, EASTERN FRONT, 1943 AND
1944.** By this time, the German Army's retreat became almost a rout. The defeat
of Germany seemed assured; and the Normandy invasion had not yet happened.

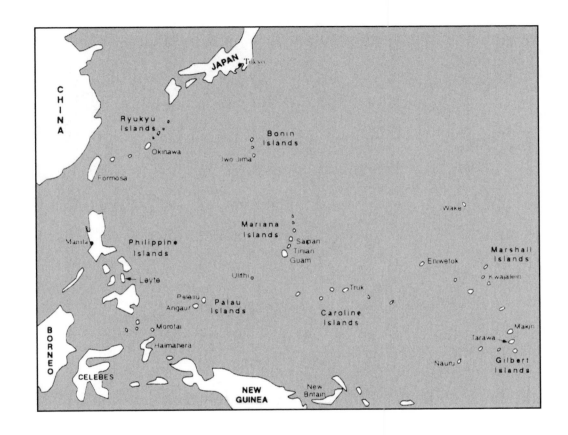

MAP 7. CENTRAL AND WEST PACIFIC ISLANDS. These were the grueling, bloody, stepping stones to Japan, scattered across the vast expanse of the Pacific Ocean that had to be conquered or, as in the case of Truk, bypassed.

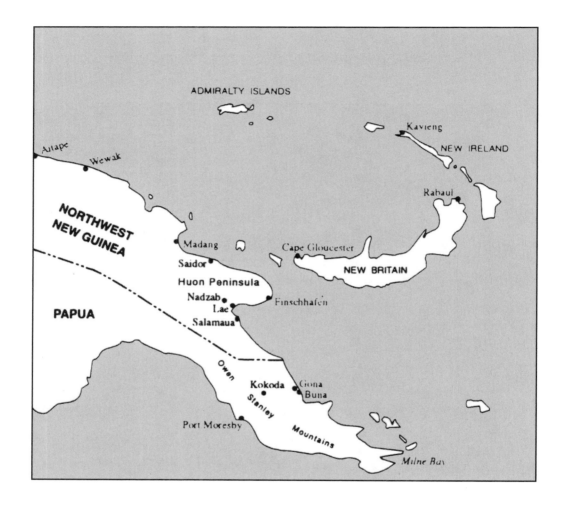

MAP 8. NEW GUINEA AND NEW BRITAIN. Although Buna-Gona appear to be close to Port Moresby on the map, the intervening Owen Stanley Mountains provided a difficult obstacle to the advancing Japanese in July, 1942. Rabaul, Japan's major military base in the South Pacific, can be seen in northern New Britain.

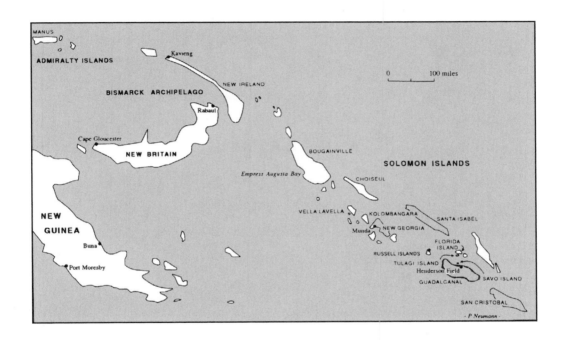

MAP 9. SOLOMON ISLANDS, INCLUDING GUADALCANAL. Here, the first major land battle was fought between the U.S. and Japanese forces from August, 1942 to February 1943.

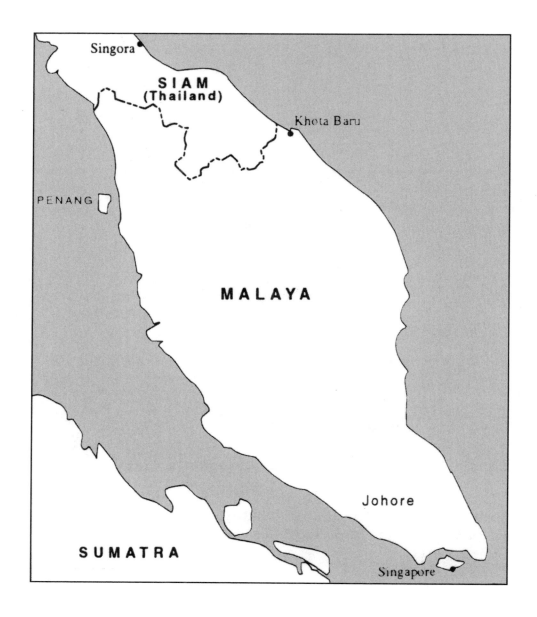

MAP 10. THE MALAY PENINSULA, THE STRAITS OF JOHORE, AND SINGAPORE. Because of its location and its sea-directed heavy artillery, Singapore, Britain's major South Pacific military base, was considered to be impregnable.

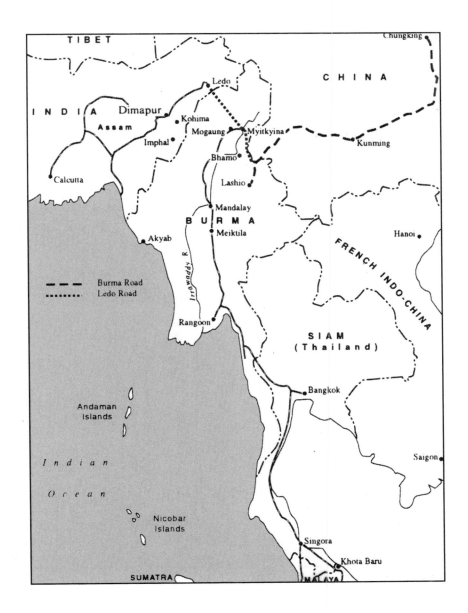

MAP 11. THE BURMA AND LEDO ROADS. These provided the only ground transport for vital supplies from the outside world (India) to China (Kunming and Chunking). Chennault's Flying Tigers were the only means of supply when these roads were held by the Japanese.

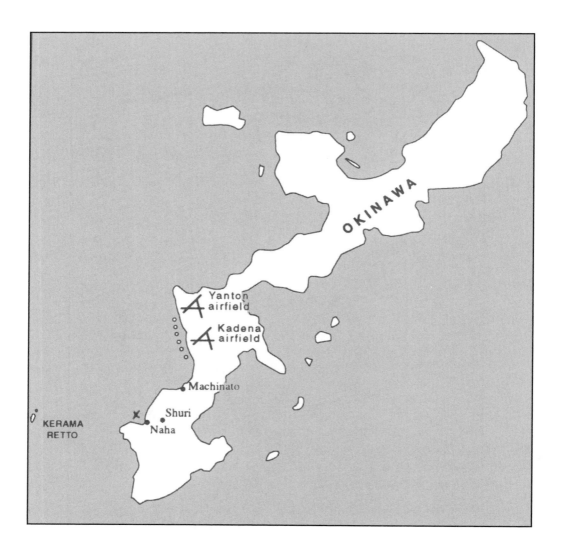

MAP 12. OKINAWA. Most of the fighting and Japan's ferocious last stand occurred in the south, below Naha. AKA-103, *Rankin*, was anchored in Naha Harbor at *X*, where 6000 tons of ammunition were unloaded from June 12 to June 24, 1945. Fighting ceased on June 21, 1945, but the *kamikaze* attacks continued.

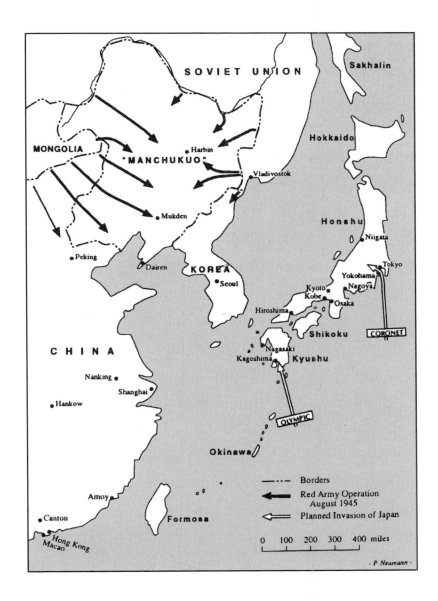

MAP 13. THE RUSSO-JAPANESE BATTLE IN MANCHURIA IN AUGUST 1945, AND THE INTENDED PLAN FOR THE INVASION OF JAPAN. *Little Boy* and *Fat Man* pre-empted the proposed invasion, ushering in the atomic age and creating our current frighteningly awesome MAD (mutual assured destruction) balance of power.

BIBLIOGRAPHY

....

Ailsby, Christopher. 1997. *Waffen-SS: Hitler's Black Guard at War*. Bristol: Siena-Parragon.

Ambrose, Stephen. 1997. *Citizen Soldiers: The U.S. Army from the Normandy Beaches to the Bulge to the Surrender of Germany: June 7, 1944–May 7, 1945*. New York: Simon and Schuster.

———. 1994. *D-Day: June 6, 1944: The Climactic Battle of WWII*. New York: Simon and Schuster.

Ballard, Robert D., and Rick Archbold. 1999. *Return to Midway*. Washington D.C.: National Geographic Society.

Berg, A. Scott. 1998. *Lindbergh*. New York: Berkley Books.

Beschloss, Michael. 2002. *The Conquerors*. New York: Simon and Schuster.

Bix, Herbert P. 2000. *Hirohito and the Making of Modern Japan*. New York: Harper and Collins.

Bradley, James. 2003. *Flyboys: A Story of Courage*. Boston, New York, London: Little, Brown and Company.

———. 2003. *Flags of Our Fathers: The Story of Iwo Jima*. Boston, New York, London: Little, Brown and Company.

Brokaw, Tom. 1998. *The Greatest Generation*. New York: Random House.

Bullock, Alan. 1962. *Hitler: A Study in Tyranny*. New York: Konecky & Konecky.

Buchanan, Patrick. 1999. A *Republic, Not an Empire: Reclaiming America's Destiny*. Washington D.C.: Regnery Publishers.

Churchill, Winston S. 1953. *Triumph and Tragedy: The Second World War*. Cambridge: Houghton Mifflin.

Clarke, Thurston. 1991. *Pearl Harbor Ghosts: A Journey to Hawaii Then and Now*. New York: William Morrow and Company.

Collier, Richard. 1992. *D-Day: 06.06.1944*. New York, London, Paris: The Abbeville Group.

Deighton, Len. 1993. *Blood, Tears and Folly: An Objective Look at WWII*. New York: Harper and Collins.

Elson, Robert T., and eds. 1977. *Time Life Series—World War II*. Alexandria: Time-Life Books, Inc.

Fleming, Peter. 1957. *Operation Sea Lion: The Projected Invasion of England in 1940*. New York: Simon and Schuster.

Fussell, Paul. 2003. *The Boy's Crusade: The American Infantry in Northwestern Europe, 1944–1945*. New York: A Modern Library Chronicles Book.

Goltz, Thomas. 2003. *Chechnya Diary: A War Correspondent's Story of Surviving the War in Chechnya*. New York: Thomas Dunne Books, St. Martin's Press.

Goodwin, Doris Kearns. 1994. *No Ordinary Time*. New York: Touchstone.

Hamilton, Nigel. 1957. *Monty: The Making of a General 1887–1942*. New York: McGraw-Hill.

Hastings, Max. 1985. *Victory in Europe: D-Day to V-E Day*. London: Little, Brown and Company.

Hitler, Adolph. 1999. *Mein Kampf*. Translated by Ralph Manheim. New York: Houghton Mifflin.

Huntington, Samuel. 1997. *The Clash of Civilizations and the Remaking of World Order*. New York: Simon Schuster.

Jenkins, Roy. 2001. *Churchill: A Biography*. New York: Farrar, Straus and Giroux.

Johnston, Stanley. 1942. *Queen of the Flat-Tops: The USS Lexington and the Coral Sea Battle*. New York: E.P. Dutton.

Kershaw, Alex. 2000. *The Longest Winter: The Battle of the Bulge and the Epic Story of World War II's Most Decorated Platoon*. Cambridge: De Capo Press.

Lewis, Jon E. 1993. *War: A Classic Collection of 56 Great War Stories of Our Time*. New York: Galahad Books.

Loftus, John, and Mark Aarons. 1994. *The Secret War Against the Jews*. New York: St. Martens Press.

Lord, Walter. 1957. *Day of Infamy: December 7, 1941*. New York: Henry Holt and Company.

Macksey, Kenneth. 1993. *Military Errors of World War II*. London: Arms and Armour Press.

Manchester, William. 1988. *The Last Lion: Winston Spencer Churchill, Vol. II, Alone, 1932–1940*. Boston: Little-Brown,

McCollough, David. 1992. *Truman*. New York: Simon & Schuster.

McConahey, William M., MD. 1998. *Battalion Surgeon*. Rochester: Private printing.

Montross, Lynn. 1960. *War Through The Ages*. New York: Harper & Row.

Natkiel, Richard and Robin L. Sommer. 1985. *Atlas of World War II*. New York: Military Press and Crown.

North, Oliver, with Joe Musser. 2001. *Heroism in the Pacific*. Washington D.C.: Regnery Publishing, Inc.

Parsinnen, Terry. 2003. *The Oster Conspiracy of 1938: The Unknown Story of the Plot to Kill Hitler and Avert World War II*. New York: Harper and Collins.

Persico, Joseph E. 1979. *Piercing the Reich: The Penetration of Nazi Germany by American Secret Agents during World War II*. New York: Barnes & Noble.

Phibbs, Brendon. 1987. *Our War for the World: A Memoir of Life and Death on the Front Lines in WWII*. Guilford: The Lyons Press.

Ravenscroft, Trevor. 1973. *The Spear of Destiny*. Boston: Weiser Books.

Read, Anthony, and David Fisher. 1993. *The Fall of Berlin*. New York: W.W. Norton and Company.

Rooney, Andy. 1995. *My War*. New York: Public Affairs-Perseus Group.

Ryan, Cornelius. 1959. *The Longest Day*. New York: Simon and Schuster.

Salisbury, Harrison E. 1969. *The 900 Days: The Siege of Leningrad*. New York: Harper and Row.

Salmaggi, Cesare, and Alfredo Pallavisini. 1977. *2194 Days of War: An Illustrated Chronology of the Second World War*. New York: Barnes & Noble.

Samuel, Wolfgang W.E. 2000. *German Boy: A Child in War*. Jackson: University Press of Mississippi.

Selkirk, Errol. 1991. *World War II for Beginners*. New York: Writers and Readers Publishing.

Shirer, William. 1960. *The Rise and Fall of the Third Reich*. New York: Simon and Schuster.

———. 1984. *The Nightmare Years—1930 to 1940*. Boston, Toronto: Little, Brown and Company.

Sledge, E.B. 1981. *With the Old Breed at Peleliu and Okinawa*. New York, Oxford: Oxford University Press.

Stinnett, Robert B. 2000. *Day of Deceit*. New York, London, Toronto: Simon and Schuster

Sulzberger, C. L. 1969. *World War II*. Boston: Houghton Mifflin.

———. 1966. *The American Heritage Picture History of WWII*. New York: America Heritage-Bonanza Books.

Time Life. 1989. *History of World War II*. Alexandria: Time-Life.

Tute, Warren, John Costello, and Terry Hughes. 1975. *D-Day*. London: Pan Books.

VFW Magazine. 1995. *Faces of Victory: Pacific—The Fall of the Rising Sun*. Kansas City: Addox Publishing Group and VFW-U.S.

Walzer, Michael. 1977. *Just and Unjust Wars*. New York: Harper and Collins.

Weinberg, Gerhard. 1994. *A World at Arms: A Global History of World War II.* NewYork: Cambridge University Press.

Weintraub, Stanley. 1991. *Long Days' Journey into War: December 7, 1941.* New York: Truman Talley Books-Dutton.

Wheal, Elizabeth-Ann, Stephen Pope and James Taylor. 1989. *Encyclopedia of the Second World War.* New Jersey: Castle Books.

Widen, Peter. 1984. *Day One: Before Hiroshima and After.* New York: Simon and Schuster.

World War II. *Encyclopaedia Britannica.* 1967 ed.

About the Author

....

Dr. Linner is a graduate of Gustavus Adolphus College, St. Peter, Minnesota, and the University of Minnesota Medical School. He interned on a Harvard Service at the Boston City Hospital in 1944. He is a Clinical Professor Emeritus, Surgery, at the University of Minnesota.

He has served as president of the Minnesota Medical Society, the Minneapolis Surgical Society, and the American Society of Bariatric and Metabolic Surgery, where he received the Outstanding Achievement Award and the Distinguished Member Award. He has written a textbook, <u>Surgery for Morbid Obesity</u>, published by Springer Verlag Publishing Company, NY in 1984.

He married Evodia Larson in 1948; they have five daughters and nine grandchildren. John and Evodia live in Edina, Minnesota and Rio Verde, Arizona.